THE CYCLADES

Cadogan Books plc
London House, Parkgate Road, London SW11 4NQ

The Globe Pequot Press
6 Business Park Road, PO Box 833, Old Saybrook, Connecticut 06475–0833

Copyright © Dana Facaros 1994
Contributors: Guy Dimond, Stephanie Ferguson and Sarah Hey

Illustrations © Pauline Pears 1986, Suzan Kentli 1993 and Horatio Monteverde 1994

Design by Animage
Cover illustration by Toby Morrison
Maps © Cadogan Guides, drawn by Thames Cartographic Ltd
Macintosh: Jacqueline Lewin and Typography 5

Editing: Guy Dimond
Managing: Vicki Ingle
Editorial Assistant: Emma Johnson
Proofreading: Stewart Wild

Series Editors: Rachel Fielding and Vicki Ingle

ISBN 0–947754–80–6

A catalogue record for this book is available from the British Library
Library of Congress Cataloging-in-Publication-Data available

Printed and bound by Scotprint Ltd,
Musselburgh, Scotland.

About the Author

Dana Facaros is a professional travel writer. Over the past ten years she has lived in several countries, concentrating on the Mediterranean area. In collaboration with her husband Michael Pauls she has written more than a dozen Cadogan Guides on, amongst others, Italy, Spain, France and Turkey. Her roots, however, are in the Greek Islands; her father comes from Ikaria. Dana's guide to all the Greek Islands, now in its fifth edition, was first published in 1979.

About the Contributors

Guy Dimond is a freelance travel writer and editor. He has visited most of the islands featured in this guide, and is editor of the series of Cadogan Guides to the Greek Islands. Freelance journalist and travel writer **Stephanie Ferguson** has travelled extensively throughout Greece and hopped round more than 40 islands. She fell under the spell of the country after a holiday in the Peloponnese in 1976, and since then has contributed to two guide books and has written features on Greece for a number of UK national publications. **Sarah Hey**, former editor of the English-language newspaper the *Corfu News*, has delivered yachts between the Ionian Islands and Mainland Greece and is currently feature-writer on the *Yorkshire Evening Post*.

Author's Acknowledgements

I would like to thank the many members of the National Tourist Organization of Greece for their kind assistance in writing this guide, and the following people without whose moral, physical and financial assistance it would not have been possible: my parents and my grandmother, Mrs Despina Facaros, Joseph Coniaris, Sotiros S. Kouvaras of Ithaki, Filia and Kosta Pattakos, Carolyn Steiner and Julie Wegner. A special thanks goes to my better half, Michael, who added the bull; to my aunt, and Ikariote informant, Toula Cavaligos; and to Guy, Stephanie and Sarah for their invaluable amendments and additions.

Contents

Travel   1–20

Practical A–Z   21–44

Modern History, Art and Architecture 45–56

Topics 57–66

Athens and Piraeus 67–91

The Islands   92–196

Maps

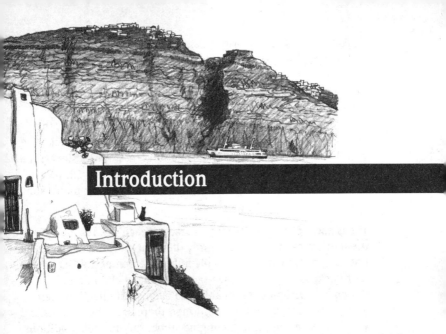

Introduction

What weighs the bosom of Abraham and the immaterial spectres of Christian paradise against this Greek eternity made of water, rock and cooling winds?

Kazantzakis

There's nothing like the Greek islands to make the rest of the world seem blurred, hesitant and grey. Their frontiers are clearly defined by a sea that varies from emerald and turquoise to indigo blue, with none of the sloppiness of a changing tide; the clear sky and dry air cut their mountainous contours into sharp outline; the whiteness and simplicity of their architecture is both abstract and organic. Even the smells, be they fragrant (lemon blossoms, incense, wild thyme, grilling fish) or whiffy (donkey flops, caique diesel engines, plastic melted cheese sandwiches) are pure and unforgettable. In such an environment, the islanders themselves have developed strong, open characters; they have bright eyes and are quick to laugh or cry or scream in fury, or inquire into the most intimate details of your personal life and offer unsolicited lectures on politics, how to brush your teeth properly or find a good husband.

Since the 1970s this clarity has been a magnet to tourists from the blurred, hesitant, grey world beyond. After shipping, tourism is Greece's most important source of income, to the extent that swallows from the north have become a regular fixture in the seasonal calendar: first comes Lent and Greek Easter, then the tourists, followed by the grape harvest, and in December, the olives. From June to September, ferries and flights are packed with holidaymakers, both Greek and foreign. Popular sites and beaches are crowded by day, and often by night as well, by visitors unable to find a room—they've been booked for months in advance.

Yet as each island has its own character, each has responded to the tourism cash cow in a slightly different way. On some, resort hotels have toadstooled up willy-nilly in search of the fast package-tour buck; some islands have sacrificed many charming old customs, environmental health, and even sanity itself in their desire to please all comers. And then there are other islands and villages, more self-reliant, clinging stubbornly to their traditions and doing all they can to keep outside interests from exploiting their coasts. Others, including some of the most visited islands, are enjoying a renaissance of traditional arts and customs, often led by the young who are pained to see their centuries-old heritage eroding into Euro-blandness.

If this book has any real purpose, it's to help you find the island of your dreams, whether you want all the mod-cons of home, sports facilities and disco dancing until dawn, or want to visit the ancient sites, study Byzantine frescoes and hone up on your Greek, or perhaps just escape to a secluded shore, where there's the luxury of doing nothing at all. Or perhaps you want a bit of each. For, in spite of all the rush to join the 20th century, the Greek islands have retained the enchantment that inspired Homer and Byron—the wine-dark sea, the scent of jasmine at twilight and nights alive with shooting stars. The ancient Greeks dedicated the islands to the gods, and they have yet to surrender them entirely to us mortals. They have kept something pure and true and alive. Or as the poet Palamas wrote, 'Here reigns nakedness. Here shadow is a dream.'

The Cyclades

Say Greek island, and many people picture one of the Cyclades: barren rock rising from a crystal sea, little villages with asymmetrical white houses and labyrinthine streets fit only for dwarfs, a pocket-sized church squeezed in at every corner. As the Cyclades are close together, one can visit a variety of the islands without losing much of the holiday in transit; in the summer there are daily communications between them. Within the Cyclades (the 'circling' islands, around sacred Delos) you'll find such constant favourites as Mykonos, Santorini and Paros, but also Heraklia and Anafi, among the least spoiled islands in Greece.

Choosing Your Island

The 3000 islands of Greece (of which a mere 170 or so are inhabited) are divided into seven major groupings: the Cyclades in the Aegean, surrounding the holy island of Delos; the Dodecanese, lying off the southwest coast of Asia Minor; the Northeastern Aegean islands, stretching from Thassos to Ikaria; the Ionian islands, sprinkled between Greece and Italy; the Saronic islands, in the Saronic Gulf; the Sporades, spread off the coast of Thessaly and Evia; and Crete, the largest island in Greece. An overall picture of the Cyclades may help you pinpoint likely destinations. You may want to head for a lively cosmopolitan place, followed by a few days of absolute peace and quiet (say, Mykonos and then Tinos). Below are thumbnail sketches, starting with the liveliest, trendiest and most touristy.

Mykonos still manages to retain an air of class, despite the hordes that it attracts. This is as jet-setty as you can get. Great beaches and the best nightlife, and a short boat ride from the holy Delos, now an outdoor archaeological museum. In Ios you'll feel old at 25; the emphasis here is definitely on pubbing and beachlife. The lovely islands of **Paros** and **Naxos** have lost much of their original character under the strain of mass package tourism, but there's plenty going on to keep you amused: Paros has paradoxically retained its island charm, despite being one of the top destinations for backpackers of all ages. Volcanic **Santorini** has a lot to live up to as almost everyone's favourite, and is the number one spot for backpackers from both hemispheres, visiting cruise boats and practically every first-timer to Greece. If you tire of the breathtaking views and chi-chi bars in Fira, the main town, you can escape to smaller villages.

Arguably the best type of island holiday can be found on islands where there are enough tourists to ensure more than basic facilities—places with a choice of decent tavernas, a bar or two for an evening drink, and most of all, a place to sit out and watch life idle by. **Serifos**, **Sifnos** and **Syros** fall happily into this category; all have a mixture of rugged island scenery, typical villages, good restaurants and swimming. There are special gems like little **Tinos**, mecca for pilgrims and popular with Greeks and families. Stand-offish **Andros** is still largely tourist free (Batsi excepted). The islands of **Kea** (Tsia) and **Kythnos**, while close to Athens, are seldom visited except by passing yachtsmen and Greek tourists.

There remain a few islands that come under the heading of 'almost away from it all'—not quite your desert island in that they have several places to stay, eat and explore, but beyond that not a lot to do after a couple of days, unless you are resourceful—**Folegandros**, **Milos**, and **Amorgos**.

If, however, you genuinely want to get away from it all and don't mind eating in the same little taverna every night, then head for the cluster of islands east and south of Naxos: **Koufonissia**, **Keros**, **Skhinoussa** and **Iraklia**. On any of these islands you can treat yourself to some serious introspection and brush up on your modern Greek with the locals.

When to Go

When choosing your island(s), the time of the year is of paramount importance, and from mid-July to 20 August you can expect nothing but frustration on the more popular islands, or the smaller ones with a limited number of beds. Don't assume that the more isolated the island the cheaper the accommodation, as supply and demand dictate the prices. You could well pay more for a room in Folegandros, for example, than on Paros, where rooms are far more plentiful. Out of season you can pick and choose, and places with a high percentage of Greek tourists (Kythnos, Kea) who tend to go for a 6-week burst in the height of summer, are a bargain.

The climate, more than anywhere else in Greece, is influenced by the winds. Winter is plagued by the *voreas,* the north wind that turns ship schedules into a fictional romance. After March the sirocco blows from the south, warming islands still green from the winter rains. By July many of the Cyclades look brown and parched, except where there are sources of underground water. From July to September the notorious *meltemi* from the Russian steppes huffs and puffs like the big bad wolf, quadrupling sales of dramamine in the ports. If you're really a land-lubber you can fly: Paros, Mykonos, Milos, Santorini, Naxos and Syros have airports.

Water continues to be a problem on some islands, and it may be turned off for part of the day. However, since these islands are so popular with visitors (and thus important to the national economy) efforts have been made to ensure that they and their new hotels have ample water supplies, even in August. Before the advent of tourism, the population of the Cyclades dropped to an all time low; it was simply too hard to make a living from the dry, rocky soil. Even now, the winter months can be lonely as many islanders retreat to flats in Athens.

History

Archaeological evidence suggests that the Cyclades have been inhabited since at least 6000 BC, the first settlers arriving from what is now Karia in Asia Minor and speaking a non-Greek language. At the beginning of the Bronze Age (3000–2000 BC) the islanders developed a culture known as Early Cycladic, which if nothing else had a staggeringly modern sense of design, at least in their elegant, almost abstract marble figurines.

In myth, King Minos of Crete conquered the Aegean Islands in order to rid himself of his overly-just brother Rhadamanthys, whom he sent to administer the new Cretan colonies. This corresponds to the Minoan influence that marks the prosperous Middle Cycladic period, when artists adopted a more natural style. The Late Cycladic period coincides with the fall of Crete and the rise of the Mycenaeans. When the Mycenaeans in turn fell to the uncouth Dorians, the islands dropped out of history for hundreds of years. The luckier islands fell under the sway of the Ionians and at the end of the 8th century BC, were part of the Ionian cultural rebirth called the Archaic period.

The rise of the Persians forced the Ionians to flee westwards to Attica, leaving the islands in Persian hands; several islands sided with the Persians at Marathon and Salamis, and were subsequently punished by Athens. To prevent future break-aways, Athens obliged the islands to enter into the new maritime league at Delos in 478 BC, replacing an older Ionian council, or Amphictyony. But what began as a league of allies gradually turned into vassals paying tribute to the Athenians, whose fleet was the only one capable of protecting the islands from the Persian menace. Cycladic resentment often flared into open revolt, and the Athenians had to work ever harder to extort the islands' annual contribution of money and ships.

During the Peloponnesian War the islands tended to side with the front-runner at any given time, and many jumped at the chance to support Sparta against their Athenian oppressors. But when Athens recovered from the war in 378 BC, it was only to form a second Delian league, again subjugating the Cyclades. Most of the islands turned to Philip of Macedon as a saviour from the Athenian bullies, only to be fought over a generation later by the generals of Alexander the Great. Only the 2nd-century BC Roman conquest brought the Cyclades peace, except for the islands given to Rhodes, a less kindly ruler than distant Rome. The fall of Rome spelt centuries of hardship; although the Cyclades were officially part of the Byzantine Empire, Constantinople could not protect them from marauders prowling the high seas, and the islanders were left to fend for themselves, building villages in the most inaccessible places possible.

When Constantinople fell in 1204, the Frankish conquerors allotted the Aegean to the Venetians, and the Archipelago, as the Venetians called it, became a free for all between grasping young noblemen and pirates (often one and the same). The Cyclades became the special territory of Marco Sanudo, nephew of the leader of the Fourth Crusade, Doge Enrico Dandolo. Marco Sanudo declared himself Duke of Naxos and ruled that island and Paros, and gave his faithful thugs the smaller islands as fiefs. The Sanudos gave way to the Crispi dynasty in 1383, but threatened by pirates and the growing Ottoman Empire, Venice herself stepped in to police the Cyclades at the end of the 15th century. There was little even Venice could do against the fierce renegade admiral Khair-ed-din-Barbarossa, who systematically decimated the islands. By the mid-16th century they were under Turkish domination, ruled by a puppet Duke of Naxos.

Venetian priests had converted many of the Greeks on the Cyclades to Catholicism, in particular on Syros, Tinos, Santorini and Naxos, and despite the Ottoman occupation both Orthodox and Catholic monasteries thrived. Turkish rule in the Archipelago was harsh only in economic terms and most of the islands were spared the cruelties inflicted on Crete. From 1771–74, one of the more outlandish episodes in Greek history brought a brief interlude from the Ottomans: Russia and Turkey were at each other's throats over Poland, so Catherine the Great decided to open a second front in the war by capitalizing on Greek discontent. Her fleet in the Aegean led an insurrection against the Sultan and occupied some of the Cyclades. By the time the Russians gave it up and went home, they had made themselves unpopular with all concerned.

When the Greek War of Independence broke out, the Cyclades offered naval support and provided a safe harbour for refugees; the islands with Catholic populations were brought under the protection of the French and remained neutral in the conflict. Nevertheless, the Cyclades were soon incorporated in the new Greek state, and Syros became the country's leading port until Piraeus took over with the advent of the steamship. Today Syros' capital, Ermoupolis, is still the largest town and administrative centre of the Cyclades.

By Air

Charter Flights

Charter flights have fixed outward and return dates, with the return date in less than one month. They are sold either with a package holiday or through 'consolidators' (travel agents) as a flight only. Charter flights to Athens and occasionally to the islands are frequent in the summer from European and North American capitals. Charters direct to Athens are available from Birmingham, Glasgow, Luton, Newcastle and Manchester. In London many travel agents offer cheap last-minute flights, and 'bucket shops' have made spare charter tickets their speciality (a return to Athens for £125 is possible). Look through publications such as *Time Out*, the *Evening Standard* or the Sunday papers for cheap deals. **Americans and Canadians** with more time than money may well find their cheapest way of getting to Greece is to take a trans-Atlantic economy flight to London and from there to buy a last-minute ticket to Greece. This may be difficult in July or August, however. Trans-Atlantic bargains can still be found, but bear in mind that the peak season runs from late May to mid-September. Many charters go direct to the Cyclades—Paros, Mykonos, and Santorini—as well as to Athens and Thessaloniki, but scheduled flights rarely go from London directly to the islands.

There are several rules about charters to Greece. One is that a charter ticket is valid for a minimum of two nights and a maximum of four weeks. Visitors to Greece using a charter flight may visit Turkey or any other neighbouring country for the day, but must not stay overnight; the Turkish officials usually stamp your passport showing the dates of entry and exit. Even if you intend to stay longer than four weeks or travel to other countries, using just half a charter ticket may still work out less than a scheduled flight, so shop around.

When you buy a **flight-only charter ticket**, you will be issued with an accommodation voucher, which entitles you to stay at a (sometimes fictitious) hotel. This strange formality is a left-over from the days when charter tickets were only sold with accommodation included. It's unlikely the Greek customs officials will ask to see this voucher, but keep it handy until you're out of the airport just in case. Student or youth charters are exempt from the voucher system and are allowed to be sold as one-way tickets. Travelling this way you can stay for over a month as long as you are under 26 or a full-time, card-carrying student under 32.

Basic travel insurance is sometimes sold with charter tickets to Greece by travel agents. It is not compulsory to buy this, no matter what they might tell you. If they insist, look elsewhere.

Scheduled Flights

Scheduled flights offer greater flexibility than charter flights, but generally cost more. There are flights direct to Athens daily from London and New York. KLM flies via Amsterdam from Toronto, Montréal, Calgary and Halifax. While the basic carriers from the United States are Olympic Airways, TWA and Delta (via Frankfurt), from London it's Olympic Airways, British Airways or Virgin Atlantic. London offers the greatest variety of flights and the prices are often competitive close to the departure time if you book through a consolidator (travel agent) instead of directly with the airline. It's advisable to shop around and see which offers the best deal. Superpex flights offer substantially reduced fares, with flights from London to Athens ranging from £180 low season to £280 high season. They must, however, be paid for on the spot and are not refundable or flexible. American economy fares range from around $900 New York–Athens in low season to $1300 high season.

Olympic Airways	© (071) 409 3400/493 3965 (London);
	© (212) 838 3600 (New York);
	© (01) 926 7251 (Athens).
British Airways	© (081) 897 4000 (London).
Virgin Atlantic	© (0293) 747747; info, (0293) 511581 (London).
Delta	© (800) 241 4141/(800) 221 1212 (New York).
Aer Lingus	© (0232) 245151 (Dublin).
KLM	© (514) 933 1314 (Montréal).
TWA	© (800) 892 4141 (New York).

Bona-fide students under 26 are sometimes eligible for discounts, especially with Olympic Airways who currently offer 25% discount to ISIC card holders on all connecting flights from Athens to the islands, even when booked from London; **Trailfinders**, 42–50 Earls Court Road, W8 6EJ, © (071) 937 5400, **STA Travel**, 86 Old Brompton Road, London SW7 or 117 Euston Road, WC1, © (071) 937 9962; and **Campus Travel**, 52 Grosvenor Gardens, SW1, © (071) 730 8111 can get you some of the best current deals. Returning from Greece, it is advisable to confirm your return flight a few days prior to departure.

Flights from Athens to the Islands

Connecting flights from Athens to the islands are available on **Olympic Airways**, 11 Conduit Street, London W1R 0LP, ℭ (071) 493 3965. Americans who do not have an Olympic Airways office in their town can call a toll-free no., ℭ (800) 223 1226, for information. At the time of writing, an additional flat fare of £50 will allow you to connect a flight landing at Athens to Kefalonia, Zakynthos, Milos, Syros, Paros, Mykonos, Naxos, Thira, Kastellirozo, Leros, Kos, Rhodes, Karpathos and a handful of other Greek island airports, connections permitting. To be assured of a seat, especially in the summer, you should book your ticket as far in advance as possible. Infants up to 2 years old receive a 90% discount, and children of 2–12 years a 50% discount. Students only receive a 25% discount if the flight is a connecting one.

Olympic Airways (Athens)

6 Othonos: ℭ 929 2555 (International), 929 2444 (Domestic).
Also 96 Leoforos Syngrou; ℭ 929 2333.

East Airport   ℭ 969 9317.
West Airport   ℭ 989 2111.

Getting to and from Ellinikon Airport, Athens

Ellinikon Airport is divided into two: East (international airlines) and West (Olympic Airlines, both international and domestic flights). Double decker blue-and-yellow express buses leave for either terminal (but not both, so be sure you are getting on the right one) from Amalias Avenue, at the top of Syntagma Square, every 20 minutes between 6am and 9pm, every ½-hour between 9pm and 2am, and every hour from 2am to 6am. The fare is 160 dr. from 6am to midnight, 270 dr. otherwise. At the time of writing, this bus stop was being dug up for the new metro station, and the buses temporarily suspended. The alternative, until these buses are reinstated, is the public bus no. 133 from Othonos St, Syntagma Square (5.40am–midnight, every 15 minutes), or no. 122 from Vass. Olgas (5.30am–11.30pm, every 15 minutes); both go to the West terminal only. The fare is 75 dr. The East terminal may be reached by public bus no. 121 from Vass. Olgas Avenue (6.50am–10.50pm, every 40 minutes; 75 dr.). From Piraeus, express bus no. 19 goes to both the East and West terminals (160 dr.).

The metro is an important means of getting across Athens, especially from Piraeus. It runs to Kifissia stopping at Thissio, Monastiraki, Omonia and Plateia Viktorias. Trolley buses run throughout the city centre from the Larissis station to Omonia and Syntagma and out to Koukaki, or linking Syntagma and Omonia with Patission and the National Archaeological Museum.

Taxis from Athens Airport

A taxi between Athens and the airport should cost you about 1100 dr. (more at night). Piraeus is particularly prone to cowboys preying on unsuspecting tourists heading from and to the ferries. Travellers should make sure they take proper yellow taxis with meters and official licence numbers. The tricksters hassle you (especially at Piraeus, less so at the airport) and charge 2–3,000 dr. for the journey; it should be around half that. If there's no meter, watch out. Prices are only double from 1-6am and on holidays such as Easter. You will have to pay surcharges on luggage, 50 dr. a piece, plus a 100 dr. supplement for an airport or Piraeus run.

In Athens cabs are difficult to find during the rush hour, when the drivers are knocking off for lunch, and when everyone is going back to work in the evenings. Hailing a cab is not for the faint-hearted. You almost have to hurl yourself in front of it and yell out your destination. Sharing is common and you all pay the full fare. Just check the meter reading when you get in so you don't get overcharged. Sharing (at full price) is also common on the islands.

By Train

There are no longer any direct trains from London to Athens, partly because of the civil war in former Yugoslavia. It is still possible to get to Athens by train, changing en route, if you really want to travel that way; it takes over three days. Call British Rail International in London ℗ (071) 834 2345. The route goes through Italy, either to Ancona or further south to Bari or Brindisi, and involves taking the ferry over to Corfu and Patras; these are now quite busy routes. British people under the age of 26 can travel by **InterRail** youth passes, which currently cost £249 for a month's rail travel in Europe—which gets you there and back via most places in Europe the train goes (excluding the UK, channel ferries and Spain). InterRail passes are also available to British residents over 26 for either 15 days or a month. Americans and Canadians can buy 2-month **Eurail** and **Youth Eurail** passes before leaving home. However, the Eurail Pass is no bargain if you're only going to Greece, which has a limited rail service. For people over 60, the **Rail Europ** senior card saves up to 30% on rail fares in Greece and several other European countries, in Germany, and on most sea crossings. It costs £5 and can be purchased from British Rail by holders of a British Rail card.

The sad truth is that since the war in Yugoslavia, travelling by train is no longer an inexpensive, pleasant or easy method of getting to Greece; it's now cheaper, and a lot more comfortable, to fly. The train does have its uses though if you want to stop off and see some of the rest of Europe en route.

For further information telephone the OSE (Hellenic Railways Organization): 522 2491 or 362 4402/6. Recorded timetables can be obtained by dialling 145 (for Greece) or 147 (for the rest of Europe).

By Bus

London to Athens

Taking a bus from London to Athens is always a possible alternative for those who are averse to air or train travel. It isn't usually much cheaper than a standby flight. But with 2½ days (or more) on the road and Adriatic ferry, adventures are practically included in the ticket price. **Eurolines**, 52 Grosvenor Gardens, Victoria, London SW1 0AU, © (071) 730 8235 offer 3-day journeys from London to Athens whch cost around £218 return if you're over 26; there's a £12 saving if you're under 26. **Olympic Bus Ltd**, 70 Brunswick Centre, London WC1 1AE, © (071) 837 9141 offer 2½-day journeys from London to Athens via Brussels and Italy for a mere £50 one-way, or £100 return, departing London on Friday evenings. In Greece, you'll find agencies selling bus tickets on the most obscure islands, as well as in Athens; Filellinon St near Syntagma Square is Athens' budget travellers' boulevard, so check there for other possibilities.

Domestic Bus Services

The domestic bus service in Greece is efficient and regular, if not always a bargain. Each bus is decorated at the whim of its drivers, with pin-ups, saints, wallpaper, tinsel, tassels, and plastic hands which wave violently when the bus falls into a pothole. Local buses can be great fun; long-distance journeys are more testing.

During the summer it is advisable to reserve seats in advance on the long-distance buses. Tickets for these journeys must normally be bought before one boards the bus. There are never enough buses on the islands in the summer nor is it customary to queue. However, you will not be left behind if it is humanly possible for you to squeeze on. If you can wake up in time, you will find that buses are rarely crowded early in the morning.

Within the Athens area the bus fare is 75 dr. You must buy a ticket or book of ten tickets in advance from a kiosk or newsagent, then stamp one to validate it on boarding the bus—if you can fight your way to the machine, that is. If you don't then get caught, you're liable for a fine 20 times the prevailing fare. The trolley buses operate in the same way as normal buses, but on fixed routes.

The most common sea route to Greece is from Italy, with daily ferry services from Ancona, Bari, Brindisi, Otranto and Venice. The most popular of these is the daily service from Brindisi, which leaves at 10pm (connecting with the train from Rome) and arrives in Corfu the next morning. Passengers are allowed a free infinite stopover in Corfu if that island is not their ultimate destination, before continuing to Igoumenitsa or Patras, but make sure it is noted on your ticket. If you plan to sail in the summer, it's advisable to make reservations in advance, especially if you bring a car (most travel agents can do this for you). Students and young people can get a discount of up to 20%. Discounts of up to 20% are also offered when buying a return ticket. The quality of service among the different lines varies, of course; some ships are spanking clean and are plushly furnished— one at least even has a laser disco—while others have been in service so long that they creak. However, the sullen demeanour of the crews seems to be uniform, unless you try a few words of Greek.

Boats to the Islands

The daily newspaper *Naftemboriki* lists all the activities of the port at Piraeus and publishes weekly ship schedules. The National Tourist Office also publishes a monthly list of ship departures, both abroad and to the islands.

A little travelling through the islands will soon show you that each boat is an individual. The many new ones are clean and comfortable and often air-conditioned. The older boats may lack some modern refinements but nevertheless they can be pleasant if you remain out on deck. The drinking water is never very good on the boats, but all sell beer, Coca Cola and lemon or orange soda. Biscuits and cigarettes complete the fare on the smaller boats, while the larger ones offer sandwiches, cheese pies or even full meals. Snacks tend to be pricier and of inferior quality to what you'll find on shore. If you're lucky, you'll have souvlaki sellers and pedlars offering nuts and *koulouria* (ringed biscuits) as the boat moves from island to island. The smallest boats which ferry you along the coast from beach to beach are called caiques, and usually have no facilities at all.

All the boats are privately owned and although the Greek government controls the prices some will be relatively more expensive, depending on the facilities offered, speed, etc. In most cases children under the age of 4 travel free, and between 4 and 10 for half-fare. Over 10 they are charged the full fare. In the summer it is wise to buy tickets in advance, to guarantee a place but you can always buy the ticket on board if you haven't had the time. Refunds are rarely given unless the boat itself never arrives, perhaps stuck in Piraeus for tax delinquencies. Boats will arrive late or divert their course for innumerable reasons, so if you have to catch a flight home allow for the eccentricities of the system and leave a day early to be safe.

When purchasing a ticket, either in Piraeus or on the islands, it's always best to do so from your ship's central agency. Other agencies may tell you that the boat is full, when in truth they've merely sold all the tickets allotted them by the central agency. On many islands, agents moonlight as bartenders or grocers and may only have a handwritten sign next to the door advertising their ship's departures.

Because Piraeus is so busy there's a new trend to use smaller mainland ports, especially Rafina and Lavrion. Neither of these is far from Athens, and bus connections are frequent; the bus stop is at Mavromateion. They are a bit of a bother for most tourists, though, which means that islands mainly served by these outlying ports are often quieter, if you take the trouble to go.

Most inter-island ferries have three or four classes: the first class, with an air-conditioned lounge and cabins (and often as expensive as flying); the second class, often with its own lounge as well, but smaller cabins; tourist class, with no cabins; and deck class, which is the norm, and usually gives you access to the typically large, stuffy rooms full of 'airline seats' and the snack bar area. As a rule the Greeks go inside and the tourists stay out—on summer nights in particular this is perhaps the most pleasant alternative if you have a sleeping bag.

You'd do well always to keep your ticket with you on a Greek ship, at least until the crew enacts its 'ticket control', a comedy routine necessitated by the fact that Greeks don't always check tickets when passengers board. Instead, after one or two pleas on the ship's loudspeaker system for passengers without tickets to purchase them forthwith, you suddenly find all the doors on the boat locked or guarded by a bored but obdurate sailor, while bands of officers rove about the boat checking tickets. Invariably mix-ups occur: children are separated from their parents, others have gone to the wc, someone has left a ticket with someone on the other side of the immovable sailor, crowds pile up at the doors, and stowaways are marched to the purser's office. In the worst cases, this goes on for an hour; on smaller ships it's usually over in 15 minutes.

Prices, though no longer cheap, are still fairly reasonable for passengers, rather dear for cars.

The following is a list of some of the more popular scheduled connections from Athens (Piraeus). Duration of each boat trip and official guidelines for prices (supplied by the Greek tourist authorities in February 94) are given in drachmas but are subject to change without notice, and will vary between boats.

Piraeus to	2nd Class (dr.)	Tourist Class (dr.)	3rd Class (dr.)	Duration (hours)
Anafi	7366	6787	4389	18
Folegandros	6006	4503	3594	12
Ios	5483	4255	3595	10
Kythnos	3297	2553	2097	4
Limnos	7007	n/a	4447	18
Milos	4360	3526	n/a	8
Mykonos	n/a	3420	2897	6
Naxos	n/a	3482	2994	7
Paros	3852	n/a	2664	6
Santorini (Thira)	5483	4255	3595	10
Serifos	3670	2859	2313	5
Sifnos	3976	3177	2760	6
Sikinos	7027	5483	4155	10
Syros	n/a	2995	2654	4
Tinos	n/a	3293	2897	5

Not included in the above prices are port taxes (350dr. approx) and VAT (currently 8%).

Hydrofoils

'Flying Dolphins' and ILIO hydrofoils run from the mainland to the Cyclades and between the islands, weather permitting. Hydrofoils as a rule travel twice as fast as ships and are twice as expensive (in some cases as much as a plane). In the peak season they are often fully booked, so buy tickets as early as you can. In a choppy sea a trip may leave you saddle-sore, and if the weather is very bad, they don't leave port. All the hydrofoils run throughout the year but are less frequent in winter. Timetables and routes change almost monthly, but some of the more reliable routes include:

Rafina—Andros—Tinos—Mykonos—Paros—Naxos (ILIO Hydrofoils);
Rafina—Kea—Kythnos—Serifos—Sifnos (Flying Dolphins);
Piraeus (Zea)—Kea—Kythnos (ILIO Hydrofoils).

Tourist Excursion Boats

These are generally slick and clean, and have become quite numerous in recent years. They are more expensive than the regular ferries or steamers, but often have schedules that allow visitors to make day excursions to nearby islands (though you can also take them one way), and are convenient, having largely taken the place of the caique operators, many of whom now specialize in excursions to remote beaches instead of island-hopping on request. They may be the only transport available to the most remote islands, but do enquire about scheduled ferries. Friendly yachtsmen may give you a lift—it never hurts to ask.

For the most recent information on Greek sea connections, get a copy of *Greek Travel Pages* by International Publications in Athens, or *Key Travel Guide*, which is updated every week. Travel agents and the Greek National Tourist Offices sometimes have spare copies, and they're easy to find in Greece itself. Better still, the *Thomas Cook Guide to Greek Island Hopping* (£9.99) is excellent for details of ferry services.

By Car

Driving from **London to Athens** (and taking the ferry from Italy to Greece) at a normal pace takes around 3½ days, which is why one sees so few British cars in Greece. Unless you are planning to spend a few weeks covering large distances on land, a car is not really worth the expense and trouble of bringing it to Greece. There are many car hire companies on the mainland and the islands, if you feel a car is necessary; prices are, if anything, higher than the rest of Europe. An **International Driving Permit** is not required by EC citizens carrying an EC driving licence. Other nationals can obtain an International Driving Permit at home, or at one of the Greek Automobile Touring Club offices (ELPA, who charge around £10 for this), by presenting a national driving licence, passport, photograph—and fee of 5000dr. In practice, tourists with bona-fide US, Australian or European driving licences can usually hire a car without fuss. The minimum age for driving is 18 years; 21 to 25 years for hire. If you're taking your own car, **The Motor Insurance Bureau** at 10 Xenofontos St, Athens, ℂ (01) 323 6733, can tell you which Greek insurance company represents your own, or can provide you with additional cover for Greece.

Customs formalities for bringing in a car are very easy and usually take very little time. A Green Card (international third party insurance) is essential and you will get a carnet stamped in your passport. If your vehicle has EC number plates, you are allowed unlimited free use of your car in Greece. Non-EC vehicles have six months of free use in Greece, and after that you need to apply for a 9-month extension. If you leave Greece without your car, you must have it withdrawn from circulation by a customs authority. ELPA has a list of lawyers who can offer free legal advice on motorcars. They also have a 24-hour recording of information useful to foreign motorists, ℂ 174.

Parking in the centre of Athens is forbidden outside designated parking areas. The traffic situation there is so bad that only cars with even number plates can park one day, cars with odd number plates the next. Local radio and newspapers tell drivers if they're on an odd or even day. Some families cheat by owning two cars. Police can unscrew the licence plates of illegally parked cars, and often do.

While driving in the centre of Athens may be a hair-raising experience, most of the rest of Greece (busy towns and rough trails excepted) is easy and pleasant. There are few cars on most roads, even in summer, and all signs have their Latin equivalents. Traffic regulations and signalling comply with standard practice on the European Continent (i.e. driving on the right). Flocks of goats or sheep, old ladies on donkeys, and slow-moving lawnmower jitneys are some of the more interesting 'obstructions'. Crossroads and low visibility in the mountains are probably the greatest hazards. Where there are no right of way signs at a crossroads, give priority to traffic coming from the right, and always beep your horn on blind corners. Take special care when approaching an unguarded railway level crossing. It is also advisable to take a spare container of petrol along with you, as petrol stations are inconsistent in their frequency. There is a speed limit of 50kph (30mph) in inhabited areas: other speed limits are indicated by signposts in kilometres. Horn blowing is prohibited in Athens and other big cities, though you'd never guess it from the cacophony that starts when the red light changes to green. The Greek Automobile Touring Club (ELPA) operates a breakdown service (free if you've brought your AA/RAC membership card with you) within 60km (40 miles) of Athens or Patras: dial 104.

Greek Automobile Touring Club

Athens: 2–4 Messogion St, Tower of Athens, ℂ (01) 779 1615
Patras: Astingos & 127 Korinthou, ℂ (061) 425411/426416

By Motorbike, Moped or Scooter

Safety considerations aside, mopeds, scooters and motorbikes are almost ideal for the islands in the summer. It almost never rains and what could be more pleasant than a gentle thyme-scented breeze freshening your journey over the mountains? Mopeds are both more economical and more practical than cars. They can fit into almost any boat and travel paths where cars fear to tread. Many islands have scooter rentals which are not expensive, and include third party coverage in most cases. To hire mopeds of under 125cc, you usually just have to leave your passport as security. For larger motorbikes of over 125cc, you must also show a valid car driving licence. For the largest motorbikes (over 250cc) you will need to show a full motorbike licence—assuming that you can find a large motorbike for hire. Most of those smart-looking, 'born-to-be-wild' bikes on display outside hire shops belong to the staff and are left there as lures; they are not for hire. Check the mechanical condition of the bike you're hiring; they are often badly maintained and only given a cursory check between customers. It pays to hire early in the day, because the oldest and ropiest machines will be hired out last.

Be warned that moped accidents are one of the most common ways that tourists get injuries in Greece—just look around the beach for evidence of grazed knees, scuffed elbows and legs in plaster, and they're the ones that were lucky. Greece has the second-worst road accident statistics in Europe (after Portugal), and Greek driving skills are not all they should be. So be very, very careful if you're not an experienced motorcyclist. Make sure your travel insurance policy covers moped accidents before you go on holiday—many policies exclude mopeds, or include them under additional cover—and try and avoid damaging the bike too, because the 'insurance' hire places offer is barely more than the legal minimum of third-party, and you'll be expected to pay for any damage more extensive than a puncture. Many British tour operators won't insure you for mopeds at all.

By Bicycle

Cycling has not caught on in Greece, either as a sport or as a means of transport, though you can usually hire a cheap (and badly-maintained) mountain bike in most major resorts. If you can put up with an ill-fitting bike with gears that crash and brakes that squeal, they can be a pleasant enough way to get around on short journeys. If you're a keen cyclist, it's a much better idea to take your own bike with you. Check with your airline before flying; the usual stipulations apply, i.e. cover your bike with a cardboard 'bike box' (free from your local bike shop), turn the handlebars, take the pedals out (to prevent them from damaging other luggage), and let the tyre pressures down to half the usual pressure (to prevent the inner tubes exploding at altitude). There is seldom any charge for carrying a bike on a plane, though you may be surcharged if the bike and your other luggage exceed the usual weight limit (most of the time bemused airline staff turn a blind eye). Trains in Greece carry bicycles for a small fee, and Greek boats generally take them along, for nothing. On the islands you will find fresh water, places to camp, and a warm and surprised welcome in the villages. Make sure both you and your bike have comprehensive accident insurance before you go.

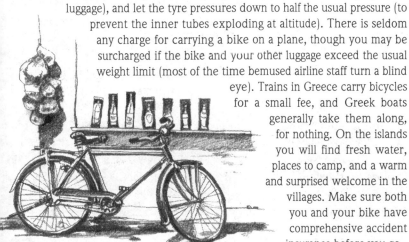

Hitch-hiking

With the rarest of exceptions, hitch-hiking, or 'autostop' as it is known in Greece, is perfectly safe and common practice on the islands and remote villages. However, the lack of cars makes it a not particularly speedy mode of transport. The Greek double standard produces the following percentage chances for hopeful hitch-hikers:

Single woman: 99% of cars will stop. You hardly have to stick out your hand. But be careful. Go for a car with a family or couple, and avoid single male drivers to be on the safe side.

Two women: 75% of cars will find room for you.

Woman and man: 50%; more if the woman is pretty.

Single man: 25% if you are well dressed with little luggage; less otherwise.

Two men: start walking.

The best time for soliciting a ride is when you disembark from a ship. Ask your fellow passengers, or better still write your destination on a piece of paper (in Greek if possible) and pin it to your shirt with a naïve and friendly smile. What you lose in dignity you will generally gain in a lift. Strictly speaking hitching is illegal in Greece (though tolerated), so don't be offended if a truck driver sets you and your conspicuous backpack down just before a police checkpoint.

Specialist Holidays

A list of tour operators including specialist ones is available from the **National Tourist Organization of Greece**, ℰ (071) 734 5997 (London), (212) 421 5777 (New York), (312) 782 1084 (Chicago), (213) 626696 (Los Angeles).

American School of Classical Studies at Athens, 41E 72nd St, New York, NY 10021. Offers archaeological tours organized from the USA.
ℰ (212) 861 0302 (New York)

British Museum Tours, 46 Bloomsbury Street, London, WC1B 3QQ. Offers a ten-day archaeological tour of Santorini and Crete in October, costing from £1290.   ℰ (071) 323 8895 fax 580 8677 (London)

Explore Worldwide, 1 Frederick Street, Aldershot, Hants, GU11 1LQ. Walking holidays.   ℰ (0252) 344161/319448 fax 343170

Filoxenia Tours, Sourdock Hill, Barkisland, Halifax, West Yorks HX4 0AG. Nature and historical holidays in many parts of Greece. They also run OPUS 23, for disabled travellers.   ℰ (0422) 375999

Peregrine Holidays, 40-41 South Parade, Summertown, Oxford, OX2 7JP. Nature and wildlife tours to the islands, plus Crete and the Peloponnese.
ℰ (0865) 511642

Ramblers Holidays, Box 43, Welwyn Garden City, Hertfordshire, AL8 6PQ. Walking holidays with emphasis on archaeology and wildflowers.
ℰ (0707) 331133

Swan Hellenic Ltd, 77 New Oxford Street, London, WC1A 1PP. The cruise ship 'Orpheus' is the best choice for culture seekers; it sails to the ancient sites of the Mediterranean, including the Greek Islands. 14-day cruises cost around £1500 to £2000, but that includes meals, excursions, port taxes and even tips.   ℰ (071) 831 1515 (London)
ℰ (617) 266 7465 (Boston, MA)

Waymark Holidays, 44 Windsor Road, Slough, SL1 2EJ. Walking holidays.
ℰ (0753) 516477

Customs and Immigration

The formalities for foreign tourists entering Greece are very simple. American, Australian and Canadian citizens can stay for up to 3 months in Greece simply on presentation of a valid passport. However, unless you are entering with a car, immigration officials no longer stamp EC passports. South Africans are permitted 2 months.

If you want to extend your stay in Greece, you must report to the police 10 days before your visa runs out. (If you are staying in Athens, register at the **Athens Alien Dept**, 173 Alexandras Ave, 115 22 Athens, © (01) 646 8103). Take your passport, four photographs, and bank exchange receipts. The rules vary from province to province, but you will most likely receive a slip of paper authorizing you to stay for a period of up to 6 months; this will cost you 11,000 dr. This has to be renewed at the end of every 6 successive months that you remain in Greece.

If you are about to visit Turkish-occupied North Cyprus, make sure the Turkish authorities stamp a removeable piece of paper in your passport; visitors to North Cyprus since the Turkish occupation are not allowed re-entry to Greece.

Yachting

One of the great thrills of sailing the Greek waters is the variety of places to visit in a relatively short time, with the bonus that nowhere in Greece is far from safe shelter or harbours with good facilities for yachtsmen. There is little shallow water, except close to the shoreline, few currents and no tides or fog. The 100,000 miles of coastline, and a collection of islands and islets numbering three thousand, provide a virtually inexhaustible supply of secluded coves and empty beaches, even at the height of the tourist season. Equally, there are berthing facilities in the most popular of international hotspots— it's all there beneath the blue skies and bright sunshine. The Greek National Tourist Organization has

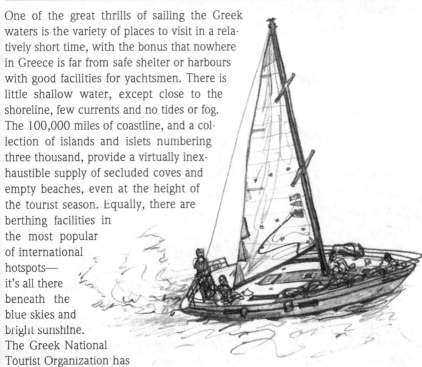

initiated a programme of rapid expansion in the face of mounting competition from Turkey and Spain; facilities are being improved and new marinas are being constructed throughout the country.

Greek weather guarantees near-perfect sailing conditions, the only real problem being the strong winds in parts of the country at certain times of the year, notably April to October, when most yachtsmen are at sea.

The Ionian Sea and the west coast of the Peloponnese are affected by the *maistros*, a light-to-moderate northwest wind which presents itself in the afternoon only. Less frequently there are westerly winds, from moderate to strong, to the west and south of the Peloponnese. To the south of Attica, and east of the Peloponnese, the sea is to a great extent sheltered by land masses and it is not until summer that the menacing *meltemi* blows. The Aegean Sea is affected by a northwest wind in the south, and a northeasterly in the north, and when the *meltemi* blows in August and September, it can reach force eight, testing all your skills at the helm. The Turkish coast has light, variable breezes which are rudely interrupted by the forceful *meltemi*.

This chart shows average wind speeds (in knots) during the months April to October.

Area	Apr	May	Jun	Jul	Aug	Sep	Oct
N.E. Aegean	NE	NE	NE	NE	NE	NE	NE
(Limnos)	10.2	8.2	8.2	10.2	10.2	10.2	11.4
Thrakiko	NE	NE	NE	NE	NE	NE	NE
(Thassos)	1.4	1.4	1.4	1.4	1.4	1.6	2.3
Kos–Rhodes	WNW	WNW	NW	NW	NW	NW	WNW
(Kos)	13.6	13.0	13.0	13.6	13.6	13.0	11.4
S.W. Aegean	N	SW	N	N	N	N	N
(Milos)	9.0	6.6	6.6	8.6	8.6	8.6	9.8
W. Cretan	SW	NNW	NWN	NNW	N	N	N
(Chania)	5.0	4.4	4.4	4.4	4.1	4.1	3.8
E. Cretan	NW	NW	NW	NW	NW	NW	NW
(Herakleon)	6.6	4.4	6.2	8.2	7.4	6.6	5.8
E. Cretan	NW	NW	NW	NW	NW	NW	NW
(Sitia)	6.6	5.0	7.0	8.6	8.2	6.6	5.0
Kythera	NE	W	W	NE	NE	NE	NE

(Kythera)	9.8	8.2	7.8	7.4	8.2	9.0	10.6
Samos Sea	NW	NW	NW	NW	NW	NW	NW
(Samos)	9.4	7.8	9.4	11.0	10.2	8.6	7.0
W. Karpathion	W	W	W	W	W	W	W
(Karpathos)	6.6	6.2	8.6	10.6	9.4	8.2	6.2
N. Ionian	SE	WSE	W	NW/W	NW	SE	SE
(Corfu)	2.9	2.6	2.9	2.6	2.6	2.3	2.6
N. Ionian	NW	NW	NW	NW	NW	NW/N	NW/NE
(Argostoli)	5.8	5.0	5.4	5.8	5.4	4.4	5.0
S. Ionian	N	NE/N	NE	N	NNE	N	NE
(Zakynthos)	9.8	9.4	9.8	10.2	9.8	9.0	10.2
S. Ionian	W	W	W	W	W	W	NE
(Methoni)	11.8	11.0	11.4	11.8	11.0	10.2	9.8

If you wish to skipper a yacht anywhere within the Greek seas, you must consult the *Compile Index Chart of Greek Seas*, otherwise known as *XEE*, published by the Hellenic Navy Hydrographic Service. Basically it is a map of Greece divided into red squares, each with an index number, from which you can select the appropriate charts and order them accordingly (cost approx. 1500 dr.). For non-Greeks, 2500 dr. will buy you what is known as *XEE 64*, a booklet of abbreviations explaining the signs on the charts, with texts in English and Greek. You also need one of the *Pilot* series books, which cost 2500 dr. each and cover the following areas in great detail:

Pilot A: South Albania to Kythera; Ionian Sea, Corinthian Gulf and North Peloponnese shores.

Pilot B: Southeastern Greek shores; Crete, Eastern Peloponnese, Saronic Gulf and Cyclades.

Pilot C: Northeastern Greek shores; Evoikos, Pagassitikos, Sporades, Thermaikos, Chalkidiki.

Pilot D: North and Eastern Aegean shores; Eastern Macedonia, Thrace, Limnos, Lesbos, Chios, Samos, the Dodecanese and Asia Minor.

These describe geographical data, possible dangers, and the present state of transportation and communication. All ports and marinas are mentioned, including where to obtain fresh water and fuel, and there are descriptions of visible inland features. The Hydrographic Service constantly updates the books and sends additional booklets to authorized sellers and to all port authorities, where you may consult them. The nautical charts are updated using the latest most sophisticated methods, and follow standardized dimensions. They are on a 1:100,000 scale for bigger areas and 1:750,000 for ports. Heights and depths are given in metres with functional conversion tables for feet and fathoms.

Further information is provided in booklets called *Notes to Mariners*, published monthly and available for consultation at port authorities. These give information on any alterations to naval charts you have purchased for your voyage. Besides all this there is the Navtex service. A special department of the Hydrographic Service keeps you informed about the weather or any special warnings for the day, through telex, or Navtex. The text is in Greek and English, and there are four retransmission coastal stations covering the Greek seas. Weather forecasts for yachtsmen are broadcast at intervals throughout the day on VHF Channel 16 (in Greek and English); security warnings are also broadcast on this channel, e.g. dangerous wrecks, lights not in operation, etc.

Bunkering Ports and Supply Stations

These are some of the ports where fuelling facilities and provisions may be obtained:

Adamas (Milos)*, Aegina, Ag. Nikolaos (Kea), Ag. Nikolaos (Crete)*, Chios*, Ermoupolis (Syros)*, Gythion*, Chania (Crete)*, Fira (Santorini), Kamares (Sifnos), Kapsali (Kythera), Kastro (Andros), Katapola (Amorgos), Kimi (Evia), Monemvasia, Mykonos*, Naxos, Parikia (Paros), Skala (Patmos)*, Zea Marina.

* indicates official ports of entry and exit, where there are port, customs and health authorities, as well as immigration and currency control services.

Main Port Authorities

Piraeus	✆ (01) 451 1311
Herakleon	✆ (081) 244912
Chios	✆ (0271) 23097

Yachts entering Greek waters must fly the code flag 'Q' until cleared by entry port authorities. Upon arrival the **port authority** (*Limenarkion*) issues all yachts with a transit log, which entitles the yacht and crew to unlimited travel in Greek waters. It also allows crew members to buy fuel, alcohol and cigarettes duty free. It must be kept on board and produced when required, and returned to the customs authorities on leaving Greece at one of the exit ports. Permission is normally given for a stay of 6 months, but this can be extended. Small motor, sail or rowing boats do not require a 'carnet de passage', and are allowed into Greece duty free for 4 months. They are entered in your passport and deleted on exit. For more information, apply to the **Greek National Tourist Organization**, 4 Conduit Street, London, W1R 0DJ, ℭ (071) 734 5997, who produce a useful leaflet *Sailing the Greek Seas.*

Anyone taking a yacht by road is strongly advised to obtain boat registration documentation from the **DVLA**, Swansea, SA99 1BX, ℭ (0792) 783355. The **Royal Yachting Association**, R.Y.A. House, Romsey Road, Eastleigh, Hampshire, SO5 4YA, ℭ (0703) 629962, is a useful source of information.

Monthly Mooring Rates (dr.):

In Alimos Marina (Athens)	*summer*	*winter*
Up to 7m	3300	2800
8–17m	3600	2900
18m and above	3700	3000

Yacht Charter

Chartering yachts is very popular these days, and as the promotional literature says, can be cheaper than staying in a hotel (if you have enough friends or family to share expenses). Between the various firms (the National Tourist Organisation has a list) there are over a thousand vessels currently available in all sizes, with or without a crew (though without a crew—bareboat charter—both the charterer and another member of the party must show proof of seamanship: a sailing certificate or letter of recommendation from a recognized yacht or sailing club). There are various options: motor yachts (without sails), motor sailors (primarily powered by motor, auxiliary sail power) and sailing yachts (with auxiliary motor power). Charters can be arranged through licensed firms of yacht brokers, or by contacting yacht owners directly. The **Yacht Charter Association**, 60 Silverdale, New Milton, Hampshire, BH25 7DE, ℭ (0425) 619004 supplies a list of its recognized yacht charter operators and offers advice on chartering overseas. For more information on chartering in Greece, write to:

The Hellenic Professional Yacht Owners Association, 43 Freatidos St, Zea Marina, 18536 Piraeus.   ℭ (01) 452 6335

Greek Yacht Brokers and Consultants Association, 7 Filellinon St, 105 57 Athens.   ℭ (01) 323 0330

Greek Yacht Owners Association, 10 Lekka St, 185 37 Piraeus.
                                    ℭ (01) 452 6335

One of the largest and most reputable firms is **Valef**, located at 22 Akti Themistokleous, Piraeus, ℰ (01) 428 1920, fax 428 1926 (in the USA: 7254 Fir Rd, PO Box 391, Ambler, PA 19002). They have more than 300 craft, accommodating 4–50 people in comfort.

Yacht Charter Operators Based in England

Bareboat yacht charter prices start from around £350–£400 per week for a 31ft boat in low season and £2,500 for a 48ft boat in high season. Prices peak during July and August and are lower during the spring and autumn months.

BUOYS Cruising Club, 8 Chase Side, Enfield, Middlesex, EN2 6NF.
    Offers charters from Athens.   ℰ (081) 367 8462

Creative Holidays & Cruises, 36 Chalton Street, London, NW1 1JB.
    Offers charters from Piraeus.   ℰ (071) 383 4243

Marinair, 188 Northdown Road, Cliftonville, Kent, CT9 2QN.
    Offers charters from Corfu, Rhodes, Kos and Athens.   ℰ (0843) 227140

McCulloch Marine, 60 Fordwych Road, London, NW2 3TH.
    Offers charters from Athens.   ℰ (081) 452 7509

World Expeditions Ltd, 8 College Rise, Maidenhead, Berkshire, SL6 6BP.
    From Athens and a number of Greek islands.   ℰ (0628) 74174

A number of English-based flotilla companies offer one or two-week sailing holidays, the airfare being included in the total cost. High season prices for a fortnight's holiday range from £550 per person to £1000 per person, depending on the number of people per yacht; expensive enough, but much cheaper than a yacht charter. The yachts have 4–6 berths, are supervized by a lead boat, with experienced skipper, engineer and hostess. **Flotilla companies** based in England include:

Sovereign Sailing, Astral Towers, Betts Way, Crawley, West Sussex, RH10 2GX.
                                            ℰ (0293) 599944

Odysseus Yachting Holidays, 33 Grand Parade, Brighton, BN2 2QA.
                                            ℰ (0273) 695094

Practical A–Z

Average Daily Temperatures

	ATHENS		CRETE (HERAKL'N)		CYCLADES (MYKONOS)		DODECS (RHODES)		IONIAN (CORFU)		N.E. AEGEAN (MYTILINI)		SARONIC (HYDRA)		SPORADES (SKYROS)	
	F°	C°	F°	C°	F°	C°	F°	C°	F°	C°	F°	C°	F°	C°	F°	C°
JAN	**48**	**11**	54	12	**54**	**12**	54	12	50	10	50	10	53	12	51	10
FEB	**49**	**11**	54	12	**54**	**12**	54	13	51	10	48	10	53	12	51	10
MAR	**54**	**12**	58	14	**56**	**13**	58	14	52	12	52	12	56	13	52	11
APR	**60**	**16**	62	17	**60**	**17**	60	17	60	15	60	16	61	16	58	15
MAY	**68**	**20**	68	20	**68**	**20**	66	20	66	19	68	20	68	20	66	19
JUN	**76**	**25**	74	24	**74**	**23**	73	21	71	21	74	24	76	25	74	23
JUL	**82**	**28**	78	26	**76**	**25**	78	26	78	26	80	27	82	28	77	25
AUG	**82**	**28**	78	26	**76**	**25**	79	27	78	26	80	27	81	28	78	26
SEP	**76**	**25**	76	24	**74**	**23**	78	25	74	23	74	23	76	25	71	22
OCT	**66**	**19**	70	21	**68**	**20**	72	21	66	19	66	19	71	21	65	19
NOV	**58**	**15**	64	18	**62**	**17**	66	17	58	15	58	15	62	17	58	15
DEC	**52**	**12**	58	14	**58**	**14**	58	14	52	12	52	12	58	15	51	12

Two Greek measurements you may come across are the *stremma*, a Greek land measurement (1 stremma = ¼ acre), and the *oka*, an old-fashioned weight standard, divided into 400 *drams* (1 *oka* = 3 lb; 35 *drams* = ¼ lb, 140 *drams* = 1 lb).

The **electric current** in Greece is mainly 220 volts, 50 Hz; plugs are continental two-pin.

Greek time is Eastern European, 2 hours ahead of Greenwich Mean Time.

Embassies and Consulates

Australia	37 D. Soutsou St, 115 21 Athens, ℭ 644 7303
Austria	26 Leof. Alexandras, 106 83 Athens, ℭ 821 1036
Canada	4 I. Gennadiou St, 115 21 Athens, ℭ 723 9511
France	7 Vass. Sofias, 106 71 Athens, ℭ 361 1665
Germany	10 Vass. Sofias, 151 24 Athens, ℭ 369 4111
Ireland	7 Vass. Konstantinou, 106 74 Athens, ℭ 723 2771
Japan	Athens Twr., 2–4 Messogion St, 115 27 Athens, ℭ 775 8101

New Zealand	15-17 Tsoha Street, Athens, © 641 0311–5
South Africa	124 Kifissias & Iatridou, 115 10 Athens, © 692 2125
United Kingdom	1 Ploutarchou St, 106 75 Athens, © 723 6211
USA	91 Vass. Sofias, 115 21 Athens, © 721 2951
United Nations	36 Amalias Ave, Athens, © 322 9624

Food and Drink

Eating Out

Eating establishments in Greece are categorized into Luxury, A, B, and C classes. Prices are controlled by the Tourist Police, who also enforce sanitary and health regulations.

The menu in Luxury restaurants is often 'international', with little to reveal that you're in Greece; in others you will find the more basic and authentic Greek cuisine. This is steeped in rich golden olive oil and the ingredients are fresh and often produced locally. It is quite usual in all but the snootiest eating places to examine the dishes (on display behind glass, or in the kitchen) before making a choice. There is usually a menu posted on the door with an English translation, listing the prices, but it's better still to see what the dish of the day is. The availability and variety of fish depends on the catch. Sadly, seafood has become one of the most expensive meals you can order. A combination of increased demand, marketing to Athens, and greedy, unsound fishing practices (such as illegal dynamiting) has decreased the fish population in the Mediterranean, so that what was once common and cheap is now costly and in some places quite rare. Each type of fish has its own price, then your portion is costed by its weight. Restaurants which specialize in fish are called *psarotavernas*.

Pork has taken the place of lamb as the most common meat in Greek tavernas since the country joined the European Community. Almost all *souvlaki* (the ubiquitous chunks of meat grilled on a stick) you get these days is pork, though lamb, roasted or stewed, is still widely available. Beef and chicken are often stewed in a sauce of tomatoes and olive oil, or roasted, accompanied by potatoes, spaghetti or rice. Village feasts, or *paniyiri*, often feature wild goat meat with rice or potatoes. A Greek salad can be just tomatoes or just cucumbers, or village-style *horiatiki* with tomatoes, cucumbers, black olives, peppers, onions and *feta* cheese—a small one for one person and a big one for two or three. You eat this during the meal, dipping your bread in the olive oil. Desserts are not generally eaten in Greece, but in the summer dinner is generally followed by melon or watermelon.

Restaurants (*estiatórion*) serve baked dishes and often grills as well. Restaurants serving just a grill and roasts are called *psistariá*. *Tavernas* may serve baked dishes or a grill or both, and is less formal than a restaurant. Don't be alarmed if food arrives tepid; Greeks believe this is better for the digestion. A sweet shop, or *zacharoplasteíon,* offers honey pastries, cakes, puddings and drinks and sometimes home-made ice cream. Many also serve breakfast, along with the less common dairy shops, or *galaktopoleíon* which sell milk, coffee, bread, yoghurt, rice pudding and custard pies. Cheese pastries (*tyropitta*) and 'tost' can appear almost anywhere. Lager beer is now common in most restaurants, Amstel and Heineken being the most popular, and wine is popular with most meals.

Prices on Greek menus are written first without, then with, service and tax charges. If you are served by a young boy (*mikró*), give him something or leave it on the table—tips are generally all he earns. If you've been given special service, you may leave a tip for your waiter on the plate. The amount varies; up to 10% is quite sufficient in most places.

Wine

The best-known wine of Greece, *retsina*, has a very distinctive taste of pine resin, dating from the time when Greeks stored their wine in untreated pine casks. It is an acquired taste, and many people can be put off by the pungent odour and sharp taste of some bottled varieties. Modern retsinas show increasingly restrained use of resin; all retsinas are best appreciated well-chilled. Draught retsina (*retsina varelisio*) can be found only on some islands, but in Athens it is the accepted, delicious accompaniment to the meal. Any taverna worth its salt will serve it, and if

it's not available you're in the wrong place, unless you've chosen a foreign or fairly exclusive Greek restaurant. In cases of desperation, where no barrelled retsina is on offer, the wine house Kourtakis produce a very acceptable bottled version at a low price. Retsina is admirably suited to Greek food, and after a while a visitor may find non-resinated wines a rather bland alternative. Traditionally it is served in small tumblers, and etiquette requires that they are never filled to the brim or drained empty; you keep topping up your colleagues' glasses, as best you can. There is a great deal of toasting throughout the meal (*stin yamas*—to our health, *stin yassas*—to your health), and by all means clink glasses with someone else, but on no account bring your glass down on another person's (unless your intentions for the evening are entirely dishonourable).

Ordinary red and white house wines are often locally-produced bargains—*krasi varelisio* or *krasi heema*, *krasi* meaning wine, *varelisio* from the barrel; *heema*, means 'loose'. The customary way of serving these is in small, copper-anodized jugs, in various metric measures (500ml and 250ml being the most common; a standard wine bottle holds 750cl). These are generally fine, though you may be unlucky and get one that's a stinker.

Greece has an ample selection of medium-priced red and white wines, often highly regionalized with each island and village offering their own unique wines. There are many indigenous Greek grape varieties which avoid the tyranny of Cabernet Sauvignon and Chardonnay. All the principal wine companies—Boutari, Achaia-Clauss, Carras, Tsantali, Kourtaki—produce acceptable table wines at very affordable prices. These large Greek wine producers have been investing heavily in new equipment and foreign expertise over the last decade, and it shows; even that humblest of bottles (and Greece's best-seller) *Demestika* has become very acceptable of late, and bears little resemblance to the rough stuff that earned it some unflattering, sound-alike nicknames. Look out for the nobler labels; Boutari *Naoussa* is an old-style, slightly astringent red, while Boutari's *Grande Réserve* is their best red; *Lac des Roches* is their most popular white on the islands. *Peloponnesiakos* from Achaia-Clauss is an easy-drinking, light white wine which is faddishly popular at the moment anywhere within exportable distance of the Peloponnese. From Carras, *Château Carras* is a Bordeaux-style red wine made from the Cabernet Sauvignon and Merlot grapes; if you're lucky you might find *Carras Limnio,* a good dinner wine. Boutari's *Santorini* is their finest island white, while in Rhodes CAIR supplies Greece with its sparkling *méthode traditionelle* white, *Cair.* There are various local spirits too, such as the wonderful *Kitron* from Naxos, a sweet citrus liqueur.

In recent years small wine producers have become very fashionable with the wine-drinking elite of Greece. Some of these island wine-makers are superb, such as the Boutari white produced on Santorini; others deserve obscurity. But for the most part, you are unlikely to come across them in the average taverna. If you're a wine buff, it's worth seeking them out from local recommendations in off-licences and high-class restaurants; or better still, consult Maggie McNie of the Greek Wine Bureau in London © (071) 823 3799, who is a Master of Wine and probably the best-qualified expert on Greek wines; she can tell you what to try, or what to bring back with you.

Cafés

Cafés or *kafeneíons* (in small towns these are frequented almost exclusively by men, who discuss the latest news, and play cards or backgammon) serve Greek coffee (*café hellinikó*), which is the same stuff as Turkish coffee. There are 40 different ways to make this, although *glykó* (sweet), *métrio* (medium) and *skéto* (no sugar) are the basic orders. It is always served with a glass of water. Nescafé with milk has by popular tourist demand become available everywhere, though Greeks prefer it iced, with or without sugar and milk, which they call *frappé*. Soft drinks and *ouzo* round out the average café fare. Ouzo—like its Cretan cousin *raki*—is a clear anise-flavoured aperitif which many dilute (and cloud) with water. It can be served with a little plate of snacks called *mezédes* which can range from grilled octopus through nuts to cheese and tomatoes, though these days you must request *mezédes*, especially in tourist areas.

Brandy, or Metaxa (the Greeks know it by the most popular brand name), is usually a late-night treat. The more stars on the label (from three to seven) the higher the price, and in theory at least, the better the quality. In tourist haunts, milkshakes, fruit juices, cocktails and even capuccino are readily available; in the backwaters you can usually get ice cream and good Greek yoghurt.

Bars

In the last few years the influx of tourists has resulted in the growth of trendy bars, usually playing the latest hit records and serving fancy cocktails as well as standard drinks. These establishments come to life later in the evening, when everyone has spent the day on the beach and the earlier part of the evening in a taverna. They close at 3 or 4am, although amid protest, the Greek Government plans to make this 2am (the Goverment claims the nation is nodding off at work after a night on the tiles). In general they're not cheap, sometimes outrageously dear by Greek standards, and it can be disconcerting to realise that you have paid the same for your Harvey Wallbanger as you paid for the entire meal of chicken and chips, salad and a bottle of wine, half an hour before in the taverna next door. Cocktails have now risen to beyond the 1000 dr. mark in many bars, but before you complain remember that the measures are triples by British standards. If in doubt stick to beer, ouzo, wine and Metaxa (Metaxa and coke, if you can stomach it, is generally about half the price of the better-known Bacardi and coke). You may have difficulty in finding beer, as the profit margin is so small that many bars stop serving it in the peak season, thus obliging you to plump for the higher-priced drinks. One unfortunate practice on the islands is the doctoring of bottles, whereby some bar owners buy cheaper versions of spirits and use them to refill brand name bottles. The only way to be sure is to see the new bottle being opened in front of you.

A list of items which appear frequently on Greek menus is included in the language section at the end of the guide.

Health

In theory there is at least one doctor (*iatrós*) on every island, whose office is open from 9am to 1pm and from 5pm to 7pm. On many islands too there are hospitals which are open all day, and usually have an outpatient clinic, open in the mornings. British travellers are often urged to carry a Form E111, available from DSS offices (apply well in advance on a form CM1 from post offices), which admit them to the most basic IKA (Greek NHS) hospitals for treatment; but this doesn't cover medicines or nursing care, which still have to be paid for. In any case, the E111 seems to be looked on with total disregard outside of Athens. Private doctors and hospital stays can be very expensive, so you should take out a travel insurance policy, then claim your money back on return to the UK. Greek General Practitioners' fees are, however, usually reasonable.

If you have a serious injury or illness, consider leaving Greece for treatment back home if you are well enough to travel, because even the best hospitals (in Athens) lag many years behind northern Europe or the USA in the modernity of their methods of care and treatment. It's quite common for families to bring food in for the patient. So make sure your holiday insurance also has adequate repatriation cover.

Most doctors pride themselves on their English, as do their friends the pharmacists (found in the *farmakeio*), whose advice on minor ailments is good, although their medicine is not particularly cheap. If you forgot to bring your own condoms and are caught short, they are widely available from *farmakeio* and even kiosks, with lusty brand names such as 'Squirrel' or 'Rabbit'. If you can't see them on display, the word *kapotes* (condom) gets results. You can also get the Pill, *xapi antisiliptiko*, morning-after Pill and HRT over the pharmacy counter without a prescription. Be sure to take your old packet to show them the brand you use.

A few hints: Coca Cola or retsina reduces the impact of the oil in Greek foods. Fresh parsley can also help stomach upsets.

Money

The word for bank in Greek is *trápeza*, derived from the word *trapezi*, or table, used back in the days of money changers. On all the islands with more than goats and a few shepherds there is some sort of banking establishment. If you plan to spend time on one of the more remote islands, however, it is safest to bring enough drachma with you. On the other hand, the small but popular islands often have only one bank, where exchanging money can take a long time. Waiting can be avoided if you go at 8am, when the banks open (normal banking hours are 8–2, 8–1 on Fri). Most island banks are closed on Saturdays and Sundays. Better still, **post offices** will exchange cash, travellers's cheques and Eurocheques; they also charge less commission than banks, and the queues are usually shorter. The numbers of 24-hour **automatic cash-tellers** are growing in Athens and large resorts.

Credit cards can be used to withdraw cash at banks; put your account into credit before going abroad, and this will often be the cheapest way to transfer money. The Commercial Bank of Greece will allow you to withdraw money by Visa, and the National Bank of Greece will exchange on Access (MasterCard). Money can also be withdrawn from some automatic tellers (24 hours daily).

Bank cards There are increasing numbers of cash dispensers for Eurocheque cards, Cirrus and Plus cards in Athens and the big tourist resorts.

Eurocheques are accepted in banks and post offices.

Traveller's cheques are always useful even though commission rates are less for cash. The major brands of traveller's cheques (Thomas Cook and American Express) are accepted in all banks and post offices; take your passport as ID, and shop around for commission rates.

Running out? Athens and Piraeus, with offices of many British and American banks, are the easiest places to have money sent by cash transfer from someone at home if you run out—though it may take a few days. If there's no bank on the island you're on, the shipping agent will change money, and the post office will change Eurocheques.

The **Greek drachma** is circulated in coins of 100, 50, 20, 10, 5, 2 and 1 drachma and in notes of 100, 500, 1000 and 5000 drachma.

Museums

All significant archaeological sites and museums have regular admission hours. Nearly all are closed on Mondays, and open other weekdays from 8 or 9am to around 2pm, though outdoor sites tend to stay open later, until 4 or 5pm. As a rule, plan to visit cultural sites in the mornings to avoid disappointment, or unless the local tourist office can provide you with current opening times. Hours tend to be shorter in the winter. Students with a valid identification card get a discount on admission fees; on Sundays admission is generally free for EC nationals.

If you're currently studying archaeology, the history of art or the Classics and intend to visit many museums and sites in Greece, it may be worth your while to obtain a free pass by writing several weeks in advance of your trip to the Museum Section, Ministry of Science and Culture, Aristidou 14, Athens, enclosing verification of your studies from your college or university. Entrance fees for sites or museums are not listed in this book. Count on 400–600 dr. in most cases; exceptions are the Acropolis and National Archaeology Museum in Athens at 1500 dr.

Music and Dancing

Greek music is either city music or village music. The music of the city includes the popular tunes, *rembetika* (derived from the hashish dens of Asia Minor) and most bouzouki music, whereas village music means traditional tunes played on the Greek bagpipes (*tsamboúna*), the clarinet (*klaríno*), the violin and sometimes the dulcimer (*sandoúri*). Cretan music specializes in the lyre (*lyra*) and is in a category of its own.

On the islands you can hear both city and village music, the former at the *bouzoukia*, or Greek nightclubs, which usually feature certain singers. Many play records or washed-out muzak until midnight as the customers slowly arrive. Smaller, rougher night clubs are called *boites* or *skilakia* — 'dog' shops. You generally buy a bottle of white wine and fruit and dance until 4 in the morning, though expect to pay a pretty drachma for the privilege. To hear traditional music, you must go into the villages, to the festivals or weddings. In many places Sunday evening is an occasion for song and dance. Village music is generally modest and unpretentious, while city music is the domain of the professional singers, although any bold member of the audience with a good voice can get up to sing a few songs. After a few hours of drinking, a particular favourite or a good dancer is liable to make the enthusiasts forget the law against *spásimo*, or plate breaking, and supporters may end up paying for missing place settings. If the mood really heats up, men will dance with wine glasses or bottles on their heads, or even sink their teeth into a fully-set table and dance without spilling a drop. When the matrons begin to belly-dance on the table, you know it's time to leave.

In the tavernas you're liable to hear either city or village music. Some put on permanent shows, and others have music only occasionally. Athens is awash with tourist shows and discotheques during the summer but starts pulsating to all kinds of Greek music in November, when Plaka is returned to the Athenians. Most musicians on the islands go to Athens in the winter.

The lyrics to most Greek songs deal with the ups and downs of love; *s'agapoh* that you hear in nearly every song means 'I love you'. Serious composers (Mikis Theodorakis is the best known) often put poetry to music, providing splendid renderings of the lyrics of George Seferis and Yannis Ritsos. The guerrillas (*partizanis*) and the Communists have a monopoly on the best political songs, many by Theodorakis. Cretan songs are often very patriotic (for Crete) and many are drawn from the 17th-century epic poem, the *Erotókritos*, written in the Cretan dialect by Vitzentzios Kornáros.

Every island in Greece has its special dance, although today it is often only the young people's folkdance societies that keep them alive, along with the island's traditional costumes. The best time to find them dancing is on each island's Day of Liberation from the Turks or any other anniversary of local significance. One of the best-known professional folkdance companies, based in Athens, is **Dora Stratou Greek Folk Dances**, Dora Stratou Theatre, Philopappou Hill, © (01) 324 4395 or © 921 4650. From beginning of May to end of September. Shows begin at 10pm every day, with an additional show at 8pm on Wednesdays and Sundays. Tickets average 1200 dr.; 700 dr. for students.

Although these shows are beautiful and interesting, there's nothing like getting up to dance yourself—a splendid way to work off the big dinner just consumed at a *paniyiri*. For a brief overview of the most popular dances, *see* p. 59

see p. 59

National Holidays

Note that most businesses and shops close down for the afternoon before and the morning after a religious holiday. If a national holiday falls on a Sunday, the following Monday is observed. The Orthodox Easter is generally a week or so after the Roman Easter.

1 January	New Year's Day	*Protochroniza;* also *Aghios Vassilis* (Greek Father Xmas)
6 January	Epiphany	*Ta Fórce/Epifania*
circa 14 March	'Clean Monday' (precedes Shrove Tuesday, and follows a three-week carnival)	*Kathari Deftéra*
25 March	Greek Independence Day	*Evangelismós*
circa 29 April	Good Friday	*Megáli Paraskevi*
circa 1 May	Easter Sunday	*Páscha*
circa 2 May	Easter Monday	*Theftéra tou Páscha*
circa 3 May	Labour Day	*Protomaya*
15 August	Assumption of the Virgin	*Koímisis tis Theotókou*
28 October	'Ochi' Day (in celebration of Metaxas' 'no' to Mussolini)	
25 December	Christmas	*Christoúyena*
26 December	Gathering of the Virgin	*Sinaxi Theotóku*

In Greece, Easter is the big national holiday, the equivalent of Christmas and New Year in northern climes and the time of year when far-flung relatives return to Greece to see their families back home; it's a good time of year to visit for atmosphere, with fireworks and feasting. On Kalymnos and Symi they even throw dynamite. After the priest has intoned: *'O Christos Aneste!'*—Christ has risen!—families return home with lighted candles, mark the sign of the cross on the doorpost, and tuck into a special meal of *mayaritsa* soup. On Easter Sunday the Paschal lamb is spit-roasted and music and dancing goes on day and night. After Easter and May 1, spring (*anixi*—the opening) has offically come, and the tourist season begins.

Festival dates for saints' days vary over a period of several given days, or even weeks, due to the Greek liturgical calendar; we have given the 1994 dates when known, but check these locally, if you can, for following years.

Packing

Even in the height of summer, evenings can be chilly in Greece, especially when the *meltemi* wind is blowing. Always bring at least one warm sweater and a pair of long trousers. Those who venture off the beaten track into the thorns and rocks should bring sturdy and comfortable shoes—trainers (sneakers) are good. Cover the ankles if you really like wilderness, where scorpions and harmful snakes can be a problem. Plastic beach shoes are recommended for rocky beaches, where there are often sea urchins; you can easily buy them near any beach if you don't want to carry them around with you.

Summer travellers following whim rather than a pre-determined programme should bring a sleeping bag, as lodgings of any sort are often full to capacity. Serious sleeping-baggers should also bring a Karrimat or similar insulating layer to cushion them from the gravelly Greek ground. Torches are very handy for moonless nights, caves and rural villages.

On the pharmaceutical side, seasickness pills, insect bite remedies, tablets for stomach upsets and aspirin will deal with most difficulties encountered. Women's sanitary towels and sometimes Tampax are sold from general stores, but on remote islands you'll need to seek out the *farmakeio;* if there's no pharmacy, you've had it. Soap, washing powder, a clothes line and especially a towel are necessary for those staying in class C hotels or less. Most important of all, buy a universal-fitting sink plug if you like sinks full of water; Greek sinks rarely have working ones. A knife is a good idea for *paniyiria*, where you are often given a slab of goat meat with only a spoon or fork to eat it with. A photo of the family and home is always appreciated by new Greek friends.

On all the Greek islands except for the most remote of the remote you can buy whatever you forgot to bring. Toilet paper and mosquito coils are the two most popular purchases on arrival. However, special needs such as artificial sweeteners, contact lens products and so on can generally be found in Athens and the more popular islands.

Let common sense and the maxim 'bring as little as possible and never more than you can carry' dictate your packing; work on the theory that however much money and clothing you think you need, halve the clothing and double the money.

Photography

Greece lends herself freely to beautiful photography, but a fee is charged at archaeological sites and museums. For a movie camera of any kind, including camcorders, you are encouraged to buy a ticket for the camera; with a tripod you pay per photograph at sites, but cameras (especially tripod-mounted ones) are not allowed in museums, for no particular reason other than the museum maintaining a monopoly on its own (usually very dull) picture stock. 35mm film, both print and slide, can be found in many island shops, though it tends to be expensive and the range of film speeds limited (100ASA and 64ASA are easily available though if you take slides). Disposable and underwater cameras are on sale in larger holiday resorts. Large islands even have 24-hour developing services, though again this costs more than at home.

The light in the summer is often stronger than it seems and is the most common cause of ruined photographs; opting for slow film (100 ASA or less) will help. Greeks usually love to have their pictures taken, and although it's more polite to ask first, you should just go ahead and take the photo if you don't want them to rush off to beautify themselves and strike a pose. You should avoid taking pictures of the aircraft, military installations and barracks, communications systems on mountain tops, and Army look-out posts. The Photography Forbidden sign shows a camera with a cross through it and speaks for itself.

If you bring an expensive camera to Greece, it never hurts to insure it. Above all, never leave it alone 'for just a few minutes'. Although Greeks themselves very rarely steal anything, other tourists are not so honest.

Post Offices

Signs for post offices *(tachidromío)* as well as postboxes *(kourti)* are bright yellow and easy to find. Many post office employees speak English. Stamps can also be bought at kiosks and in some tourist shops, although they charge a small commission. Stamps are *grammatósima*. Postcards can take up to three weeks to arrive at their destinations, or only a week if you're lucky; letters sent abroad are faster, taking just over a week, depending on the route. If you're really in a hurry you can send letters *Express* for extra cost.

If you do not have an address, mail can be sent to you *Poste Restante* to any post office in Greece, and can be picked up with proof of identity. After one month all unretrieved letters are returned to sender. If someone has sent you a parcel, you will receive a notice of its arrival, and you must go to the post office to collect it. You will have to pay a handling fee of 650dr, and customs charges and duties should the parcel contain dutiable articles. 'Fragile' stickers attract scant attention. In small villages, particularly on the islands, mail is not delivered to the house but to the village centre, either a café or bakery. Its arrival coincides with that of a ship from Athens.

If you want to mail a package, any shop selling paper items will usually wrap it for a small fee.

Sports

Watersports

Naturally these predominate in the islands. All popular beaches these days hire out pedal boats and windsurf boards; some have paragliding and jet skis. Water-skiing prevails on most islands and large hotel complexes. Several islands offer sailing and windsurfing instruction. For more details contact:

Hellenic Yachting Federation, 7 Akti Navarchou Kountourioti, Piraeus, © 413 7351.

Greek Windsurfing Association, 7 Filellinon St, Piraeus, © 323 3696.

Nudism is forbidden by law in Greece, except in designated areas, such as the more remote beaches of Mykonos. In practice, however, many people shed all in isolated coves, at the far ends of beaches, or ideally on beaches accessible only by private boat. On the other hand, topless sunbathing is now legal on the majority of popular beaches *away* from settlements. Do exercise discretion. It isn't worth wounding local sensibilities, no matter how prudish other people's attitudes may seem. You could be arrested on the spot and end up with three days in jail or a stiff fine. Canoodling on public beaches in broad daylight can also offend.

Underwater activities with any kind of breathing apparatus are strictly forbidden to keep divers from snatching any antiquities and to protect marine life. However, snorkelling is fine, and Mykonos has diving schools where, even if you already know how to dive, you have to go out with their boats.

Average Sea Temperatures

Jan	Feb	Mar	Apr	May	Jun	Jul	Aug	Sep	Oct	Nov	Dec
59°F	59°F	59°F	61°F	64°F	72°F	75°F	77°F	75°F	72°F	64°F	63°F
15°C	15°C	15°C	16°C	18°C	22°C	24°C	25°C	24°C	22°C	18°C	17°C

Land Sports

Tennis is very popular in Athens with numerous clubs from Glyfada to Kiffissia. Otherwise there are courts at all major resort hotels, where, if you are not a resident, you may be allowed to play in the off season.

Organized horse riding is offered by many small riding stables. In Athens, call The Riding Club of Greece, Paradissos, ✆ 682 6128 and Riding Club of Athens, Gerakos, ✆ 661 1088.

Telephones

The *Organismos Telepikoinonia Ellathos*, better known as *OTE*, has offices in the larger towns and at least one on every island that has a telephone service; these are the best place to make international calls. You can call both direct and collect (reverse charges), although the latter usually takes at least half an hour to put through. On the larger islands you may dial abroad direct (for Great Britain dial 0044 and for the USA 001 before the area code). A 3-minute call to the UK will cost about 750 dr., to the US 1600 dr. You should also use OTE for calling other places in Greece. Telegrams can be sent from OTE or the post office.

Payphones don't exist as such; the few that there were have been replaced with cardphones during the summer of 1993. Calls can be made from kiosks (more expensive), *kafeneíons*, and shops (always ask first). Phonecards have now come to Athens and the busier resorts but some islands only have the blue booths without the phones *in situ* yet. Buy a card when you arrive at the airport, or get one from a *periptero* at 1000 dr for 100 units or *monades*.

It is often impossible to call Athens from the islands in mid-morning; chances improve in the evening. To defeat the beeps, whirrs, and buzzes you often get instead of a connection, wait for the series of six clicks after the area code is dialled before proceeding.

It's customary in Greece to put the used toilet paper in a special wastebasket beside the toilet (which is emptied regularly); this is a habit left over from the days when toilet paper blocked the inadequate plumbing. However, Greek plumbing has improved remarkably in the past few years, especially in the newer hotels and restaurants. Nevertheless, public toilets and those in cheaper hotels and pensions often have their quirks. Tavernas, *kafeneíons*, and sweet shops almost always have facilities (it's good manners to buy something before you excuse yourself).

In older pensions and tavernas, the plumbing often makes up in inventiveness for what it lacks in efficiency. Do not tempt fate by disobeying the little notices 'the papers they please to throw in the basket'—or it's bound to lead to trouble. Also, a second flush in immediate succession will gurgle and burp instead of swallow. Many places in Greece have only a ceramic hole. Women who confront this for the first time should take care not to wet their feet: squat about halfway and lean back as far as you can. Always have paper of some sort handy.

If you stay in a private room or pension you may have to have the electric water heater turned on for about 20 minutes before you take a shower, so if you were promised hot water but it fails to appear, ask the proprietor about it. In most smaller *pensions*, water is heated by a solar panel on the roof, so the best time to take a shower is in the late afternoon, or the early evening (before other residents use up the finite supply of hot water). In larger hotels there is often hot water in the mornings and evenings, but not in the afternoons. Actually 'cold' showers in the summer aren't all that bad, because the tap water itself is generally lukewarm, especially after noon. A good many showers are of the hand-held variety; sinks in Greece rarely have plugs.

Greek tap water is perfectly safe to drink, but on some islands like Halki and Kalymnos it's very salty and undrinkable. Big plastic bottles of spring water are widely available, even on ships, and taste better than tap water. On dry islands, remember to ask what time the water is turned off.

Tourist Information

If the Greek National Tourist Organisation (in Greek the initials come out: EOT) can't answer your questions about Greece, at least they can refer you to someone who can.

In Athens

EOT Information Desk: National Bank of Greece, Syntagma Square, 2 Karageorgi Servias St, ✆ (01) 322 2545, 323 4130.
EOT, East Airport: ✆ (01) 969 9590.
Head Office: 2 Amerikis St, Athens 10564, ✆ (01) 322 3111; fax 322 2841.

In Australia

51–57 Pitt St, Sydney, NSW 2000, ✆ 241 1663/4; fax 235 2174.

In Canada

1300 Bay St, Toronto, Ontario, ✆ (416) 968 2220, fax 968 6533.
1233 De La Montagne, Montreal, Quebec, ✆ (514) 871 1535, fax 871 1535.

In the UK

4 Conduit St, London W1R ODJ, ✆ (071) 734 5997, fax 287 1369.

In the US

Head Office: Olympic Tower, 645 Fifth Ave, 5th Floor, New York, NY 10022, ✆ (212) 421 5777; fax 826 6940.
168 N. Michigan Ave, Chicago, Ill. 60601, ✆ (312) 782 1084; fax 782 1091.
611 West Sixth St, Suite 2198, Los Angeles, Calif. 90017, ✆ (213) 626 6696; fax 489 9744.

Islands without a branch of the EOT often have some form of local tourist office; if not, most have **Tourist Police** (often located in an office in the town's police station). You can always tell a Tourist Policeman from other policemen by the little flags he wears on his pocket, showing which languages he speaks. They have information about the island, and can often help you find a room. In Athens there are four Tourist Police stations, and a magic telephone number—171. The voice on 171 not only speaks good English, but can tell you everything from ship departures to where to spend the night.

Tourist Police in Athens

Dimitrakopoloulou 77, Veikou (the new home of 171).
Larissa Train Station, ✆ 821 3574.
West Airport, Olympic Airways, ✆ 981 4093.
East Airport, ✆ 969 9523.
At **Piraeus:** Akti Miaouli, ✆ 452 3670/418 4815.

Travelling with Children

Greece is one of the best Mediterranean countries to bring a child, as children are not barely tolerated as they are in more 'sophisticated' holiday resorts, but are generally enjoyed and encouraged. Depending on their age, they go free or receive discounts on ships and buses. You can also save on hotel bills by bringing sleeping bags for the children. However, if they're babies, don't count on island pharmacies stocking your baby's brand of milk powder or baby foods—they may have some, but it's safest to bring your own supply. Disposable nappies, especially Pampers, are widely available, even on the smaller islands. Travelling with a baby is like having a special passport. Greeks adore them, so don't be too surprised if your infant is passed round like a parcel. Greek children usually have an afternoon nap, so do their parents, so it's quite normal for Greeks to eat *en famille* until the small hours. The attitude to children is very different to the British one of being seen but not heard—Greek children are spoiled rotten. Finding a babysitter is never a problem.

Superstitions are still given more credit than you might expect; even in the most cosmopolitan of households, you'll see babies with amulets pinned to their clothes or wearing blue beads to ward off the evil eye before their baptism. Beware of commenting on a Greek child's intelligence, beauty or whatever, as this may call down the jealous interest of the old gods. The response in the old days was to spit in the admired child's face, but these days, superstitious grannies will say the ritual 'phtew—phtew—phtew', as if spitting, to protect the child from harm.

Where to Stay

Hotels

All hotels in Greece are divided into six categories: Luxury, A, B, C, D and E. This grading system bears little relationship to the quality of service or luxury; it's more to do with how the building is constructed, size of bedrooms, etc. If the hotel has a marble-clad bathroom it gets a higher rating. For this reason, some D and C class hotels can be better than Bs. You may come across government-run hotels, *Xenias*, many of which look like barracks. Some of these are better than others.

Prices are set and strictly controlled by the Tourist Police. Off season you can generally get a discount, sometimes as much as 40%. In the summer season prices can be increased by up to 20%. Other charges include an 8% government tax, a 4.5% community bed tax, a 12% stamp tax, an optional 10% surcharge for stays of only one or two days, an air conditioning surcharge, as well as a 20% surcharge for an extra bed. All of these prices are listed on the door of every room and authorized and checked at regular intervals. If your hotelier fails to abide by the posted prices, or if you have any other reason to believe all is not on the level, take your complaint to the Tourist Police.

1994 hotel rate guideline in drachma for mid-high season (1/5/94–30/9/94)*

	L	A	B	C	D
Single room with bath	9–30,000	6.7–15,000	6.7–10,000	4.5–8000	2.7–5000
Double room with bath	13.1–35,000	9.9–17,000	5.7–14,000	4.6–10,000	4–6000

* 1994 maximum prices were still not confirmed at the time of writing, as the change of Government in late 1993 disabled the civil service and EOT for months; the above prices are based on the most up-to-date information available in Spring 1994.

Prices for E hotels are about 20% less than D rates.

During the summer, hotels with restaurants may require guests to take their meals in the hotel, either full pension or half pension, and there is no refund for an uneaten dinner. Twelve noon is the official check-out time, although on the islands it is usually geared to the arrival of the next boat. Most Luxury and class A, if not B, hotels situated far from the town or port supply buses or cars to pick up guests.

Hotels down to class B all have private bathrooms. In C most do. In D you will be lucky to find a hot shower, and in E forget it. In these hotels neither towel nor soap is supplied, although the bedding is clean.

The importance of reserving a room in advance, especially during July and August, cannot be over-emphasized. Reservations can be made through the individual hotel or:

The Hellenic Chamber of Hotels, 24 Stadiou St, 105 61 Athens, © (01) 323 6962 (from Athens: between 8am and 2pm); fax (01) 322 5449.

In the 'Where to Stay' sections of this book, accommodation is listed according to the following **price categories**. Please note that prices quoted are always for **double rooms**.

luxury	15,000 dr. and above
expensive	8–15,000 dr.
moderate	4–8000 dr.
cheap	4000 dr. and below

Rooms (Domatia) in Private Homes

These are for the most part cheaper than hotels and are sometimes more pleasant. On the whole, Greek houses aren't much in comparison to other European homes mainly because the Greeks spend so little time inside them; but they are clean, and the owner will often go out of his or her way to assure maximum comfort for the guest. Staying in someone's house can also offer rare insights into Greek domestic taste, which ranges from a near-Japanese simplicity to a clutter of bulging plastic cat pictures that squeak when you touch them; lamps shaped like ships, made entirely of macaroni; tapestries of dogs shooting pool; and flocked sofas covered in heavy plastic that only the Patriarch of the Orthodox Church is allowed to sit in. Increasingly, however, rooms to rent to tourists are built in a separate annexe and tend to be rather characterless.

While room prices are generally fixed in the summer—the going rate in high season is now 4000 dr.—out of season they are always negotiable (with a little finesse), even in June.

Prices depend a lot on the island; fashionable ones like Mykonos or Santorini are very expensive. Speaking some Greek is the biggest asset in bargaining, although not strictly necessary. Claiming to be a poor student is generally effective. Always remember, however, that you are staying in someone's home, and do not waste more water or electricity than you need. The owner will generally give you a bowl to wash your clothes in, and there is always a clothes line.

The Tourist Police on each island have all the information on rooms and will be able to find you one, if you do not meet a chorus of Greeks chanting 'Rooms? Rooms?' as you leave the boat. Many houses also have signs.

Youth Hostels

Some of these are official and require a membership card from the Association of Youth Hostels, or alternatively an International Membership Card (about 2500 dr.) from the Greek Association of Youth Hostels, 4 Dragatsaniou St, Athens, © (01) 323 4107; other hostels are informal, have no irksome regulations, and admit anyone. There is an official youth hostel on the island of Santorini. Most charge extra for a shower, sometimes for sheets. Expect to pay 600–1200 dr. a night, depending on the quality of facilities and services offered. The official ones have a curfew around midnight.

Camping Out

The climate of summertime Greece is perfect for sleeping out of doors. Unauthorized camping is illegal in Greece, although each village on each island enforces the ban as it sees fit. Some couldn't care less if you put up a tent at the edge of their beach; in others the police may pull up your tent pegs and fine you. All you can do is ask around to see what other tourists or friendly locals advise. In July and August you only need a sleeping bag to spend a pleasant night on a remote beach, cooled by the sea breezes that also keep hopeful mosquitoes at bay. Naturally, the more remote the beach, the less likely you are to be disturbed. If a policeman does come by and asks you to move, though, you had best do so; be diplomatic. Many islands have privately-operated camping grounds—each seems to have at least one. These are reasonably priced, though some have only minimal facilities. The National Tourist Office controls other, 'official', campsites which are rather plush and costly.

There are three main reasons behind the camping law: one is that the beaches have no sanitation facilities for crowds of campers; secondly, forest fires are a real hazard in summer; and thirdly, the law was enacted to displace gipsy camps, and is still used for this purpose. If the police are in some places lackadaisical about enforcing the camping regulations, they come down hard on anyone lighting any kind of fire in a forest, and may very well put you in jail for 2 months; every year forest fires damage huge swathes of land.

National Tourist Office of Greece **camping rates** per day during high season

	dr.		
Adult:	600	–	800
Child (4–12):	300	–	500
Caravan:	1000	–	1300
Small tent:	500	–	650
Large tent:	900	–	1200
Car:	150	–	200

Renting a House or Villa

On most islands it is possible to rent houses or villas, generally for a month or more at a time. Villas can often be reserved from abroad: contact a travel agent or the National Tourist Organisation (NTOG) for names and addresses of rental agents. In the off season houses may be found on the spot with a little enquiry; with luck you can find a house sleeping 2–3 people, and depending on the facilities it can work out quite reasonably per person. Islands with sophisticated villa rentals (i.e. with a large number of purpose-built properties with all the amenities, handled by agents in Athens, Great Britain and North America) are Mykonos, and Paros. The NTOG has a list of agents offering villas and apartments. Facilities normally include a refrigerator, hot water, plates and utensils, etc. Generally, the longer you stay the more economical it becomes. Things to check for are leaking roofs, creeping damp, water supply (the house may have a well) and a supply of lamps if there is no electricity.

Self-catering Holidays

Greek Sun Holidays, 1 Bank Street, Sevenoaks, Kent, TN13 1UW. Apartments and studios on Mykonos, Paros, Serifos, Sifnos, Sikinos and Tinos.

© (0732) 740317

Ilios Island Holidays, 18 Market Square, Horsham, West Sussex, RH12 1EU. Villas and apartments on Tinos and Naxos.   © (0403) 259788

Sunvil Holidays, 7–8 Upper Square, Old Isleworth, Middlesex, TW7 7BJ. Small resorts on Andros, Tinos, Naxos, Syros, Santorini, Milos, Sikinos, Folegandros and Amorgos.   © (081) 568 4499

Traditional Settlements in Greece

This is a programme sponsored by the National Tourist Organisation of Greece to preserve old villages and certain buildings while converting their interiors into tourist accommodation with modern amenities. Often these are furnished with handmade furniture and weaving typical of the locale. The aim is to offer visitors a taste of rural life while improving the economy in these areas. So far guesthouses are available on Santorini, and in several villages on other island groups and the mainland; more are planned for the future. Prices are quite reasonable (especially when compared with the going rate for villas) and information may be had by writing to the nearest Greek National Tourist Organisation/EOT. You can then book direct, or through EOT.

Art Centres of the School of Fine Arts

An annexe of the Athenian School of Fine Arts is located on Mykonos. It provides inexpensive accommodation for foreign artists (for up to 20 days in the summer and 30 in the winter) as well as studios, etc. One requirement is a recommendation from the Greek embassy in the artist's home country. Contact its Press and Information Office for further information.

Women Travellers

Greece is fine for women travellers but foreign women travelling alone can be viewed as an oddity in some places. Be prepared for a fusillade of questions. Greeks tend to do everything in groups or *pareas* and can't understand people who want to go solo. That said, Greece is a choice destination for women travelling on their own. Out of respect Greeks on the whole refrain from annoying women as other Mediterranean men are known to do, while remaining friendly and easy to meet; all the Greek men from sixteen to sixty like to chat up foreign women, but extreme coercion and violence such as rape is rare. Men who try to take advantage of women or chase tourists are generally looked down on and have bad reputations. While some Greek men can't fathom what sexual equality might mean—they are usually the same who hold the fantasy that for a woman a night without company is unbearable mortification of the flesh—they are ever courteous and will rarely allow even the most liberated female (or male) guest to pay for anything.

In the major resorts like Rhodes, tourist women are considered fair game, fish to be harpooned in more ways than one by the local lads throughout the season. A *kamaki* is a harpoon in Greek, and also the name given to the Romeos who usually roar about on motorbikes, hang out in the bars and cafés, and hunt in pairs or packs. Their aim is to collect as many women as possible, notching up points for different nationalities. There are highly professional *kamakis* in the big resorts, gigolos who live off women tourists, gathering as many foreign hearts plus gold chains and parting gifts as they can; they overwinter all over the world with members of their harem. Other Greeks look down on them, and consider them dishonourable and no good.

Many young Greek women are beginning to travel alone—that leggy blonde with the rucksack could just as well be Greek as Swedish nowadays—but this is no indication that traditional values are disappearing. Although many women in the larger towns now have jobs, old marriage customs still exert a strong influence, even in Athens. Weddings are sometimes less a union of love than the closing of a lengthily negotiated business deal. In the evenings, especially at weekends, you'll see many girls of marriageable age join the family for a seaside promenade, or *volta*, sometimes called 'the bride market'. A young man, generally in his late twenties or early thirties, will spot a likely girl on the promenade or will hear about her through the grapevine. He will then approach the father to discover the girl's dowry—low wages and high housing costs demand that it contains some sort of living quarters from the woman's father, often added on top of the family house. The suitor must have a steady job. If both parties are satisfied, the young man is officially introduced to the daughter, who can be as young as 16 in the villages. If they get along well together, the marriage date is set. The woman who never marries and has no children is sincerely pitied in Greece. The inordinate number of Greek widows (and not all wear the traditional black) is due to the traditional 10- to 20-year age difference between husband and wife.

Because foreign men don't observe the Greek customs, their interest in a Greek woman will often be regarded with suspicion by her family. Although the brother probably won't brandish a knife at a man for glancing at his sister, he is likely to tell him to look elsewhere.

Working

If you run out of money in Greece, it usually isn't too difficult to find a temporary job on the islands, ranging from polishing cucumbers to laying cement. The local *kafeneíon* is a good place to enquire. Work on yachts can sometimes be found by asking around at the Athenian marinas. The theatre agents, for work as extras in films, are off Academias Ave, by Kanigos Square. Teachers may apply to one of the seven English/American schools in Athens, or apply to work as an English teacher in a *frontistirion*, a poorly-paid, private school. The *Athens News*, the country's English daily, and *The Athenian*, a monthly publication, often have classified advertisements for domestic, tutorial, and secretarial jobs.

Modern History, Art and Architecture

Unless you're one of those dullards who unplug themselves from their earphones and novels only to take photographs of donkeys, then you'll want to meet the Greeks. Although the massive influx of foreign visitors in recent years has had an inevitable numbing effect on the traditional hospitality offered to strangers, you will find that almost everyone you meet is friendly and gracious, and the older islanders—especially in the small villages—full of wonderful stories.

And rare indeed is the Greek who avoids talking about politics. It was Aristotle, after all, who declared man to be a political animal and if Greeks today have any link with their Classical past it is in their enthusiasm for all things political. An enthusiasm especially evident during an election, when all means of transport to the Greek islands are swamped with Athenians returning to their native villages to vote. Some knowledge of modern history is essential in understanding current Greek views and attitudes, and for that reason the following outline is included. Ancient and Byzantine history, which touches Greece less closely today, is dealt with under Athens and the individual islands.

The Spirit of Independence

From ancient times to the end of the Byzantine Empire, Greek people lived not only within the boundaries of modern-day Greece but throughout Asia Minor, in particular that part of Asia Minor now governed by Turkey. Constantinople was their capital, and although founded as a new Rome by Constantine, it was Greek. Not even during the 400-year Turkish occupation did these people and their brethren in Europe stop considering themselves Greeks—and the Turks, for the most part, were content to let them be Greek as long as they paid their taxes.

The revolutionary spirit that swept through Europe at the end of the 18th and beginning of the 19th centuries did not fail to catch hold in Greece, by now more than weary of the lethargic inactivity and sporadic cruelties of the Ottomans. The Greek War of Independence was begun in the Peloponnese in 1821, and it continued for more than six years in a series of bloody atrocities and political intrigues and divisions. In the end the Great Powers, namely Britain, Russia and France, came to assist the Greek cause, especially in the decisive battle of Navarino (20 October 1827) which in effect gave the newly formed Greek government the Peloponnese and the peninsula up to a line between the cities of Arta and Volos. Count John Capodistria of Corfu, ex-secretary to the Tsar of Russia, became the first President of Greece. While a king was sought for the new state, Capodistria followed an independent policy which succeeded in offending the pro-British and pro-French factions in Greece—and also the powerful Mavromikhalis family who assassinated him in 1831. Before the subsequent anarchy spread too far, the Great Powers appointed Otho, son of King Ludwig I of Bavaria, as King of the Greeks.

The Great Idea

Under Otho began what was called The Great Idea of uniting all the lands of the Greek peoples with the motherland, although Athens lacked the muscle to do anything about it at the time. Otho was peaceably ousted in 1862 and the Greeks elected William George, son of the King of Denmark, as 'King of the Hellenes'. By this they meant all the Greek people, and not merely those within the borders of Greece. The National Assembly drew up a constitution in 1864 which made the nation officially a democracy under a king, a system that began to work practically under Prime Minister Kharilaos Trikoupis in 1875. With the long reign of George I, Greece began to develop with an economy based on sea trade. The Great Idea had to wait for an opportune moment to ripen into reality.

In 1910 the great statesman from Crete, Eleftherios Venizelos, became Prime Minister of Greece for the first time. Under his direction the opportune moment came in the form of the two Balkan Wars of 1912–13, as a result of which Crete, Samos, Macedonia and southern Epirus were annexed to Greece. In the meantime King George was assassinated by a madman, and Constantine I ascended to the throne of Greece. Constantine had married the sister of Kaiser Wilhelm and had a close relationship with Germany, and when the First World War broke out, so did a dispute as to whose side Greece was on. Venizelos supported the Allies and Constantine the Central Powers, although he officially remained neutral until the Allies forced him to mobilize the Greek army. Meanwhile, in the north of Greece, Venizelos had set up his own government with volunteers in support of the Allied cause.

After the war to end all wars The Great Idea still smouldered, and Venizelos made the blunder of his career by sending Greek forces to occupy Smyrna (present-day Izmir) and advance on Ankara, the new Turkish capital. It was a disaster. The Turks, under Mustapha Kemal (later Ataturk) had grown far more formidable after their defeat in the Balkan War than the Greeks had imagined. In August 1922 the Greek army was completely routed at Smyrna, and many Greek residents who could not escape were slaughtered. Constantine immediately abdicated in favour of his son George II, and died soon afterwards. The government fell and Colonel Plastiras with his officers took over, ignobly executing the ministers of the previous government. Massive population exchanges were made between Greece and Turkey to destroy the rationale behind Greek expansionist claims, and the Greeks were confronted with the difficulties of a million Anatolian refugees.

In 1929 a republic was proclaimed which lasted for ten shaky years, during which the Greek communist party, or KKE, was formed and gained strength. After the brief Panglos dictatorship, the Greeks elected Venizelos back as President. He set the present borders of Greece (except for the Dodecanese Islands, which belonged to Italy until 1945). During his term of office there was also an unsuccessful uprising by the Greek Cypriots, four-fifths of the population of what was then a British Crown Colony, who desired union with Greece.

World War–Civil War

The republic, beset with economic difficulties, collapsed in 1935, and King George II returned to Greece, with General Metaxas as his Prime Minister. Metaxas took dictatorial control under the regime of 4 August, which crushed the trade unions and all leftist activities, exiling the leaders. Having prepared the Greek army long in advance for the coming war, Metaxas died in 1941 after his historic 'No!' to Mussolini. In 1940, with Italian troops on the Albanian border, Greece was the first Allied country voluntarily to join Britain against the Axis. The Greek army stopped the Italians and then pushed them back into Albania.

But by May 1941 all of Greece was in the hands of the Nazis, and George II was in exile in Egypt. The miseries of Occupation were compounded by political strife, fired by the uncertain constitutionality of a monarch who had been acting for so many years without parliamentary support. The Communist-organized EAM, the National Liberation Front, attacked all the competing resistance groups so rigorously that they came to support the monarchy as a lesser evil than the Communists. These Monarchists were supported in turn by the British. Nothing could be done, however, to prevent Civil War from breaking out three months after the liberation of Greece. The army of the EAM almost took Athens before the King finally agreed not to return to Greece without a plebiscite.

After the World War and the Civil War the country was in a shambles, economically and politically. Americans began to supersede the British in Greek affairs, and acted as observers in the elections of March 1946. A few months later the King was officially welcomed back to Greece, although he died a year later to be succeeded by his brother Paul.

Recovery and the Issue of Cyprus

Recovery was very slow, despite American assistance. Stalin also became very interested in the strategic location of Greece. In a roundabout way this caused the second Civil War in 1947 between the Communists and the government. The Americans became deeply involved defending the recent Truman Doctrine (on containing Communism, especially in Greece) and government forces finally won in October 1949, allowing the country to return to the problems of reconstruction.

With the Korean War in 1951 Greece and Turkey became full members of NATO, although the Cyprus issue again divided the two countries. In 1954, the Greek Cypriots, led by Archbishop Makarios, clamoured and rioted for union with Greece. Either for military reasons (so believe the Greeks) or to prevent a new conflict between Greece and Turkey, the Americans and British were hardly sympathetic to Cyprus' claims. Meanwhile Prime Minister Papagos died, and Konstantinos Karamanlis replaced him, staying in office for eight years. The stability and prosperity begun under Papagos increased, and agriculture and tourism began to replace Greece's traditional reliance on the sea. The opposition to Karamanlis criticized him for his pro-Western policy, basically because of the Cyprus bugbear, which grew worse all the time. Because of the island's one-fifth Turkish population and its strategic location, the Turks would not agree on union for Cyprus—the independence or partitioning of the island was as far as they would go. Finally in 1960, after much discussion on all sides, Cyprus became an independent republic and elected Makarios its first President. The British and Americans were considered to be good friends again.

Then once more the economy began to plague the government. The royal family became unpopular, there were strikes, and in 1963 came the assassination of Deputy Lambrakis in Thessaloniki (see the film *Z*) for which police officers were tried and convicted. Anti-Greek government feelings rose in London, just when the King and Queen were about to visit. Karamanlis advised them not to go, and their insistence sparked off his resignation. George Papandreou of the opposition was eventually elected Prime Minister. King Paul died and Constantine II became King of Greece.

In 1964 violence broke out in Cyprus again, owing to the disproportional representation in government of the Turkish minority. A quarrel with the King led to Papandreou's resignation resulting in much bitterness. The party system deteriorated and on 21 April 1967 a group of colonels established a military dictatorship. George Papandreou and his son Andreas were imprisoned, the latter charged with treason. Col. George Papadopoulos became dictator, imprisoning thousands without trial. In 1967 another grave incident occurred in Cyprus, almost leading to war. King Constantine II fled to Rome.

Moral Cleansing

The proclaimed aim of the colonels' junta was a moral cleansing of 'Christian Greece'. Human rights were suppressed, and the secret police tortured dissidents—or their children. Yet the British and American governments tolerated the regime, the latter very actively because of NATO. The internal situation went from bad to worse, and in 1973 students of the Polytechnic school in Athens struck. Tanks were brought in and many were killed. After this incident popular feeling rose to such a pitch that Papadopoulos was arrested, only to be replaced by his arrester, the head of the military police and an even worse dictator, Ioannides. The nation was in turmoil. Attempting to save his position by resorting to The Great Idea, Ioannides tried to launch a coup in Cyprus by assassinating Makarios, intending to replace him with a president who would declare the long-desired union of Cyprus with Greece. It was a fiasco. Makarios fled, and the Turkish army invaded Cyprus. The dictatorship resigned and Karamanlis returned to Athens from Paris where he had been living in exile. He immediately formed a new government, released the political prisoners and legalized the Communist party. He then turned his attention to Cyprus, where Turkish forces had occupied 40% of the island. But the Greek army was not strong enough to take on the Turks, nor did the position taken by the British and the American governments help.

Today's Republic

On 17 November 1974 an election was held, which Karamanlis easily won. The monarchy did less well and Greece became the republic it is today. In 1977 Archbishop Makarios died leaving the Cyprus issue unresolved in the minds of the Greeks, although the Turks seem to consider it well nigh settled. This remains one of the major debating points in Greek politics. The desire for social reform and an independent foreign policy were to be the ticket to Andreas Papandreou's Socialist victories in the 1980s. His party, PASOK, promised withdrawal from NATO and the removal of US air bases, along with many other far-reaching reforms. In practice, the new government found these impossible to implement, and the arrogant Papandreou succeeded in alienating nearly all of Greece's allies while overseeing a remarkable economic boom, thanks to the growth of tourism and EC loan money. In the end, scandals and corruption brought PASOK down; Papandreou's open affair with a much younger woman—Dimitri Liani, now his wife—and the Bank of Crete corruption scandal didn't go down well in an essentially conservative country. This led to PASOK losing power in 1990.

Mitsotakis and the New Democracy (ND) conservatives took a slim majority in the elections to grapple with Greece's economic problems. ND immediately launched a wave of austerity measures which proved even more unpopular than Papandreou—a crackdown on tax evasion, which is rife in Greece; a wage freeze for civil servants; privatisation of most state-run companies, including Olympic Airways; and steep increases in charges for public services. This sparked off a wave of strikes in 1991 and 1992. By late 1992 Mitsotakis was also involved in political scandals, and in 1993 a splinter party formed, Political Spring, led by Antonis Samaras. The principal effect of this was to split the votes and thereby topple ND when a general election was held in October 1993.

PASOK, led again by the ageing Andreas Papandreou, won the election, and proceeded to build a political dynasty that would make Bill Clinton jealous; he appointed his young wife as chief of staff, made his son the deputy foreign minister, and even made his own doctor the minister of health. 75-year-old Papandreou's own health is poor, and most Greeks doubt his ability to administer the medicine Greece needs. The big issues on the agenda for the next year or so are the continuing economic problems, the rising foreign debt, the influx of Albanian refugees, and the Macedonian question, on which Greece seems prepared to defy all of her allies, even at the risk of igniting an all-out Balkan war.

A Brief Outline of Greek Art and Architecture

Neolithic to 3000 BC

The oldest known settlements on the Greek islands date back to approximately 6000 BC—Knossos, Phaistos and the cave settlements of **Crete**, obsidian-exporting Phylokope on **Milos**, sophisticated Paleochoe on **Limnos** and Ag. Irene on **Kea**. Artistic finds are typical of the era elsewhere—dark burnished pottery, decorated with spirals and wavy lines and statuettes of the fertility goddess in stone or terra cotta.

Bronze Age: Cycladic and Minoan styles (3000–1100 BC)

Contacts with Anatolia and the Near East brought Crete and the Cyclades to the cutting edge of not only Greek, but European civilization. Around 2600 BC Cycladic dead were buried with extraordinary white marble figurines, or idols that border on the modern abstract (in the museums in **Naxos** and **Athens**). In the same period the first Minoans in Crete were demonstrating an uncanny artistic talent in their polychrome pottery—Kamares ware—and their stone vases (carved to resemble ceramic) and gold jewellery. They buried their dead in round *tholos* tombs up to 18 m in diameter. Hieroglyphs, learned from the Egyptians, were used to keep track of the magazines of oil, wine and grain stored in huge *pithoi* which characterize Minoan palaces and villas.

By the Middle Minoan period (2000–1700 BC) Crete ruled the Aegean with its mighty fleet. The Minoan priest-kings were secure enough from external and internal threats to build themselves unfortified palaces and cities, inevitably centred around a large rectangular courtyard. They installed a system of canals and drains which suggests that the Romans were hardly the first to take regular baths. Hieroglyphic writing was replaced by the still undeciphered script Linear A. Cretan civilization reached its apogee in the Late Minoan period (1700–1450 BC), when the Minoans had colonies across the Aegean and their elegant ambassadors figured in the tomb paintings of the Pharaohs; their own palaces at **Knossos, Phaistos, Zakros, Mallia** and at their outpost of Akrotiri on the island of **Santorini** were adorned with elegant frescoes of flowers, animals, human figures and bull dancers and other treasures now in the archaeology museums of **Herakleon** and **Athens**.

Built mostly of wood and unbaked brick, the Minoan palaces collapsed like card castles in a great natural disaster when the volcanic island of Santorini exploded *c.* 1450 BC. The Achaeans of Mycenae rushed in to fill the vacuum of power and trade in the Aegean, taking over the Minoan colonies; their influence extended to the language of Linear B, which has been deciphered as a form of early Greek. The Achaeans adopted the Minoans' artistic techniques, especially in goldwork and ceramics. Little of this ever reached the islands, although many have vestiges of the Achaeans' stone walls, known as *cyclopean* after their gigantic blocks. As impressive as they are, they failed to keep out the northern invaders known as the Dorians, who destroyed Aegean unity and ushered in one of history's perennial Dark Ages.

Geometric (1000–700 BC) and Archaic (700–500 BC)

The break-up of the Minoan and Mycenaean world saw a return to agriculture and the development of the *polis* or city-state. In art the Geometric period refers to the simple, abstract decoration of the pottery; traces of Geometric temples of brick and wood are much rarer. The temple of Apollo at **Dreros** on Crete and the first Temple of Hera on **Samos** were built around the 8th century, although both pale before the discovery in 1981 of the huge sanctuary at **Lefkandi** on Evia, believed to date from *c.* 900 BC. The most complete Geometric town discovered so far is Zagora on **Andros**.

The Archaic Period is marked by the change to stone, especially limestone, for the building of temples and a return to representational art in decoration. The first known stone temple—and a prototype of the Classical temple with its columns, pediments and metopes—was **Corfu**'s stout-columned Doric Temple of Artemis (580 BC), its pediment decorated with a formidable 10-ft Medusa (now in Corfu's museum). The beautiful Doric Temple of Aphaia on **Aegina** was begun in the same period and decorated with a magnificent 6th-century pediment sculpted with scenes from the Trojan war (now in Munich). The excavations at Emborio, on **Chios**, are among the best extant records we have of an Archaic town; the 6th-century Efplinion tunnel at Pythagorio, **Samos** was the engineering feat of the age.

This era also saw the beginning of life size—and larger—figure sculpture, inspired by the Egyptians: poses are stiff, formal, and rigid, one foot carefully placed before the other. The favourite masculine figure was the *kouros*, or young man, originally one of the dancers at fertility ritual (see the marble quarries of **Naxos** and the *Kriophoros* of **Thassos**); the favourite feminine figure was the *kore*, or maiden, dressed in graceful drapery, representing Persephone and the return of spring. The Archaeology Museum in **Athens** has the best examples of both. The 7th century also saw the development of regional schools of pottery, influenced by the black-figured techniques of Corinth: **Rhodes** and the Cycladic islands produced some of the best.

Classic (500–380 BC)

As Athens became the dominant power in the Aegean, it attracted much of the artistic talent of the Greek world and concentrated its most refined skills on its showpiece Acropolis, culminating with the extraordinary mathematical precision and perfect proportions of the Parthenon, the greatest of all Doric temples, yet built without a single straight line in the entire building. Nothing on the islands approaches it, although there are a few classical-era sites to visit: **Limen** on Thassos and **Eretria** on Evia, **Lindos, Kamiros** and **Ialysos** on Rhodes.

Hellenistic (380–30 BC)

This era brought new stylistic influences from the eastern lands, conquered and hellenized by Alexander the Great and his lieutenants. Compared to the cool, aloof perfection of the Classical era, Hellenistic sculpture is characterized by a more emotional, Mannerist approach, of windswept drapery, violence, and passion. Much of what remains of **Samothrace**'s Sanctuary of the Great Gods, and the Louvre's dramatic *Victory of Samothrace* are from the Hellenistic period. Ancient Rhodes was at the height of its powers, and produced its long-gone Colossus, as well as the writhing *Laocoon* (now in the Vatican museum) and Aphrodite statues in the **Rhodes** museum. Houses became decidedly more plush, many decorated with mosaics and frescoes as in the commercial town of **Delos** and in the suburbs of **Kos**.

Roman (30 BC–529 AD)

The Pax Romana ended the rivalries between the Greek city-states and pretty much ended the source of their artistic inspiration, although sculptors, architects, and other talents found a ready market for their skills in Rome, cranking out copies of Classic and Hellenistic masterpieces. The Romans themselves built little in Greece: the stoa and theatre of Heroditus Atticus (160 AD) were the last large monuments erected in ancient Athens. On the islands, the largest site is **Gortyna**, the Roman capital of Crete.

Byzantine (527–1460)

The art and architecture of the Byzantine Empire began to show its stylistic distinction under the reign of Justinian (527–565), and the immediate post-Justinian period saw a first golden age in the splendour of Ag. Sofia in Istanbul and the churches of Ravenna, Italy. On the islands you'll find only the remains of simple three-naved basilicas—with two important exceptions: the 6th-century Ekatontapyliani of **Paros** and 7th-century Ag. Titos at **Gortyna**, Crete.

After the austere anti-art puritanism of the Iconoclasm (726–843) the Macedonian style (named the Macedonian emperors) slowly infiltrated the Greek provinces. The old Roman basilica plan was jettisoned in favour of what became the classic Byzantine style: a central Greek-cross plan crowned by a dome, elongated in front by a vestibule (narthex) and outer porch (exonarthex) and in the back by a choir and three apses. **Dafni** just outside Athens and Nea Moni on **Chios** with its massive cupola, are superb examples; both are decorated with extraordinary mosaics from the second golden age of Byzantine art, under the dynasty of the Comnenes (12th–14th centuries). As in Italy, this period marked a renewed interest in antique models: the stiff, elongated hieratic figures with staring eyes have more naturalistic proportions in graceful, rhythmic compositions; good examples are at **Dafni**. The age of the Comnenes also produced some fine painting: the 12th-century frescoes and manuscripts at the Monastery of St John on **Patmos**; the beautifully-frescoed early 13th-century Kera Panayia at **Kritsa**, near Ag. Nikolaos on Crete. Crete's occupation by Venice after 1204 marked the beginning of an artistic cross-fertilization that developed into the highly-esteemed Cretan school of icon painting, most conveniently seen in the Byzantine museums in Ag. Katerina in **Herakleon** and in **Athens**.

What never changed was the intent of Byzantine art, which is worth a small digression because in the 14th century Western sacred art went off in an entirely different direction—so much so that everything before is disparagingly labelled 'primitive' in most art books. One of the most obvious differences is the strict iconography in Byzantine painting: if you know the code you can instantly identify each saint by the cut of beard or his or her attribute. Their appeal to the viewer, even in the 11th century when the figures were given more naturalistic proportions, is equally purely symbolic; a Byzantine Christ on the Cross, the Virgin *Panayia*, the 'all-holy', angels, saints and martyrs never make a play for the heartstrings, but reside on a purely spiritual and intellectual plane. As Patrick Leigh Fermor wrote: 'Post-primitive religious painting in the West is based on horror, physical charm, infant-worship and easy weeping.' Icons and Byzantine frescoes never ask the viewer to relive vicariously the passion of Christ or coo over Baby Jesus; Byzantine angels never lift their draperies to reveal a little leg; the remote, wide-eyed Panayia has none of the luscious charms of the Madonna. They never stray from their remote otherworldliness.

And yet, in the last gasp of Byzantine art under the Paleologos emperors (14th–early 15th centuries), humanist and naturalistic influences combined to produce the Byzantine equivalent of the Late Gothic/early Renaissance painting in Italy, in Mistras in the Peloponnese. It is the great might-have-been of Byzantine art: after the Turkish conquest the best painters took refuge on Mount Athos, or on the islands ruled by Venice, but none of their work radiates the same charm or confidence in the temporal world.

Turkish Occupation to the Present

The Turks left few important monuments in Greece, and much of what they did build was wrecked by the Greeks after independence. **Rhodes** town has the best surviving mosques, hammams, houses and public buildings, not only because the Turks loved it well, but because it only became Greek in 1945. **Crete** and **Corfu** have a number of fine Venetian relics: impressive fortifications and gates, fountains, public buildings and town houses. Elsewhere, islands with their own fleets, especially **Hydra**, **Spetses** and **Symi** have impressive captain's mansions, while other islands continued traditional architectural styles: the whitewashed asymmetry of the Cyclades, the patterned sgraffito in the mastic villages of Chios, the Macedonian wooden upper floors and balconies of the northernmost islands.

In the 19th century, public buildings in both Athens and **Syros** (briefly Greece's chief port) are fairly bland neo-Classical works; a host of neo-Byzantine churches went up, while many older ones were unfortunately tarted up with tired bastard painting, Byzantine in iconography but most of it no better than the contents of a third rate provincial museum in Italy.

On the whole, the less said about 20th century architecture on the islands the better: the Fascist architecture left by the Italians on the Dodecanese islands has a sense of style, which is more than can be said of the cheap concrete slabs that have gone up elsewhere. Prosperity in the 1980s has brought an increased interest in local architecture and historic preservation: following the lead of the National Tourist Organization's traditional settlement programme, private individuals have begun to restore old monasteries, abandoned villages, and captains' mansions, while many of the newest resort developments are less brash and more in harmony with local styles. One individual who won't be restoring any of his Palaces is ex-King Constantine of Greece, whose properties were expropriated by the Papandraeus Government in 1994.

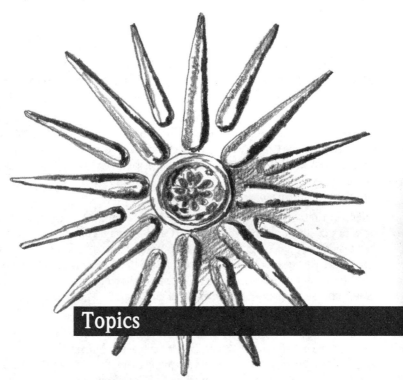

Topics

Macedonia

The signs at Athens Airport proclaim: Macedonia is Greek. If that doesn't sink in, then the slogans on the new phonecards drive the message home: Macedonia is One and Only and it is Greek. And don't think you can escape hearing about the issue by flying off to the distant islands; the Greeks are obsessed with the subject, and it's worth knowing some historical background in case you become embroiled in a discussion about it.

The Greek government, and the nation, emphatically denies recognition of the independent Republic of Macedonia in the former Yogoslavia. Ever since the province bordering Greek Macedonia declared itself independent and adopted the M-word in April 1993, nationalistic fervour has broken out and the Greeks are outraged, wearing lapel pins featuring the symbol of Alexander the Great, Macedonia's most famous son.

Ironically Greece, host nation of the EU in 1994, is pitting itself against EC moves to recognize the former Yugoslav state. Campaigners argue that Macedonia has been Greek for 3,000 years (some claim 4,000 years), and thus has a copyright on the name. They fear borders will be re-drawn, there is even threat of invasion, and say Ancient Macedonia was a Hellenistic civilisation, not a Slavic one, as the Slavs didn't settle on the Balkan peninsula until the 6th century AD.

Macedon was a backwoods kingdom on the fringes of Greek civilization until the advent of Philip II (reigned 359–336 BC), who, aided by the discovery of gold and his own unconventional military tactics, created the most effective army in Greece. As the Greek states squabbled among themselves, he annexed Thessaly (352 BC), and in 338 BC gobbled up the rest of Greece by crushing the last-minute anti-Macedonian coalition of Athens and Thebes. Philip forced the city-states into a pan-Hellenic leagues that took orders from him. The first was to raise a massive army against the Persians. Philip was assassinated, leaving the vast army to his son Alexander, who had been carefully groomed to think like a true Greek by the greatest teacher of the day—Aristotle.

Alexander had inherited all of his father's military genes, and then some. After a quick razing of Thebes to keep the quarrelsome Greeks in their place, he took his pan-Hellenic army to Persia and began his inexorable conquest that stretched to India before his army staged a sit-down strike and refused to march another step. Although much of his great empire died with him or was divided up into chunks by his generals (his Ptolemies in Egypt, the Seleucids of Syria), his greatest achievment in the eyes of the Greeks was the hellenisation (read civilisation) of his conquests. Greek became the lingua franca and the gods of Olympus usurped the temples of their barbaric brethren. Yet during his lifetime, Alexander was looked down on by the Greeks as little more than a barbarian himself.

From 215–146 BC Rome meddled increasingly in Greek affairs, at first participating in the Macedonian Wars between Philip V of Macedon and the rival Aetolian and Achaian federations. Philip was forced into an alliance with Rome in 200 BC and the Macedon kingdom was destroyed in 168 BC to become the Roman province of Macedonia; under the later Ottoman empire the population of Macedonia, a region with hazily-defined borders, was such a mixture of Greeks, Albanians, Serbs, Bulgarians and Romanians that it gave rise to the French word for salad (*macédoine*).

As the Ottoman Empire died its slow death in the early 1990s, Macedonia became a hotbed of rival nationalistic groups. When the two Balkan wars erupted in 1912 Greece gained southern Macedonia, Salonika and Kavala, just beating the Bulgarians in the rush for territory. Disagreements over the borders have rankled ever since; in the murky Balkan fruit salad names count for a lot.

Fiercely proud and defensive after centuries of domination, the Greeks believe it is an outrage for the name of Macedonia to be adopted by the former Yugoslav state. To them the golden age of their cultural history has been usurped and acceptance of any EC recognition is unlikely.

On *Kefi* and Dancing

In the homogenized European Community of the 1990s, only the Spaniards and Greeks still dance to their own music with any kind of spontaneity, and it's no coincidence that both have untranslatable words to describe the 'spirit' or 'mood' that separates going through the steps and true dancing. In Spain, the word is *duende*, which, with the hard driving rhythms of flamenco, has an ecstatic quality; in Greek, the word is *kefi*, which comes closer to 'soul'. For a Greek to give his all, he must have *kefi*; to dance without it could be considered dishonest. The smart young men in black trousers and red sashes who dance for you at dinner probably don't have it; two craggy old fishermen, in a smoky café in Crete, who crank up an old gramophone and dance for their own pleasure, do. You can feel the *kefi* at Easter when the village elders join hands and dance an elegant *kalamatiano*, or when a group of children celebrate the local saint's day in North Karpathos. Any sensitive person can't help but be moved by the atmosphere, especially in constrast with the stark, technically perfect stage performances of the dance troupes under the Acropolis or in the old fort of Corfu. If the *kefi* moves you to leap up and dance, your Greek friends will see you in a new light, your bond with Greece established, and you may find it just that bit harder to book your ticket home.

Nearly every island has its own dance, some of which are extremely difficult. Then there are the dances everyone knows, from the elementary 'one two three kick kick', or *Sta Tria*, footed in a circle with hands on shoulders. The circle is never complete, however: even in this simple dance a man or woman will lead, handkerchief in hand, setting the pace and supplying the special effects with leaps, foot slaps, kicks, little skips or whatever he or she likes. Cretans are among the most energetic leaders—some are almost contortionists.

Sta Tria often begins slowly and picks up to a furious pace towards the end. The *sýrto*, on the other hand, retains its slow graceful pace throughout. It has only six easy steps which are repeated until the end, but watch the leader for variations. This is considered the oldest Greek dance of all, dating back to Hellenistic, if not Homeric times. The *kalamatíanos*, a 12-step dance, takes some practice. If a Greek invites you to dance the *bállos*, the most common couple's dance, follow your partner's lead and hope for the best. While there are certain set steps to the *tsíftetéli*, or belly dance, it has become a free-spirited dance for the loose limbed and requires plenty of nerve (or wine) to pull off successfully.

The *zembekiko* is normally but not exclusively performed by men, a serious, deliberate solo dance with outstretched arms, evoking the swooping flight of the eagle; a companion will go down on one knee to encourage the dancer and clap out the rhythm. The *hasápiko*, better known as the Zorba dance, and traditionally performed by two men, will require some practice but is well worth learning— like Alan Bates who finally began to fathom *kefi* from Anthony Quinn at the end of the film *Zorba the Greek*. Plenty of practice and energy are the rules for joining in most Cretan dances, where the music demands furious, machine-gun fire steps and hops that go on until your adrenalin has pumped its last. But toss back another *raki*, and before you know it you'll be up dancing another *pentozal* or *podokto*.

You can get off on the right foot with *Greek Dances* by Ted Petrides (published by Lycabettus Press in Athens), supplemented by some private coaching from the Greeks—or their children, who usually have more patience.

Orthodoxy

With the exception of a handful of Catholics in the Cyclades, nearly all Greeks belong to the Orthodox, or Eastern church; indeed, being Orthodox and speaking Greek are the two most important criteria in defining a Greek, whether born in Athens, Alexandria or Australia. Orthodoxy is so fundamental that even the greatest sceptics can hardly conceive of marrying outside the church, or neglecting to have their children baptized.

One reason for this deep national feeling is that unlike everything else in Greece, Orthodoxy has scarcely changed since the founding of the church by Constantine in the 4th century. As Constantinople took the place of Rome as the political and religious capital, the Greeks believe their church to be the only true successor to the original church of Rome. Therefore, a true Greek is called a *Romiós* or Roman, and the Greek language of today is called *Romaíka*. It is considered perfect and eternal and beyond all worldly change; if it weren't, its adherents could not expect to be saved. Hence, the Greeks have been spared the changes that have rocked the West, from Vatican II to discussions over women in the clergy to political questions of abortion, birth control and so on—matters on which Orthodoxy has always remained aloof. Much emphasis is put on ceremony and ritual, the spiritual and aesthetic, with very little appeal to the emotions.

This explains the violence of Iconoclasm, the one movement to change the rules. Back in the early 8th century Byzantine Emperor Leo III the Isaurian, shamed by what his Moslem neighbours labelled idolatry, deemed the images of divine beings to be sacrilegious. Iconoclasm began the rift with Rome, that worsened in 800 when the Pope crowned Charlemagne as emperor, usurping the position of the Emperor of Constantinople. Further divisions arose over the celibacy of the clergy (Orthodox may marry before they are ordained) and the use of the phrase 'and the son' in the Holy Creed, the issue which caused the final, fatal schism in 1054 when the Pope's representative Cardinal Humbert excommunicated the Patriarch of Constantinople.

After the fall of the Byzantine Empire (that 'thousand-year-long mass for the dead' as one recent Greek writer put it), the Turks not only tolerated the Orthodox church, but they had the political astuteness to impart considerable powers to the patriarch. The church was thus able to preserve many Greek traditions and Greek education through the dark age of Ottoman rule; on the other hand it often abused this power against its own flock, especially locally. According to an old saying, priests, headmen and Turks were the three curses of Greece and the poor priests (who in truth are usually quite amiable fellows) have not yet exonerated themselves from the list they now share with the king and the cuckold.

The extraordinary quantity of churches and chapels on some islands has little to do with the priests, however. Nearly all were built by families or individuals, especially by sailors, seeking the protection of a patron saint. Some were built to keep a promise, others in simple thanksgiving. Architecturally they come in an endless variety of styles depending on the region, period and terrain, as well as the wealth and whim of the builder. All but the tiniest have an *iconostasis*, or altar screen, made of wood or stone to separate the *heiron* or sanctuary, where only the ordained are allowed, from the rest of the church. Most of the chapels are now locked up; some light-fingered tourists have decided that icons make lovely souvenirs; if you track down the caretaker, do dress discreetly (no shorts!) and leave a few drachmas for upkeep.

Almost all these chapels have only one service a year, on the name day of the patron saint (name days are celebrated in Greece more widely than birthdays: 'Many years!' *(Chrónia pollá!)* is the proper way to greet someone on their name day). This annual celebration is called a *yiortí* or more frequently *paniyiri*, and is the cause for feasts and dancing before or after the church service. If feasible, *paniyiria* take place directly in the churchyard, if not, in neighbouring wooded areas or in tavernas. The food can be superb but is more often basic and plentiful; for a set price you receive more than your share and a doggy bag full, generally of goat. *Paniyiria* (festivals) are also the best places to hear traditional island music and learn the dances, and it's sad that they're only a fond memory in most major tourist centres (although alive and well in less frequented areas).

The Assumption of the Virgin, 15 August, is the largest *paniyiri* in Greece apart from Easter, the biggest holiday. The faithful sail to Tinos, the Lourdes of Greece, and to a dozen centres connected with Mary, making mid-August a very uncomfortable time to travel among the islands, especially the Cyclades. Not only are the ships packed to the brim, but the *meltemi* wind also blows with vigour, and Greek matrons, the most ardent pilgrims of all, are the worst of all sailors.

Orthodox weddings are another lovely if long-winded ritual. The bride and groom stand solemnly before the chanting priest, while family and friends in attendance seem to do everything but follow the proceedings. White crowns, bound together by a white ribbon, are placed on the heads of bride and groom, and the *koumbáros*, or best man, exchanges them back and forth. The newlyweds are then led around the altar three times, which spurs the guests into action as they bombard the happy couple with fertility-bringing rice and flower petals. After congratulating the bride and groom guests are given a small *boboniéra* of sugared almonds. This is followed by the marriage feast and dancing, which in the past could last up to five days. If you are in the vicinity of a village wedding you may be offered a sweet cake; you may even be invited to come along to the feasting as a special guest.

Baptisms are cause for similar celebration. The priest completely immerses the baby in the Holy Water three times (unlike Achilles, there are no vulnerable spots on modern Greeks) and almost always gives the little one the name of a grandparent. For extra protection from the forces of evil, babies often wear a *filaktó*, or amulet, the omnipresent blue glass eye bead. If you visit a baby at home you may well be sprinkled first with Holy Water, and chances are there's a bit of beneficial garlic squeezed somewhere under the cradle. Compliments to the little one's parents should be kept to a minimum; the gods do get jealous.

Funerals in Greece, for reasons of climate, are carried out as soon as possible, and are announced by the tolling of the village church bells. The dead are buried for three to five years (longer if the family can pay) after which time the bones are exhumed and placed in the family box to make room for the next resident. *Aforismós*, or Orthodox excommunication, is believed to prevent the body decaying after death—the main source of Greek vampire stories. Memorials for the dead take place three, nine and forty days after death, and on the first anniversary. They are sometimes repeated annually. Sweet buns and sugared wheat and raisin *koúliva* are given out after the ceremony; children wouldn't miss them for the world.

The *Periptero* and the Plane Tree

In Greece you'll see it everywhere, the greatest of modern Greek inventions, the indispensable *periptero*. It is the best-equipped kiosk in the world, where people gather to chat, make local or international calls, or grab a few minutes' shade under the little projecting roof. The *periptero* is a substitute bar, selling everything from water to cigarettes to ice cold beer; an emergency pharmacy stocked with aspirin, mosquito killers, condoms and sticking plaster; a convenient newsagent for Greek and international publications, from *Ta Nea* to *Die Zeit*; a tourist shop offering travel guides, postcards and stamps; a toy shop for balloons, plastic swords and My Little Pony; a general store for shoelaces, batteries and rolls of film. In Athens they're at most traffic lights. On the islands they are a more common sight than a donkey. You'll wonder how you ever survived before *peripteros* and the treasures they contain.

The other great meeting centre of Greek life is the mighty plane tree, or *platanos*, for centuries the focal point of village life, where politics and philosophy have been argued since time immemorial. Since Hippocrates the Greeks have believed that plane shade is wholesome and beneficial (unlike the ennervating shadow cast by the fig) and one of the most extraordinary sights in the islands is 'Hippocrates' plane tree' on Kos, propped up on scaffolding and as protected as any national monument would be. In Greek the expression *herete mou ton platano* loosely translates as 'go tell it to the marines', presumably because the tree has heard all that nonsense before. For a Greek village the *platanos* represents that village's identity; the tree is a source of life, for it only grows near abundant fresh water; its deep roots a symbol of stability, continuity and protection—a huge majestic umbrella, even the rain cannot penetrate its sturdy leaves. Sit under its spreading branches and sip a coffee as the morning unfolds before you; the temptation to linger there for the day is irresistible.

Some Plain Old Pests

The wily mosquito tops the list for pure incivility. Most shops stock the usual defences: lotions, sprays and insect coils; or pick up one of those inexpensive electric mosquito repellents that fit right in the wall plug and don't stink as badly as the smouldering coils. The most effective repellents contain high proportions of Deet; Autan and Jungle Formula (on sale in the UK, sometimes from airport chemists) do the job. Jungle Formula contains more Deet and tends to be more effective.

Public insect enemy Number Two is the wasp, either taking bites out of that honey baklava you've just ordered, or spoiling your picnic on the beach. Dangers lurk in the sea as well: harmless pale brown jellyfish (*médusas*) may drift in anywhere depending on winds and currents, but the oval transparent model (*tsouitres*) are stinging devils that can leave scars on tender parts of your anatomy if you brush against them. Pincushiony black sea urchins live on the rocks of rocky beaches, and must be avoided. The spines may break and embed themselves, deeper still if you try to force them out; the Greeks recommend olive oil and a lot of patience to get the spine to slip out. As first aid, they suggest peeing on them to take away the sting (if you're a woman, summon a friend). They hurt like hell, so on rocky beaches it makes sense to wear sandals or plastic shoes in the water if you're likely to be putting your feet down on the rocks.

Much less common are Greece's shy scorpions, who hide out in between the rocks in rural areas; unless you're especially sensitive, their sting is no more nor less painful than a bee's. Always avoid the back legs of mules, unless you've been properly introduced. The really lethal creatures are rare: the small, grey-brown viper that lives in the nooks and crannies of stone walls, where it is well camouflaged, only comes out occasionally to sun itself. Although it is seldom seen (it prefers abandoned villages and quiet archaeological sites), the Greeks are terrified of it; the mere word *fithi* (snake) will turn the most stout-hearted villager to jelly. Mountain sheepdogs are a more immediate danger in outer rural areas; by stooping as if to pick up a stone to throw, you might keep a dog at bay.

Sharks seldom prowl near the coastal regions of Greece. Blood attracts them, so if you are wounded, swim for shore without delay. Divers should ask their Greek confrères about other dangerous fish in the area, such as the weaver, an unlikely delicacy whose razor-sharp fins can kill.

Shirley Valentines

Know thyself

—inscription over the gate of the oracle at Delphi

There isn't an island without at least one Shirley Valentine, drawn years ago by something special, a holiday romance perhaps that turned into a love affair with a place rather than a person, an enjoyment of living in a country where eccentrics are welcomed rather than scorned. Shirley Valentines come in all shapes and sizes, male or female, young or old, cynical or innocent, birdwatchers or bartenders, pensioners from New York, English gym teachers and marine insurance agents, lost souls from Hamburg, Dutch advertising execs, an occasional black sheep or social misfit; all characters who have found their Atlantis, and can now only live as strange birds in foreign nests.

These people have become part of island daily life and, as far as many locals are concerned, add a missing ingredient. They know their island well, and are usually a good source of information, whether it be tracking down the friendliest watering hole, or blackmailing the builder who promised to turn up weeks ago. Björn from Stockholm has been there for years, married a local girl and can outswear the locals. Penny from Bath can drink the village boys under the table. She has her reasons for doing so; her heart is broken with regularity, and every day brings tears and laughter, but turning Ipanemian brown under the Greek sun, far from the monochrome office blocks, and watching the sun set at the most beautiful time of the day brings a serenity and happiness previously unknown.

'Greece' once remarked President Karamanlis, 'reminds me of an enormous madhouse'. True or not, whether the Shirley Valentines have a streak of madness in them, Greece has allowed them to invent for themselves a way of living their fantasies, of building a new personality that was just under the surface anyway.

When You've Gone

As the days shorten and the cafés close, the last forlorn tourists sit on the deserted waterfront, and the empty echoes of summer fade away. There's now a chill to the wind as the waiters collect up the tables and chairs, no longer needed for the rest of the year, and the island returns to normality. The discotheques, not long ago throbbing to Right Said Fred, close down; the bouzouki replaces the electric guitar, boogie gives way to the *zembekiko* and the overall tempo of life changes. The real Greece re-emerges, the islanders claim back their island. Plastic cafés are re-transformed into lively little *ouzeri*, and it is time to sit and reflect on the summer, count the precious drachmas and lick wounds. The evening stroll, or *volta* returns with full intensity, and the greeting is *Kalo chimona*, or 'Have a good winter'. Wild seas reclaim the beaches; the last Coca Cola can is washed away as the pebbles are rinsed of suntan lotion. Even the swallows decamp, and head south to warmer climes. As the wind kicks up, bare-bones ferry schedules go haywire; fresh vegetables, meat and milk become scarce on many islands, and many a meal consists of beans or lentils, sardines and pasta.

Cold, wet and windy, the Greek winter takes hold of the summer paradise, and men huddle in the *cafenia* discussing politics and tourist conquests, playing cards and *tavli* (backgammon), watching blue movies. Gambling becomes a craze in the winter and fortunes made in the summer can be lost at the turn of a card. Women stay at home and do their needlework or watch soaps on TV. The sun's warmth is replaced by the warmth of the family, and grandma can now take repossession of her little room rented out on the black to backpackers. The only voices in the main street are those of the children wandering in a ragged line to the village school, clutching their schoolbags and midday snacks of bread and spam. The few hardy perennial foreign residents make a reappearance in the cafés, and the lingua franca once again returns to demotic Greek.

The summer spirit flickers briefly in winter's depths, and the gentle sun sometimes provides enough warmth to sit out by the still, sparkling blue sea, watching the caiques come in with their haul. Spring, the loveliest of all seasons in Greece, sees the trees blossom and the islands transformed into carpets of flowers, as Easter approaches. Even the most boisterous Greeks are subdued in the week preceding the Easter weekend, which erupts into a frenzy of dancing, rejoicing, eating and drinking, as fireworks light up the midnight sky. *Christos anesti!* is the greeting, 'Christ has risen!' and millions of candles are lit around the country.

Like magic any harsh memories of the previous summer are forgotten, vendettas are forgiven, and a rejuvenated population prepares itself for a new season, painting café chairs, mending shopfronts, whitewashing walls. There's a feeling of expectancy in the air as, first the swallows, then the tourists arrive, and the whole show winds up again.

Athens and Piraeus

Many travellers to the Greek islands eventually find themselves in Athens and Piraeus, but it's rarely love at first sight; Athens, with its ramshackle architecture and grubby, dusty exterior, wins no beauty prizes. Look closely, however, and you may be won over by this urban crazy quilt of villages—small oases of green parks hidden amidst the hustle and bustle; tiny family-run tavernas tucked away in the most unexpected places; the feverish pace of its nightlife and summer festivals devoted to wine and song; and best all, the Athenians themselves, whose friendliness belies the reputation of most inhabitants of capital cities.

An Historical Outline of Athens

Inhabited by pre-Hellenic tribes in the Neolithic Age (c. 3500 BC) Athens made its proper debut on the stage of history in the second millennium, when Ionians from Asia Minor invaded Attica and established several small city-states. Their main centre was Kekropia, named for the serpent god Kekrops (he later became connected with King Erechtheus, who was himself a snake from the waist down and is considered to be the original founder of Athens). The owl was sacred to Kekropia—as it was to the goddess Athena, and her worship and name gradually came to preside in the city.

In the 14th century BC Athens, as part of the Mycenaean empire of the Achaeans, invaded Crete, fought Thebes, and conquered Troy, but managed to escape the subsequent Dorian invasion which brought chaos into the Mycenaean world. Two hundred years later, however, it was Attica's turn to meet the uncouth Dorians, who brought with them Greece's first Dark Age. This endured until the 8th century BC, far too long for the sophisticated Ionians and Aeolians, who went back to their homelands in Asia Minor and settled many of the Aegean islands.

Sometime during the 8th century all the towns of Attica were peaceably united, an accomplishment attributed to the mythical King Theseus (1300 BC). Athens was then ruled by a king (the chief priest), a *polemarch* (or general), and an *archon* (or civil authority), positions that became annually elective by the 6th century. The conflict between the landed aristocracy and rising commercial classes gradually brought about the solution of democratic government, beginning under the reforms of Solon. Yet under every stone there lurked a would-be tyrant; Solon was still warm in the grave when Pisistratos, leader of the popular party, made himself boss (545 BC) and began the naval build-up that first made Athens a threat to the other independent city-states of Greece.

Pisistratos' son was followed by another reformer, Kleisthenes, who discarded Athens' ancient but unsatisfactory political classifications by dividing the population into ten tribes. Each selected by lot 50 members of the people's assembly, from which a further lot was drawn to select an archon, creating ten archons in all, one from each tribe. The head archon gave his name to the Athenian year.

Meanwhile, as Persian strength grew in the east, Ionian intellectuals and artists settled in Athens, bringing with them the roots of Attic tragedy. They encouraged Athens to aid the Ionians against the Persians, an unsuccessful adventure that landed the city in the soup when Darius, the King of Kings, turned to subdue Greece, and in particular Athens, which posed the only threat to the Persian fleet. In 490 BC Darius' vast army landed at Marathon only to be defeated by a much smaller Athenian force under Miltiades. Powerful Sparta and the other Greek states then recognized the eastern threat, but continued to leave 'national' defence primarily in the hands of the Athenians and their fleet, which grew ever mightier under Themistocles. However, it failed to keep the Persians from having another go at Greece, and in 480 BC the new king Xerxes showed up with the greatest fleet and army the ancient world had ever seen. Athens was destroyed, but the Persian navy was neatly outmanoeuvred by the Athenian ships at Salamis and the invasion was finally repelled by the Athenians and Spartans at the battle of Plataea.

Having proved her naval might, Athens set about creating a maritime empire, not only to increase her power but also to stabilize her combustible internal politics. She ruled the confederacy at Delos, demanding contributions from the islands in return for protection from the Persians. Sea trade became necessary to support the city's growing population, while the founding of new colonies around the Mediterranean ensured a continual food supply to Athens. The democracy became truly imperialistic under Pericles, who brought the treasure of Delos to Athens to skim off funds to rebuild and beautify the city and build the Parthenon. It was the golden age of Athens, the age of the sculptures of Phidias, the histories of Herodotos, the plays of Sophocles and Aristophanes, the philosophy of Socrates.

The main cause of the Peloponnesian War (431–404 BC) was concern over Athenian expansion in the west. Back and forth the struggle went, Sparta with superiority on land, Athens on the seas, until both city-states were near exhaustion. Finally Lysander captured Athens, razed the walls, and set up the brief rule of the Thirty Tyrants.

Although democracy and imperialism made quick recoveries (by 378 the city had set up its second Maritime League), the Peloponnesian War had struck a blow from which Athens could not totally recover. The population grew dissatisfied with public life, and refused to tolerate innovators and critics to the extent that Socrates was put to death. Economically, Athens had trouble maintaining the trade she so desperately needed. Yet her intellectual tradition held true in the 4th century, bringing forth the likes of Demosthenes, Praxiteles, Menander, Plato and Aristotle.

Philip II of Macedon took advantage of the general discontent and turmoil to bully the city-states into joining Macedon for an expedition against Persia. Athenian patriotism and independence were kept alive by the orator Demosthenes until Philip subdued the city (338). He was assassinated shortly before beginning the Persian campaign, leaving his son Alexander to conquer the East. When Alexander died, Athens had to defend herself against his striving generals, beginning with Dimitrios Poliorketes (the Besieger) who captured the city in 294. Alexandria and Pergamon became Athens' intellectual rivals, although Athens continued to be honoured by them.

In 168 BC Rome captured Athens, but gave her many privileges including the island of Delos. Eighty years later Athens betrayed Roman favour by siding with Mithridates of Pontos, for which Sulla destroyed Piraeus and the walls of the city. But Rome always remembered her cultural debt; leading Romans attended Athens' schools and gave the city great gifts. Conversely many Greek treasures ended up in Rome. St Paul came to preach to the Athenians in AD 44. In the 3rd century Goths and barbarians sacked Athens, and when they were driven away the city joined the growing Byzantine Empire.

Justinian closed the philosophy schools in AD 529 and changed the temples to churches and the Parthenon into a cathedral. By now Athens had lost almost all of her former importance. She became the plaything of the Franks after they pillaged Constantinople in 1204. St Louis appointed Guy de la Roche as Duke of Athens, a dukedom which passed through many outstretched hands: the Catalans, Neapolitans and Venetians all controlled it at various times. In 1456 the Turks took Athens, turning the Parthenon into a mosque and the Erechtheion into a harem. While attacking the Turks in 1687 Morosini and the Venetians blew up part of the Parthenon, where the Turks had stored their gunpowder. A year later the Venetians left, unsuccessful, and the citizens who had fled returned to Athens. In 1800 Lord Elgin began the large-scale removal of monuments from Athens to the British and other museums.

In 1834, after the War of Independence, Athens—then a few hundred war-scarred houses deteriorating under the Acropolis—was declared the capital of the new Greek state. Otho of Bavaria, the first King of the Greeks, brought his own architects with him and laid out a new city on the lines of Stadiou and El. Venezelou streets, which still boast most of Otho's neo-Classical public buildings. The rest of the city's architecture was abandoned to unimaginative concrete blocks, spared monotony only by the hilly Attic terrain. More and more of these hills are being pounded into villas and flats by the ubiquitous cement mixer; greater Athens squeezes in over three million lively, opiniated inhabitants (a third of the entire Greek population) who thanks to native ingenuity and EC membership are now more prosperous than they have been since the age of Pericles. Unfortunately this means a million cars now crawl the ancient streets, creating the worst smog problem east of Los Angeles, and one that threatens to choke this unique city.

Modern Athens currently has a new problem with ethnic tensions. The Gipsies have traditionally been looked on as the underclass in Greece, blamed for wrongdoings and thefts. But since thousands of impoverished refugees poured into northern Greece from Albania in 1990 they have become the new whipping boys, especially those who are not ethnically Greek. Albanians are blamed for an increase in street crime and burglaries in the cities.

Many Albanians have moved into Athens, adding to the unemployment problem in the eyes of Athenians. There has been an increase in housebreaking, theft from cars, and other crimes previously unknown in the suburbs of Athens; inevitably, the immigrants, with their visible poverty, have become the new scapegoats.

Orientation

Syntagma (or **Constitution**) **Square** is to all intents and purposes the centre of the the city, and it's here that the **Parliament Building** is to be found, backing on to the **National Gardens** and **Zappeion Park**, a haven of green and shade to escape the summer heat, with ducks to feed and a hundred benches useful for grabbing a few winks. The square itself is a busy roundabout with traffic whizzing past, but this doesn't seem to deter the people sitting feet away at the outdoor tables of the numerous overpriced cafés.

From Syntagma it's a short walk down to the far more interesting **Plaka**, the medieval centre of Athens at the foot of the Acropolis, where many of the older houses have been converted into intimate tavernas or bars, each tinkling away with its own electric bazouki. This is also a good place to look for mid-priced accommodation, and a fun part of the city to wander around in the evening.

During the day meander through Athens' nearby flea market district, to the west of **Monastiraki Square** (and metro), where bulging shops sell everything from good quality woollen goods and fake Caterpillar boots to furniture and second hand fridges. To reach the flea market, you'll find several streets en route that all claim to be the flea market, but are nothing more than tourist traps selling tat such as engraved souvenirs of Athens, fur coats, fake icons, and lots of t-shirts with 'Hellas' printed on them.

A 10-minute walk from Syntagma will take you to **Kolonaki Square**, Athens' Knightsbridge in miniature, complete with fancypants shops and restaurants (all of course expensive) and plenty of well-heeled Athenians to patronize them. Up from the square (it's a long haul on foot, but there's a funicular) is the hill of **Lycavitos**, illuminated like a fairytale tower at night. On the top sits the chapel of **St George**, a restaurant/bar and a cannon fired on national holidays. It offers the best panoramic views of Athens, including a sweeping vista down to the sea at Piraeus, *nefos* (Athens' special brand of smog) permitting.

A 20-minute walk from Syntagma, along Vass. Sofias, brings you to the Hilton Hotel, a useful landmark. Behind it are the essential Athenian neighbourhoods of **Ilissia** and **Pangrati**, the best place to get a feel for everyday life in the city. Lose yourself in their backstreets and you may find your own little taverna, of which there are plenty, rather than restrict yourself to the tourist haunts in the centre.

From Zappeion Park buses run frequently down to the coast and suburbs of **Glyfada**, **Voula** and **Vouliagmenis**. Glyfada, close to the airport, is a green and pleasant suburb, and the town itself has grown into a busy resort and a rival Kolonaki. Many smart city dwellers shop at the ritzy boutiques, and there are even a couple of well-designed (but small, fortunately) indoor shopping centres.

Here and further down the coast at Voula are pay beaches run by EOT, the National Tourist Organisation. The water is generally clean, but nothing like the more remote islands. There's also good swimming beyond Voula in the rocky coves at Vouliagmenis. Beyond Vouliagmenis, the road continues along the coast to **Sounion** and its **Temple of Poseidon** (440 BC), famous for its magnificent position and sunsets and where there's always at least one tourist searching for the column where Byron carved his name.

Agora Museum (the Theseum and Ancient Agora)

Open 8.30–3, closed Mon, adm.

The Agora was not only the market but the centre of Athenian civic and social life where citizens spent much of their day; here Socrates questioned their basic conceptions of life and law. In 480 BC the Persians destroyed all the buildings of the Agora, which were rebuilt in a much grander style; many suffered the wrath of the Romans and fires set by the barbarians. Only the foundations remain of the **Bouleuterion** or council house, and the neighbouring Temple of the Mother of the Gods, the **Metroon**, built by the Athenians in reparation for their slaying of a priest from the cult. The round **Tholos** or administration centre is where the administrators or *prytanes* worked, and as some had to be on call day and night, kitchens and sleeping quarters were included. Its final reconstruction took place after Sulla's rampage in 88 BC. Only a wall remains of the **Sanctuary of the Eponymous Heroes of Athens**, the ten who gave their names to Kleisthenes' ten tribes. The **altar of Zeus Agoraios** received the oaths of the new archons, a practice initiated by Solon.

The 4th-century **Temple of Apollo** was dedicated to the mythical father of the Ionians, who believed themselves descended from Ion, son of Apollo. The huge statue of Apollo in the Agora museum once stood inside the temple. Almost nothing remains of the **Stoa Basileios**, or of Zeus Eleutherios, which played a major role in Athenian history as the court of the annual archon, where trials concerning the security of the state took place. By the Stoa of Zeus stood the **Altar of the Twelve Gods**, from which all distances in Attica were measured. Alongside it ran the **Panathenaic Way**; some signs of its Roman rebuilding may be seen by the Church of the Holy Apostles. After crossing the Agora, this ceremonial path ascended to the Acropolis, where devotees celebrated the union of Attica. South of the Altar of Twelve Gods is the site of the Doric **Temple to Ares** (5th century BC). The **Three Giants** nearby were originally part the **Odeon of Agrippa** (15 BC); parts of the orchestra remain intact after the roof collapsed in AD 190. Confusingly, the site and the giants were reused in the façade of a 5th-century AD gymnasium, that served for a century as the site of the University of Athens until Justinian closed it down. Near the **Middle Stoa** (2nd century BC) are ruins of a **Roman temple** and the ancient shops and booths. On the other side of the Middle Stoa is the people's court, or **Heliaia**, organized by Solon in the 6th century BC to hear political questions; it remained active well into Roman times.

Between the **South and East Stoas** (2nd century BC) is the 11th-century **Church of the Holy Apostles** (Ag. Apostoli), built on the site where St Paul addressed the Athenians and restored, along with its fine paintings, in 1952. Across the Panathenaic Way run the remains of **Valerian's Wall** thrown up in AD 257 against the barbarian, its stone cannibalized from Agora buildings wrecked by the Romans. Between Valerian's Wall and the Stoa of Attalos are higgledy-piggledy ruins of the **Library of Pantainos**, built by Flavius Pantainos in AD 100 and destroyed 167 years later. Finds from the entire Agora are in the museum in the **Stoa of Attalos**, the 2nd-century BC portico built by King Attalos II of Pergamon, reconstructed by John D. Rockefeller.

The same ticket gets you into the mid-5th-century BC **Theseum**, nothing less than the best-preserved Greek temple in existence. Doric in order and dedicated to Hephaistos, the god of metals and smiths, it may well have been designed by the architect of the temple at Sounion. It is constructed almost entirely of Pentelic marble and decorated with metopes depicting the lives of Heracles and Theseus (for whom the temple was named). Converted into a church in the 5th century, it was the burial place for English Protestants until 1834, when the government declared it a national monument.

The Acropolis

Mon–Fri 8–5, Sat and Sun 8.30–3, adm.

The naturally-fortified **Acropolis** was inhabited from the end of the Neolithic Age. The Mycenaeans added a Cyclopean wall and the palace of their king. This was later replaced by a temple to the god of the spring, Poseidon, and to Athena. In mythology, these two divinities took part in a contest to decide who would be the patron of the new city. With his trident Poseidon struck the spring Klepsydra out of the rock of the Acropolis, while Athena invented the olive tree, which the Athenians judged the better trick.

The tyrant Pisistratos ordered a great gate constructed in the wall, but Delphi cursed it and the Athenians dismantled it. In 480 BC the temple's cult statue of Athena was hurried to the protection of Salamis, just before the Persians burnt the Acropolis. Themistocles built a new rampart out of the old Parthenon, and under Perikles the present plan of the Acropolis buildings was laid out.

The path to the Acropolis follows the Panathenaic Way, laid out at the consecration of the Panathenaic Festival in 566 BC. The Acropolis entrance is defended by the **Beulé Gate** (named after Ernest Beulé, the archaeologist who found it); the monumental stairways were built by the Romans and the two lions are from Venice. The reconstructed Panathenaic ramp leads to the equally reconstructed

Propylaia, the massive gateway replacing Pisistratos' cursed gate, built by Pericles' architect Mnesikles. The ancient Greeks considered the Proplyaia the architectural equal of the Parthenon itself, although it was never completed because of the Peloponnesian War. On either side of the Propylaia's entrance are two wings; the north held a picture gallery (Pinakotheke) while the smaller one to the south consisted of only one room of an unusual shape, because the priests of the neighbouring Nike temple didn't want the wing in their precinct. The original entrance had five doors, the central one pierced by the Panathenaic Way.

Temple of Athena Nike

The Ionic Temple of Athena Nike, or *Wingless Victory*, was built by the architect Kallikrates in 478 BC of Pentelic marble. Inside was kept the cult statue of Athena, a copy of a much older wooden statue. Its lack of wings, unlike later victory statues, gave it its second name. In 1687 the Turks destroyed the temple to build a tower. It was rebuilt in 1835 and again in 1936, when the bastion beneath it threatened to crumble away. The north and western friezes were taken to England by Lord Elgin and have been replaced by cement casts. From the temple of Athena Nike the whole Saronic Gulf could be seen in the pre-smog days, and it was here that Aegeus watched for the return of his son Theseus from his Cretan adventure with the Minotaur. Theseus was to have signalled his victory with a white sail but forgot; at the sight of the black sail of death, Aegeus threw himself off the precipice in despair.

The Parthenon

The Parthenon, the glory of the Acropolis and probably the most famous building in the world, if not the most imitated, is a Doric temple constructed between 447 and 432 BC under the direction of Phidias, the greatest artist and sculptor of the Periclean age. Originally called the Great Temple, it took the name Parthenon (Chamber of Virgins) a hundred years after its completion. Constructed entirely of Pentelic marble, it originally held Phidias' famous statue of Athena Parthenos, more than 36 ft high and made of ivory and gold. Look closely, and you'll see that the Parthenon's foundation is curved slightly to prevent an illusion of drooping caused by straight horizontals. To make the columns appear straight the architect bent them a few centimetres inward. Corner columns were made wider to complete the illusion of perfect form.

The outer colonnade consists of 46 columns and above them are the remnants of the Doric frieze left behind by the beaverish Lord Elgin: the east side portrayed the battle of giants and gods, the south the Lapiths and Centaurs (mostly in the

British Museum today), on the west the Greeks and the Amazons, and on the north the battle of Troy. Little remains of the pediment sculptures of the gods. Above the interior colonnade, the masterful Ionic frieze designed by Phidias himself shows the quadrennial Panathenaic Procession in which Athena was brought a golden crown and a new sacred garment, or *peplos*.

The Parthenon's roof was blown sky high in 1687 when a Venetian bomb hit the Turks' powder stores inside; the destruction was continued in 1894 by an earthquake and today the nefarious *nefos* smog threatens to give the kiss of death to this graceful prototype of a thousand bank buildings. Entrance within the Parthenon itself is forbidden, to save on wear and tear. What is intriguing—and sometimes you can see the work in progress—is that after all these years the Greek government has decided to pick up all the pieces lying scattered since Morosini's day, and reconstruct as much of the temple as possible.

The Erechtheion

The last great monument on the Acropolis is the Erechtheion, a peculiar Ionic temple that owes its idiosyncrasies to the various cult items and the much older sanctuary it was built to encompass. Beneath the temple stood the Mycenaean House of Erechtheus, mentioned by Homer, and the primitive cult sanctuary of Athena; on one side of this grew the Sacred Olive Tree created by Athena, while under the north porch was the mark left by Poseidon's trident when he brought forth the divine spring. The tomb of Kekrops, the legendary founder of Athens, is in the Porch of the Maidens or Caryatids, where Erechtheus died at the hand of either Zeus or Poseidon. Within the temple stood the ancient cult statue of Athena Polias, endowed with the biggest juju of them all, solemnly dressed in the sacred *peplos* and crown.

After the Persian fires, the sanctuary was quickly restored, but the marble temple planned by Pericles was not begun until 421 BC. Used as a church in the 7th century, it became a harem under the Turks, who used the sacred place of the trident marks as a toilet. Lord Elgin nicked parts of this temple as well, including one of the caryatids which you can now see in the British Museum; acidic air pollution has forced the Greek government to replace the other girls with casts.

Basically the Erechtheion is a rectangular building with three porches. Inside were two cellas, or chambers: the East Cella dedicated to Athena Polias, the smaller to Poseidon–Erechtheus. Six tall Ionic columns mark the north porch where the floor and roof were cut away to reveal Poseidon's trident marks, for it was sacrilegious to hide something so sacred from the view of the gods. The six famous maidens gracefully supporting the roof on their heads are another Ionian motif.

The Acropolis Museum

(open Tues–Fri 8–4.30, Mon 10–4.30, Sat and Sun 8.30–2.30)

The museum houses sculptures and reliefs from the temples, in particular the Erechtheion's maidens, or Kores. But frankly, the museum's contents are far less impressive than the site outside, unless you're a scholar of classics or have a big interest in archaeology.

Below the Acropolis is the **Areopagos**, or hill of Ares, the god of war. There sat the High Council, who figured so predominantly in Aeschylos' play *The Eumenides* where mercy defeated vengeance for the first time in history during the trial of the matricide Orestes. Although Pericles removed much of the original power of the High Council, under the control of the ex-archons it continued to advise on the Athenian constitution for hundreds of years.

The Theatres

*Prices vary: 800dr. is the current rate of admission to the site of the **Acropolis**, for an adult without a concession.*

On the south side of the Acropolis are two theatres. The older, the **Theatre of Dionysos**, was used from the 6th century BC when Thespis created the first true drama, and was continually modified up to the time of Nero. In this theatre the annual Greater Dionysia was held, in honour of the god of wine and patron divinity of the theatre, Dionysos. The dramatic competitions led to the premières of some of the world's greatest tragedies. The stage that remains is from the 4th century BC, while the area before the stage, the **proskenion**, is decorated with 1st century AD scenes based on the life of Dionysos. Beside the theatre stood two temples to Dionysos Eleutherios.

Above the theatre is an **Asklepieion**, a sanctuary to the god of healing. The stoa which remains is from the second rebuilding, while the first and oldest sanctuary to the west first belonged to a water goddess, but very little of it remains. Both the old and new Asklepieions were connected with the parent cult at Epidauros.

The **Theatre of Herodes Atticus** was built and named for the Rockefeller of his day in AD 161 and originally partially covered. Now it hosts the annual mid-May and September **Festival of Athens**, where the cultures of modern Europe and ancient Greece are combined in theatre, ballet, and classical music concerts performed by companies from all over the world.

Other Museums

Benaki Museum: On the corner of Vassilis Sofias and Koumbari St, *open 8.30–3, daily.* This museum holds the collection of Antonios Benaki, who spent 35 years amassing objects from Europe and Asia, Byzantine and Islamic. The Byzantine artworks (6th–14th centuries) are fascinating examples of early Christian art: icons, jewellery, ceramics, silver and embroidery, while the post-Byzantine exhibits (15th–17th century) show the influences of Islamic and Italian art. There are two icons by the Cretan-born El Greco, painted before his departure to Venice and Spain—the *Adoration of the Magi* (1560–65) and the *Evangelist Luke* (1560). The section on folk art, dating from the Ottoman occupation, contains a superb collection of costumes and artefacts from the Ionian islands to Cyprus.

National Archaeology Museum: Patission and Tossitsa Sts, *open 8–5, Sat and Sun 8.30–3, Mon 11–5, free Thurs and Sun.* The National Museum contains some of the most spectacular ancient Greek art anywhere—the Minoan-style frescoes from Santorini, gold from Mycenae (including the famous mask of Agamemnon), statues, reliefs, tomb stelae, and ceramics and vases from every period. The Cycladic collection includes one of the first known musicians of the Greek world, the sculpture of the little harpist that has become the virtual symbol of the Cyclades. The star of the sculpture rooms is a virile bronze of Poseidon (5th-century BC) about to launch his trident, found off the coast of Evia in 1928; around him are some outstanding archaic Kouros statues and the Stele of Hegeso, an Athenian beauty, enveloped by the delicate folds of her robe, seated on a throne. The museum has a shop on the lower level, with reproductions of exhibits by expert craftsmen, so accurate that each piece is issued with a certificate declaring it an authentic fake so you can take it out of the country.

National Gallery: 50 Vass. Konstantinou, across from the Athens Hilton, *open 9–3, Sun 10–2, closed Mon.* Also known as the Alexander Soustou Museum, the National Gallery concentrates on art by modern Greek artists. Works by the leading contemporary painter, Nikos Hadzikyriakos-Ghikas, are permanently displayed on the ground floor, while the lower level is used for rotating exhibitions. The museum shop has posters, cards, catalogues and jewellery, and there's a pleasant outdoor café, for when you've done the rounds.

Historical and Ethnological Museum: At the Palea Vouli (Old Parliament), Stadiou St, *open 9–1, closed Mon.* This imposing neo-Classical edifice is the guardian of Greek history, from the fall of Constantinople to the present day. The bronze warrior on horseback is Theodoros Kolokotronis, hero of the War of Independence, while exhibits within trace the history of modern Greece in paintings, sculptures, armaments (including Byron's sword and helmet), maps, folk costumes, jewellery and more covering every period, from Ottoman rule to resistance against the Nazis in 1940.

Popular Art Museum: 17 Kydathinaion St, *open 10–2, closed Mon.* The museum has a collection of Greek folk art, both religious and secular, along with paintings by naïve artists.

The Pnyx: On the hill west of the Acropolis. The Pnyx once hosted the General Assembly of Athens and the great speeches of Pericles and Demosthenes. On assembly days citizens were literally rounded up to fill the minimum attendance quota of 5000, but they were paid for their services to the state. Later the assembly was transferred to the theatre of Dionysos. On the summit of the nearby Hill of the Muses is the **Philopappos Monument**, the tomb of Caius Julius Antiochos Philopappos, a Syrian Prince and citizen of Athens. The monument was built for him by the Athenians in AD 114 in gratitude for his beneficence to the city.

Roman Agora: Located between the Agora and the Acropolis, *open 8.30–3pm closed Mon. Adm 1000dr.* Dating from the end of the Hellenistic age, the Roman Agora contains the celebrated **Tower of the Winds**, or Clock of Andronikos, built in the 1st century BC. Run by a hydraulic mechanism, it stayed open day and night so that the citizens could know the time. Its name comes from the frieze of the eight winds that decorate its eight sides, although it has lost its ancient bronze Triton weathervane. The Roman Agora also contains the **Gate of Athena Archegetis**, built by money sent over from Julius and Augustus Caesar; there is also a court and the ruins of stoae. Beside the Agora is the Fehiye Camii, the Victory or Corn Market Mosque.

Byzantine Museum: 22 Vassilis Sofias, *open 8.30–3, closed Mon.* This monumental collection of religious treasures and paintings dates from the Early Byzantine period to the 19th century—not only icons but marble sculptures, mosaics, woodcarvings, frescoes, manuscripts and ecclesiastical robes. There are three rooms on the ground floor arranged as chapels, one Early Christian, another Middle Byzantine, and the third post-Byzantine.

Museum of Cycladic Art: 4 Neoforos Douka St (between Byzantine and Benaki museums), *open 10–3.30, Sat 10–2.30, closed Tues and Sun.* This museum houses a vast collection of Cycladic figurines and objects dating back to 3200–2000 BC, illustrating everyday life. The female figurines with folded arms are unique. The newest addition is the 'Treasure of Keros', a small island near Naxos where excavations in the 1950s and 60s unearthed a wealth of figurines.

Keramikos and Museum: 148 Ermou St, *open 8.30–3, closed Mon.* The ancient cemetery or Keramikos was used for burials from the 12th century BC into Roman times, but the most impressive and beautiful finds are in the rich private tombs built by the Athenians in the 4th century BC. Large stone vases mark the graves of the unmarried dead, while others are in the form of miniature temples and stelae; the best are in the National Museum.

Temple of Olympian Zeus: Olgas and Amalias Avenues, *open 8.30–3, closed Mon.* Fifteen columns recall what Livy called 'the only temple on earth of a size adequate to the greatness of the god'. The foundations were laid by the tyrant Pisistratos, but work ground to a halt with the fall of his dynasty, only to be continued in 175 BC by a Roman architect, Cossutius. It was half finished when Cossutius' patron, Antiochos IV of Syria kicked the bucket, leaving the Emperor Hadrian to complete it in AD 131. Nearby are the ruins of ancient houses and a bath and at the far end stands **Hadrian's Arch**, neatly dividing the city of Theseus from the city of Hadrian. The Athenians traditionally come here to celebrate the Easter Resurrection.

Museum of the City of Athens: Plateia Klafthmonos, *open Mon, Wed, Fri, Sat 9–1.30; free Wed.* Located in the re-sited neo-Classical palace of King Otho, this new museum contains photos, memorabilia and a model showing Athens as it was soon after it became the capital of modern Greece.

Byzantine Churches and Monasteries in Athens

Agii Theodori: This 11th-century church in Klafthmonos Square at the end of Dragatsaniou St is most notable for its beautiful door; the bell tower and some of the decorations inside are more recent additions.

Kapnikarea: A few blocks from Agii Theodori, on Ermou St. Tiny Kapnikarea (the chapel of the University of Athens) was built in the late 11th century in the shape of a Greek cross, its central cupola sustained by four columns with Roman capitals.

Panayia Gorgoepikoos (or Ag. Eleftherios): Situated in Mitropoleos Square and known as the little Metropolitan to distinguish it from the nearby cathedral, this is the loveliest church in Athens. Built in the 12th century almost entirely of ancient marbles the builders found lying around; note the ancient calendar of state festivals embedded over the door. Curiously, the **Cathedral** (just to the north) was built in 1840–55 with the same collage technique, using bits and pieces from 72 destroyed churches.

Dafni and its Wine Festival: 10 km from Athens; take bus 282 from Eleftherios Square. The name Dafni derives from the temple of Apollo Dafneios (of the laurel), built near the Sacred Way. The site became a walled monastery in the 6th century and in 1080 a new church was built, decorated with the best Byzantine mosaics in southern Greece. These are dominated in the vault of the dome by the tremendous figure of Christ Pantokrator 'the all powerful', his eyes spellbinding and tragic, 'as though He were in flight from an appalling doom' as Patrick Leigh Fermor has written. From mid-August until September, daily 7.45pm–12.30am, the monastery park holds a festival with over 60 different Greek wines (free once you've paid the 300dr. admission at the gate) accompanied by (poor and over-priced) food, singing and dancing, an event well-attended by Athenians and visitors alike.

Where to Stay in Athens

Athens is a big noisy city, especially so at night when you want to sleep—unless you do as the Greeks do and take a long afternoon siesta. Piraeus (*see* below) may be a better bet, no less noisy but much more convenient for catching those up-at-the-crack-of-dawn ships to the islands, although women on their own may find too many sailors and working girls about to feel at ease. All accommodation fills up quickly in the summer and if you don't have a reservation, or erratic boat schedules have mangled your booking, it's best to head straight for the EOT office on Syntagma Square (in the National Bank building) and use their hotel finding service.

luxury

New luxury chain hotels are mushrooming up everywhere just outside the city centre—there's the **Ledra Marriott** at 113–115 Syngrou, ✆ (01) 934 7711, fax 935 8603, featuring a Chinese–Japanese restaurant, and a hydrotherapy pool you can soak in with a view of the Parthenon. Another addition to the scene (and one on a human scale) is the 76-room **Astir Palace Athens Hotel** on Syntagma Square, ✆ 364 3112, fax 364 2825 owned by the National Bank of Greece. While it was under construction, ancient foundations and waterpipes were uncovered and these are incor-porated into the décor of the hotel's restaurant, the **Apokalypsis**, located below street level (Greek and international cuisine). Despite its location, specially insulated glass windows keep out the hubbub below the rooms. There's a sauna, and each room features a mini bar and colour TV (with an in-house movie channel).

Directly across the square from the Astir is the **Grande Bretagne**, © 323 0251, fax 322 8034 originally built in 1862 to house members of the Greek royal family who couldn't squeeze into the main palace (the current Parliament building) up the square. The Grande Bretagne is the only 'grand' hotel in Greece worthy of the description, with a vast marble lobby, elegant rooms (now air conditioned and appointed with such modern conveniences as direct dial phones and colour TV), a formal dining room, and an appearance of grandeur and style that the newer hotels, with all their plushness, may never achieve. Having said that, on our most recent stay there (Autumn 1993) we found the service to be positively complacent, which is disappointing at the prices they charge. Even if you're not going to stay there, you may want to poke your head in (there's a pleasant bar) to see where the crowned heads of Europe lodge in Athens—and where the Nazis set up their headquarters during the Second World War. Winston Churchill spent Christmas 1944 at the Grande Bretagne and was lucky to escape a bomb meant for him, planted in the hotel's complex sewer system.

On a less exalted level, but with a far more fetching view is the **Royal Olympic Hotel** at 28 Diakou, © 922 6411, fax 923 3317, facing the Temple of Olympian Zeus and Mt Lycavitos. Rooms here are American in spirit, with a number of family-sized suites, and if you have the misfortune to get a room without a view, there's the wonderful panorama from the rooftop bar.

expensive

The **Electra Palace** at 18 Nikodimou St, © (01) 324 1401, fax 324 1875, has views of the Acropolis and a wonderful rooftop swimming pool in a garden setting—something you don't find every day in Athens. Rooms are air conditioned and there's a garage adjacent to the hotel. Halfboard is obligatory—unfortunately, because the hotel is quite close to the good tavernas of Plaka. More reasonable, and centrally located just off Syntagma Square, the **Astor**, 16 Karagiorgi Servias, © 325 5555, also has fully air conditioned rooms and a rooftop garden restaurant.

moderate

The best value in this category (and a big favourite with Americans) has long been the **Hotel Alkistis** at 18 Plateia Theatrou, © (01) 321 9811, all rooms with private baths and phones, all very modern and perfectly clean. If the Alkistis is full, a good second bet is the **Hotel Museum** at 16

Mykonos Blu

GRECOTEL

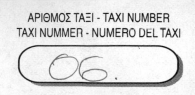

06.

TAXI

ΚΑΛΑ ΝΑ ΠΕΡΑΣΕΤΕ - HAVE A NICE TIME

VIEL VERGNUEGEN - BUON DIVERTIMENTO

Bouboulinas St, © 360 5611, right at the back of the Archaeology Museum. The rooms are about the same, but the prices are a bit higher. **Hotel Tempi**, 29 Eolou St, © 321 3175, near Monastiraki, is more downgrade, but is cheaper and has washing facilities. **Art Gallery** at Erekhthiou 5, Veikou, © 923 8376, is a pleasant place at the lower end of this price category, though it is out of the centre; Plaka is a 20-minute walk, more if you're fumbling with a map.

cheap

Most of the inexpensive hotels are around Plaka. For better or worse, the government has shut down many of the old dormitory houses that grew up in the 1960s to contain the vanguard of mass tourism in Greece—every hippy in Europe, or at least so it seemed to the amazed Greeks. Survivors of the government purge have upgraded themselves but are still a bargain—and many still let you sleep on the roof for a thousand drachmas (not an unpleasant option in the thick heat of August). Best bets in the cheaper category include:

Hotel Phaedra, 16 Herefondos St, © (01) 323 8461, just off Filellinon St, with free hot showers; unreconstructed pre-war interior, and pleasant staff (double room 6000dr, more in season).

John's Place, 5 Patroou St, © 322 9719. Around 4000dr.

Hotel Cleo, 3 Patroou St, © 322 9053, small and near Plaka.

Student Inn, 16 Kidathineon, © 324 4808, very conveniently placed in the Plaka, and ideal for the rowdy younger crowd (1.30am curfew though).

Joseph's House, 13 Markou Botsari, © 923 1204, in a quieter area on the south side of the Acropolis; washing facilities available (take advantage of it—if you're travelling in the islands for any length of time, washing clothes will be your biggest headache).

Less savoury, but also less expensive is the city's **IYHF Youth Hostel**, inconveniently located far from the centre at 57 Kypselis St, Kypseli, © (01) 822 5860. A better option, though it is not a member of the YHA, is the **Student's Hostel** at 75 Damareos St, Pangrati, © 751 9530. The nearest **campsites** to Athens are at Dafni Monastery, and down on the coast at Voula. When your make you way through the metro station at Piraeus, you're guaranteed to have fliers thrust in your hand for other rock-bottom options.

Eating Out in Athens

Athenians rarely dine out before 10 or 11pm, and they want to be entertained afterwards. If it's warm, chances are they'll drive out to the suburbs or the sea shore. **Glyfada**, near the airport, is a popular destination and on a summer evening the cool sea breeze can be a life saver after the oppressive heat of Athens. The obvious meal to choose is something from the sea, and most of the tavernas specialize in fish (especially red mullet, or *barbounia*), lobster, squid and shrimp, although, as everywhere in Greece, it's the most expensive food you can order. Remember that prices marked for fish usually indicate how much per kilo, not per portion.

Glyfada

Leading off the main square in Glyfada is a street almost entirely devoted to excellent restaurants and friendly, inexpensive bars. At reasonably priced **George's**, the steak will be cooked according to your specifications and the meatballs (*keftedes*) are a speciality. To feed the large foreign community in Glyfada, a plethora of fast food joints has grown up in the area, and now expensive Arab restaurants (complete with imported Middle Eastern singers and belly dancers) have made an appearance on the scene.

central Athens

Costayiannis, 37 Zaimi, near the National Archaeology Museum, with a succulent display of food in the glass cabinets near the entrance preparing you for a memorable culinary evening. Apart from the superb seafood, the 'ready food' is unbeatable—try the quail with roast potatoes, the roast pork in wine and herb sauce or the rabbit *stifado*, accompanied by barrelled retsina, if you've developed a taste for it. Prices here are very reasonable—3500 dr. for a full evening meal (closed lunchtimes and Sundays). As near to a traditional taverna that you'll find, the **Taverna Karavitis** is a few streets up from the old Olympic stadium, on the corner of Arkitinou and Pafsaniou and housed in a long, low white building, with barrels lining the walls. Athenians come here for a good time; the food, served by friendly young lads in jeans, is better than average, wine is served from the barrel, and it's open till late (1500 dr.). Just off Mikalakopoulou St, and not far from the Hilton Hotel is **John's Village (To Chorio tou Yianni)**, a cut above the ordinary taverna and warmly decorated with hand-woven rugs and island pottery. The accompanying music, played by a strolling minstrel, makes this a favourite spot to spend an evening without breaking the bank. There's a good variety of well-prepared dishes and a meal will cost about 3000 dr. Behind the Hilton, on Mikalakopoulou, is the Cypriot restaurant **Othello's**, with delicious, authentic cuisine at around 2500 dr. for a meal.

the Plaka

Plaka is the place to head for for pleasant restaurants and *al fresco* dining in the evening. There are scores of places catering for the passing tourist trade, and they are all very competent, though few serve true, vernacular food that you'll find on the islands (if you make the effort to look for it). Despite this, the Plaka is still the perennial favourite with both Greeks and tourists. The atmosphere at night is exciting with its crowded tavernas perched precariously on uneven steps, Greek dancers whirling and leaping on stages the size of postage stamps, light bulbs flashing and *bouzouki* music filling the air. A typical charming Plaka taverna is the rooftop **Thespes**, 100 m along from the Plaka Square, where a selection of starters, such as *tzatziki, taramasalata* and fried aubergine (eggplant) followed by lamb chops and plenty of wine won't cost you much more than 2000 dr. In some of the other tavernas you may not be as lucky and will have to pay well over the odds, particularly if there's live music, for food that rarely rises above the mediocre. One other outstanding exception is **Platanos**, the oldest taverna in the Plaka, near the Tower of the Four Winds. The food here is good and wholesome, but forget about perusing the menu—it's definitely an 'in the kitchen and point' joint, and inexpensive at 1500–2000 dr. for a meal. In the heart of Plaka, in Filomosou Square, where every visitor lands up sooner or later, you can eat well at **O Costas** or **Xynou Taverna**, 4 Geronda St, which serves excellent food in a garden setting, with strolling musicians playing traditional Greek music. It's very popular (closed on Sat and Sun), and reservations are a must (© 322 1065; 2500 dr.). Off touristy Adrianou St, with all its souvenirs, the family-run taverna **Tsegouras**, 2 Epicharmou, is in a walled garden in the shade of an enormous gum tree, with good Greek food for around 2000 dr.

While walking around Plaka, you're likely to pass **Brettos,** a small but colourfully-lit shop selling own-label *mastika* and liqueurs; try some, it beats bringing back a bottle of ouzo with you on the aeroplane.

Just outside the Plaka, two blocks south of Hadrian's arch at 5 Lembessi St, **O Kouvelos** is another typical, reliable Athenian taverna, serving excellent *meze* and barrelled retsina. They'll save you the bother of ordering the meze by planting it on the table in front of you; don't be shy to change it if you want something different (2000 dr.) In the same area (cross Makriyianni St), you could try **Socrates Prison**, 20 Mitseon St, a real favourite with locals and expats. Greek food with a flair in attractive surroundings, though the service can be variable. Bottled or barrelled wine (2000 dr., evenings only, closed Sun). A few blocks west of here, at 7 Garivaldi St, the **Greek House** has dining on a rooftop terrace with a most beautiful view of the Acropolis. Don't be put off by the name; this restaurant serves superb and reasonably priced specialities—try the 'Virginia', slices of *filet mignon* with mushrooms, or the shrimp salad. They also make wonderful spinach and cheese pies (2500 dr.). Near the Monastiraki *elektriko* (underground) station, search out **Taverna Sigalas**, a bustling place where you can soak up the least pretentious side of Athenian life; usual Greek food served at unpredictable temperatures, and Greek folk music to make you feel you never want to go home (1500–2000 dr.).

around Omonia Square

Omonia Square is a great place to try Greek street food. You can buy bags of nuts, coconut sweets, savoury pies (*tyropitta*—cheese, and *spanakopitta*—spinach), late-night souvlaki, and sandwiches, and it's all very cheap. Near Omonia Square are a number of cheap restaurants displaying cuts of roast lamb, pork and the occasional grinning sheep's head. They're really worth a try if you are watching your drachme, but feel like a 'proper' meal—a portion of chicken with rubber fried spuds and a small bottle of retsina will set you back about 1000 dr. Of the half-a-dozen or so places, try **Platanos** on Satombriandou.

ethnic cuisine

Athens is well supplied with ethnic eating places—French, Italian, Spanish, Chinese, Japanese, Mexican, American and restaurants of other nationalities are scattered around the capital. Of particular note for lovers of German food is the **Rittenburg** at 11 Formionos in Pangrati, where the boiled and grilled sausages, and pork with sauerkraut are tops. North German dishes are on the menu in the small, intimate and aptly named

Delicious in Kolonaki at 6 Zalokosta—marinated fish, *bratkartoffeln*, lovely goulash and home-made black bread (2500 dr.). Asian restaurants are all relatively expensive. The Chinese-Malaysian **Rasa Sayang**, in the seaside suburb of Glyfada, on Palea Leoforos Vouliagmenis and 2 Kiou, serves great Peking Duck and beef with mango slices, among many other items (3000 dr.). A little further down the coast at Voula, **Loon Fung Tien** does fixed-price *dim sum* (buffet) lunchtimes on Sunday. Italian restaurants are established in every major European city, and Athens is no exception. **Boschetto**, in the Evangelismos Gardens opposite the Hilton, is one of the city's best. Exquisite spaghetti with *frutti di mare*, inventive main courses (guinea hen with bacon and pomegranate sauce) and fine desserts (4000 dr.). In Kolonaki the trendy **Pane e Vino**, 8 Spefsipou, is popular for its antipasti (aubergine and Gorgonzola rolls) and pasta (tagliolini with smoked salmon), together with main dishes such as sole with mussels or scaloppine with prosciutto (4–5000 dr.) A collection of top class, expensive French restaurants have graced the Athens culinary scene for years. In Kolonaki **Je Reviens**, 49 Xenokratous, is an old favourite, with live music and outdoor seating (5000 dr.). Near the American Embassy **Balthazar**, 27 Tsoha and Vournazou, is a renovated mansion with an attractive bar and a comprehensive selection of international dishes, but it's best to book © 644 1215; 3500 dr.

hotel restaurants

Some of the luxury hotels in Athens have some swish theme restaurants (with swish prices of course). The **Ledra Marriott** (pxx76) has the 'Polynesian' **Kona Kai** in an exotic tropical setting, with all the delicacies from that other island paradise; a few blocks down, the **Athenaeum Intercontinental** also has Asian cuisine in its **Kublai Khan** restaurant.

Bars

Watering holes abound in Athens, many of them serving bar food, and most of the English-speaking community do the rounds of the **Red Lion**, the **Underground** and the **Ploughman's**, all within a stone's throw of the Hilton.

Wine bars are a fairly recent addition to Athens' nightlife. If you want to try some finer wines from Greece and Europe, the following places will oblige: **Kelari**, in the Hilton, serving Greek dishes as an accompaniment, in a friendly, warm décor; **Loutro**, 18 Feron, way north near Victoria

Square, decorated in sophisticated Roman bath style, serving imaginative dishes to accompany the French, Italian and lesser known Greek wines; **Le Sommelier d'Athènes**, Leof. Kifissias in Kifissia, in a beautiful old suburban villa, with an emphasis on French and Italian; **Strofilia**, 7 Karitsi (behind the Historical Museum), with mainly Greek labels, and an extensive salad bar.

Piraeus

The port of Athens, Piraeus—pronounced 'Pirefs'—was the greatest port of the ancient world and remains today one of the busiest in the Mediterranean. In Greece, a country that derives most of its livelihood from the sea in one way or another, Piraeus is the true capital, while Athens is a mere sprawling suburb where the bureaucrats live. Still, it takes a special visitor to find much charm in the tall grey buildings and dusty hurly-burly in the streets, although Marina Zea and Mikrolimani with their yachts, brightly-lit tavernas and bars are a handsome sight, as are the neon signs flashing kinetically as you sail to or from Piraeus in the evening. The tall, half-finished building on the waterfront was built and abandoned by the junta when they found that the foundations were mixed with sea water. Somehow its useless silhouette makes a fitting monument to that ignorant and often cruel government.

An Historical Outline

Themistocles founded the port of Piraeus in the 5th century BC when Phaliron, Athens' ancient port, could no longer meet the growing needs of the city. From the beginning Piraeus was cosmopolitan and up-to-date: the Miletian geometrician Hippodamos laid it out in a straight grid of streets that have changed little today. The centre of action was always the huge agora in the middle of the city. Under its stoae the world's first commercial fairs and trade expositions were held, some on an international scale. All religions were tolerated, and women were allowed for the first time to work outside the home.

As Piraeus was so crucial to Athens' power, the conquering Spartan Lysander destroyed the famous Long Walls that linked city and port in 404, at the end of the Peloponnesian War. Piraeus made a brief comeback under Konon and Lykurgos, who rebuilt its arsenals. After the 100-year Macedonian occupation and a period of peace, Sulla decimated the city to prevent any anti-Roman resistance, and for 1900 years Piraeus dwindled away into an insignificant village with a population as low as 20, even losing its name to become Porto Leone (after an ancient lion statue, carved from runes by Harald Hadraada and his Vikings in 1040 and carted off by Morosini as a trophy to embellish Venice's Arsenal). Since the selection of Athens as the capital of independent Greece, Piraeus has regained its former glory as the reigning port of a sea-going nation.

Getting Around

In Piraeus this usually means getting out of town as quickly as possible. **Ships** are grouped according to their destination and almost anyone you ask will be able to tell you the precise location of any vessel. The cluster of ticket agents around the port is very noisy and competitive, but prices to the islands are fixed, so the only reason to shop around is to see if there is an earlier or faster ship to the island of your choice. Beware that ticket agents often don't know or won't tell you information on lines other than the ones they carry. Only the Tourist Police on Akti Miaouli have complete information on boat schedules.

There are three **railway stations.** The half-underground Elektriko serves Athens as far north as the posh suburb of Kifissia, setting off every 10 minutes from 6am to 1.30am from the terminal opposite the quay. Stations for northern Greece and for the Peloponnese are further down the road.

Buses to Athens run day and night, the main 'Green' line (no. 040) taking you directly to Syntagma Square. The express line no. 19 bus service to East and West Airport leaves from Karaiskaki Square.

Tourist Police

Akti Miaouli, © (01) 452 3670.
Irron Politechniou, © (01) 412 0325.

The Sights

If you find yourself in Piraeus with time to kill on a Sunday morning, take a prowl through the flea market parallel to the underground (Elektriko) line, where you may well happen across some oddity brought back by a Greek Sinbad. If culture beckons, there's an **Archaeology Museum** at 31 Har. Trikoupi St, with an above average collection of antiquities (*8.30–3, closed Mon*), or perhaps the **Maritime Museum** on Akti Themistocles by Freatidos St, with intriguing plans of Greece's greatest naval battles, ship models and mementoes from the War of Independence (*8.30–1, closed Sun and Mon*). The **Hellenistic Theatre** at Zea occasionally has performances in the summer.

Beaches are not far away, although the sea isn't exactly sparkling and on most you must pay. Kastella is the closest, followed by New Phaliron which is free. Buses go to Ag. Kosmos by the airport, where you can play tennis or volleyball; at Glyfada, further down the road, there's more wholesome swimming and a golf course for duffers.

Zea, Glyfada and Vouliagmeni are the three **marinas** organized by the National Tourist Organization. Piraeus is also the place to charter yachts or sail boats, from 12-foot dinghies to deluxe twin-screw yachts, if you've missed your island connection (*see* yachting pp. 15–20).

Where to Stay in Piraeus

Hotel accommodation in Piraeus is geared towards businessmen, and unfortunately less so towards people who have arrived on a late-night ship or plan to depart on an early morning one. Brave souls sleep out in the squares, particularly in Karaiskaki, but they have to put up with lights, noise, the neighbouring discotheques and sailors of every nationality who hang around hoping for something to happen.

expensive

If you're with the kids, try the quiet and very clean **Hotel Anemoni**, at Karaoli Demetriou and Evripidou 65–67, ✆ 413 6881; since it's not directly on the port you miss the sailors and some of the racket. All rooms are air conditioned, and there's a free transfer service to the port.

moderate

If you want to be within walking distance of the docks, the **Hotel Triton**, ✆ 417 3457, is one of the best of the many in the area; its B class doubles start at 5500 dr., but go shooting up in high summer. All rooms have private bath and breakfast is available. A mediocre alternative is the **Ideal**, 142 Notara St, ✆ 451 1727, 50 m from the customs house, with air conditioning and private bath.

cheap

On the lower end of the scale there are many D & E class hotels, some of which are not as appetizing as they might be, but their rates range from 3000 dr. to around 5000 dr. Typical of these is **Achillion**, 63 Notara St, ✆ 412 4029.

Eating Out in Piraeus

Around the port the fare is generally fast food and giro spinners, while the tavernas are so greasy it's a wonder they don't slide off the street. For seafood (especially if you're on an expense account), the bijou little harbour of Mikrolimano (or Turkolimano) is the traditional place to go, although too many tourists with too much money have inflated the price to a nasty pitch. A far better idea is to forego fish and eat up at the excellent **Kaliva** in Vass. Pavlou, Kastella, with a splendid view down over the harbour (excellent meat dinners for 2500 dr.) followed by a stroll through Mikrolimano for a coffee and Metaxa on the harbour front. But if it's fish you must have, head over to Frates, around from the Zea Marina yacht harbour, where several moderately-priced places offer fresh fish and sea views. There's really not all that much to distinguish one from another; just stroll around until you find a fish that winks at you. Zea Marina itself is a vast necklace of neon, where the locals haunt the inexpensive **American Pizza**, but there are places with Greek pizza and other fare, both on the harbour and on the streets giving into it.

If you've got time between boats or flights, the stretch of coast between Piraeus and the airport has a few possibilities. Chefs from the eastern Mediterranean are undoubtedly the kings of kebab; try the **Adep Kebab**, 20 Leof. Possidonos in Paleo Phaliron, where the meat is delicately flavoured with the spices of the Levant. Specialities are the *adana* kebab, *domatesli* kebab (cooked with tomatoes on charcoal) and the succulent shish-kebab, marinated in milk, lemon juice, oil and spices. Alternatively, in Nea Smyrni, the **Tria Asteria**, 7 Melitos and 77 Plastira, is run by Armenians from Istanbul. The choice of appetizers is endless, including delicious *cli kofte*, a meatball of veal and lamb, bulgur wheat and pine nuts. This is also the only place in Athens to find *tandir* kebab, lamb which has been smoked and then baked in a red wine sauce. At either of these restaurants, count on around 3000 dr.

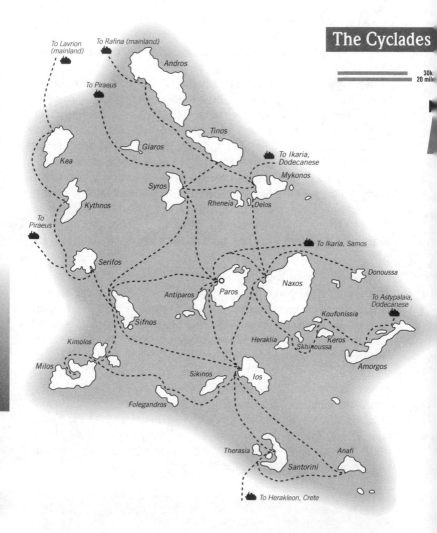

The Cyclades

30k
20 mile

To Lavrion
(mainland)

To Rafina (mainland)

Andros

To Piraeus

Tinos

Giaros

To Ikaria,
Dodecanese

Mykonos

Kea

Syros

Kythnos

Rheneia

Delos

To
Piraeus

To Ikaria, Samos

Serifos

Donoussa

Antiparos

Paros

Naxos

To Astypalaia,
Dodecanese

Sifnos

Koufonissia

Kimolos

Heraklia

Keros

Skhinoussa

Milos

Sikinos

Ios

Amorgos

Folegandros

Therasia

Anafi

Santorini

To Herakleon, Crete

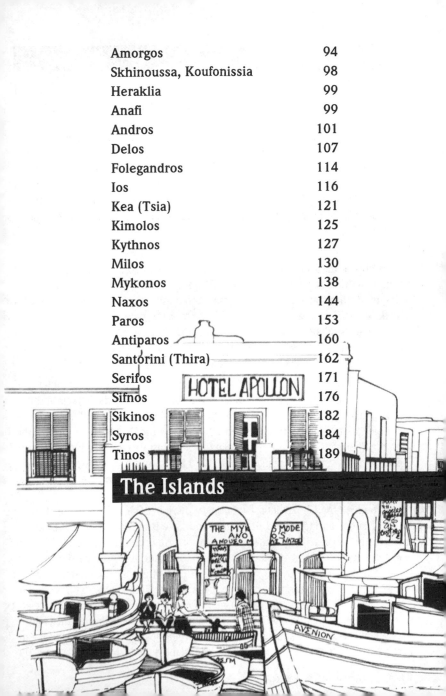

The Islands

HOTEL APOLLON

Amorgos

Easternmost of the Cyclades, Amorgos is also one of the most dramatically rugged islands. On the south coast cliffs plunge vertically into the sea, and trying to cross the island from north to south by road is so rocky a journey that most people prefer to get about by caique. For many years Amorgos was a destination for the adventurous, then all of a sudden travellers arrived en masse seeking the quiet Cycladic life of their dreams, swooping down on Amorgos by surprise until there were people literally camping out in the streets. There still aren't enough rooms to accommodate everyone who would like to stay on the island, so if you come in the height of summer without a reservation be prepared to sleep under the stars.

History

Both Amorgos and its neighbouring islet Keros were inhabited as far back as 3300 BC. In 1885 the German archaeologist Dummler uncovered 11 ancient cemeteries, producing many fine ceramics and marbles now to be seen in the museums of Oxford and Copenhagen; artefacts pointed to early trade with Milos and Egypt. Three ancient independent cities occupied Amorgos, each minting its own coins and worshipping Dionysos and Athena: Kastri (modern Arkesini) was settled by Naxians, Minoa by Samians, and Aegiali by Milians.

After Alexander the Great, Amorgos came under the Hellenistic rule of Ptolemy of Egypt who made it a centre of worship of the Alexandrian gods, Serapis and Isis. The Romans used the island as a place of exile, beginning a downhill trend which continued as the island was ravaged by Goths, Vandals and Slavs during the Byzantine period. One bright moment in this dark history came during the War of the Iconoclasts, when a miraculous icon sailed to Amorgos, set adrift, according to tradition, by a religious lady from Constantinople. As the icon showed a distinct preference for staying by the cliffs on Amorgos' south coast, Emperor Alexis Comnenus founded the Chozoviotissa monastery there in 1088. In 1209 the Duke of Naxos, Marco Sanudo, seized the island, and gave it to the Gizzi, who built the town castle. In spite of the Turkish occupation, Amorgos prospered in the 17th century, mostly from the export of exquisite embroideries made by the women, some of which are now in the Victoria and Albert Museum in London. Between the 17th and 19th centuries so many of these extraordinary pieces were sold, that a hero of the War of Independence, General Makriyiannis, threatened to declare war on Amorgos should the island send any more abroad. Rather than battle Makriyiannis, the island simply ran out of embroideries, and no one today remembers how to make them. The highlight of the island's more recent history was the filming of the cult Luc Besson 1988 movie *The Big Blue* here, which has attracted trendy tourists, especially French ones.

Connections

Six times a week with Naxos and Paros, five times a week with Syros and Piraeus, four times a week with Heraklia, Koufonissia and Skhinoussa, three times a week with Mykonos and Tinos, once a week with Astypalaia, Ios, Santorini and Anafi. Several times a week to these islands and Rafina by hydrofoil or catamaran.

Tourist Information

Information office on the quay in Katapola, ✆ (0285) 71 278; also regular police, ✆ 71 210.

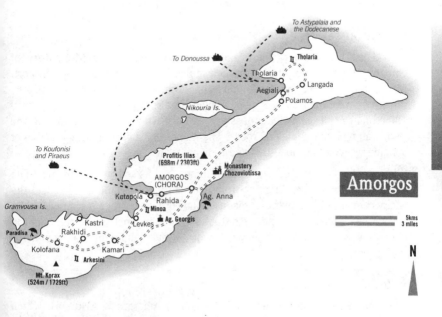

Because of the condition of the road linking the two halves of Amorgos, ships tend to call at both island ports, **Katapola** in the south and **Aegiali** in the north. Katapola isn't much: a yacht supply station, a place to swim, a couple of hotels and a few pensions, and a bus up to the capital Chora. From Katapola you can walk up the hill to the ancient city of **Minoa** where walls, part of the acropolis, a gymnasium and a few remains of a temple to Apollo can still be seen. The name Minoa comes from Minos, the King of the Mountain, or Minos, the King of Crete, although the great city states of Amorgos were closely linked to the Ionians, geographically closer to Asia Minor than the other Cyclades. East of Katapola, a 45-minute walk, is **Rahida** where the church Ag. Georgios occupies the site of an ancient oracle.

The capital of **Amorgos**, also known as Chora, is a typical white Cycladic town, perched more than 300m above sea level. A neat column of windmills (each family had its own) once laboured with the winds that rose up the dizzying precipices from the sea. In the middle of town, steps lead up the rocky mount to the well-preserved castle built by Geremia Gizzi in 1290. The locals call it **Apano Kastro**, and it affords a panoramic view of the island.

Chozoviotissa

A road has been built to the island's main sight, the grand **Monastery of Chozoviotissa** and cars have replaced mules as the easiest form of transport. Most people, however, prefer to make the 20-minute walk along the dramatic, serpentine path from the bus stop. Above the dirt track, at the foot of a steep 180m orange cliff stands the monastery—a huge white fortress, resembling one great wall built into the living rocks. The monastery is open mornings and after 5pm; be sure to dress modestly to be allowed inside.

Within are some 50 rooms, two churches and exactly three monks. The miraculous icon of the Madonna from Constantinople is still in place, and the library contains 98 hand-written manuscripts. For many years a mysterious spear, thrown by an unknown hand, was stuck in the living rock of the cliff over the monastery, and although it finally fell, worn away by time, there are still many stories about it.

Arkesini

The other ancient city in the southern half of Amorgos is **Arkesini**, which has extensive tombs, walls and houses, near the modern hamlet of **Rakhidi**, accessible on foot. A well-preserved Hellenistic tower may be seen near here at **Ag. Trias**. There are several quiet beaches (like **Paradisa**) in the south. Most people who stay in Chora swim off dark **Ag. Anna** beach, the closest to town and the monastery; the water is deep blue and crystal clear.

Aegiali

Although it's easiest to reach the north side of Amorgos by boat, a rough track braves the wild terrain, guarded on either side by an occasional tower (the walk takes about 5 hours). **Aegiali**, small and charming, is Amorgos' northern port and main resort, boasting the island's one genuine sandy beach. In some shops here, and in Chora, you can find embroidered scarves made locally, but they are nothing like the original embroideries of Amorgos. Near Aegiali you can take in the scant remains of ancient Aegiali; at **Tholaria** are Greek vaulted tholos tombs which date from the Roman period.

Festivals

The good people of Amorgos have yet to become bored by tourism, and they go out of their way to invite guests to their celebrations: 26 July, Ag. Paraskevi at Arkesini; 15 August at Langada and 21 November at the Chozoviotissa Monastery.

© (0285–)   ***Where to Stay***

expensive

In Aegiali, the **Aegialis**, © 73 244, is a smart hotel complex with pool and taverna, and a great view from the verandah.

moderate–cheap

In the port Katapola, there's the comfortable and upmarket **Hotel Minoa**, © 71 480, with reasonable rates, and several pensions, most prominently the **Pension Amorgos,** © 71 214. Other good pensions include **Pension Anna**, © 71 218; **Pension Tasia**, © 71313, also in Katapola. There are numerous rooms in Chora (there are no official pensions or hotels here), and pensions en route to Chora; **Pension Chora**, © 71 110, and **To Panorama** (no phone). In Aegiali, you can choose between the ageing **Mike Hotel**, © 71 252 (open only in the summer), or the **Pension Lakki**, with a garden. Both are on the beach, where those who can't get rooms (or don't care to) can sleep out without too many hassles. Ag. Anna beach serve a similar function on the south half of the island.

Eating Out

Amorgos has good, inexpensive, and very Greek tavernas in its main centres. In Chora the trendiest caff on the island is the **Vegera Café Bar**; **Taverna Dimitri** is good for traditional Greek food, and **Café Doza** is an authentic ouzerie. In Katapola, the deservedly most popular taverna by the sea is **Bitzentos**, where arriving late could mean missing the day's speciality; try the kid and potato casserole, stuffed aubergines with tomatoes, mushroom, parsley and onion (2000 dr.). **Taverna Minos** and **Le Grand Bleu Bar** is where tourists hangs out; they screen the Luc Besson film nightly. Aegiali boasts a whole range of good tavernas and restaurants. In Tholaria the **Panorama** is good, with a wonderful view, while the **Corali** west of the harbour specializes in fish. In Langada **Nikos** is a good taverna with rooms, © (0285) 73 310.

Skhinoussa and Koufonissia

Between Amorgos and Naxos lie a bevy of tiny islands, three of which— **Heraklia** (or Heraklia, *see* below), **Skhinoussa** and **Koufonissia**—are served by the daily boat *Skopelitis*, which rolls and buckets its way between Naxos and Amorgos, and the occasional steamer from Piraeus. These three islands all have rooms to rent; they are certainly quiet places, and not prepared to take many visitors, though it seems Heraklia is gearing up for an increase in guests. If you plan to stay any length of time, you should bring some food along, and be prepared to be sparing with the water.

Skhinoussa, a short hop from Heraklia, has a hotel in its 'capital' of the same name, and two beaches, one at the charming, miniature port, and the other across the island at **Psili Ammos**. Skhinoussa is blessed with fresh springs, and supports a species of mastic bush on its relatively flat surface.

Koufonissia is actually two islands; lower, or Kato Koufonisi, is just barely inhabited, while **Koufonisi** itself has two restaurants and two beaches, at **Harakopou** and **Pori**. From here you may be able to take a caique to **Keros**, which has the ruins of a Neolithic settlement at **Daskalio** on the west coast, and those of an abandoned medieval settlement in the north.

To reach **Donoussa**, east of Naxos, you have to take the steamer from Piraeus or the small boat from Naxos or Amorgos. A Geometric-era settlement was excavated on the island, but most of its visitors come for its fine sandy beaches near the south coast villages of Donoussa, the port, and **Mersini.**

Heraklia

Heraklia, the most westernly and the largest of the islands between Naxos and Amorgos, has rooms in its port, Ag. Georgios; from here it's a 20-minute walk to the large sandy beach at **Livadi**. The one excursion, other than to the beach, is to walk along the mule path from Ag. Georgios to the tiny hamlet of **Heraklia**, and from there to the large cave overlooking Vourkaria Bay, then back along the west coast to Ag. Georgios.

Where to Stay

moderate–cheap

In Chora, a new rooms complex is being built for 1994; otherwise, it's private *domatia*, just ask around.

Eating Out

In Ag. Georgios, **Restaurant Dimitris Gavalas** and **I Melissa** are good value. In Tholaria, try Estiatorio **Adelfi Vekri**, Kafenio-Taverna **Tholaria**, or in Livadi, **Restaurant Livadi** on the beach.

Anafi

Anafi, most southerly of the Cyclades, is a primitive island, difficult of access, its one village lacking many amenities. Visitors should bring along provisions to supplement the little fish and macaroni available locally. But if the crowds and noise seem too thick elsewhere, Anafi may be the antidote of peace and quiet you seek; here the inhabitants continue to go about their lives as they always have. Little contact with the outside world has meant that several old customs have been preserved, and some scholars have found in the Anafiotes' songs and festivals traces of the ancient worship of Apollo.

History

Apollo had a particularly strong following on Anafi; myth has it that the island rose at the god's command to shelter Jason and the Argonauts when they were besieged by a tempest, and ever since then it has kept its 28sq km-head out of the water. In the 15th century BC, however, a great deal of volcanic rock, 5m thick in some places, was added to Anafi from the explosion of Santorini, carried to the island by wind and tidal wave. The twelfth Duke of Naxos, Giacamo Crispi, gave Anafi to his brother who built a castle, but his fortification had little effect when the terror of the Aegean, Barbarossa, turned up, and enslaved the entire population. For a long time after that Anafi remained deserted, people trickling back only when it was safer. Anafiote migrant workers built houses in the island style at the foot of the Acropolis in Athens; they took advantage of the law that stated if you could erect a roof and four walls by sunrise, the place was yours.

Connections

Twice a week with Piraeus, Santorini, Ios, Naxos and Paros, once a week with Amorgos and Syros; occasional catamaran from other Cyclades islands and Piraeus.

Around the Island

The island's one village, **Chora**, with some 300 people, is a short walk up a steep hill from the landing, **Ag. Nikolaos**. A path east of Chora leads to **Katalimatsa**, with a few ruins of ancient houses, and to the island's main attraction, the **Monastery of Panayia Kalmiotissa**, built near the remains of the ancient temple to Apollo, dedicated by the grateful Jason. The **Kastro** built by Guglielmo Crispi is to the north of the village and half ruined; a path leads up to its rocky height. There are attractive **beaches** along the coast around Ag. Nikolaos.

Festivals

15 August, Panayia at the monastery, known for its authentic folkdances.

Where to Stay

The increase of tourism in the last few years has created a few new pensions in Anafi. There are a few primitive rooms to rent in Chora, and six beds in the community guest house. Ask around if you're not offered a room when you get off the ship.

The **Crazy Shrimp** bar in Chora is popular; also many tourists seem to like **Roussos** in Ag. Nikolaos, while up in Chora **Kyriakos** is the gathering spot for dinner.

Andros

One of the largest and most populated of the Cyclades, Andros is much more visited by Greeks with summer villas than by foreigners. As it's easy to reach from Rafina, Andros is popular with young Athenians and has some chic cocktail bars and the odd toga party. In the south only the narrowest of straits separates Andros from Tinos, while in the north the blustery Doro Channel, long dreaded by sailors, lies between the island and Evia. However, the same irksome wind also makes Andros, and especially its capital, one of the coolest spots in the Aegean in July and August. Lush vegetation, orchards and forests, covers the land between the rocks, and fresh water is abundant, especially commercially-exploited mineral water. It is a prosperous island, neat, well ordered, adorned with white dovecots first built by the Venetians and famed for its captains and shipowners; many from elsewhere come here to retire.

History

The name Andros is thought to be derived from the Phoenician Arados, or from Andrea, the general sent by Rhadamanthys of Crete to govern the island. In 1000 BC Ionians colonized Andros, leading to its early cultural bloom in the Archaic period. Dionysos was the most popular god worshipped at the pantheon of Palaiopolis, the leading city at the time, and a certain temple of his had the remarkable talent of turning water into wine during the Dionysia.

For most of the rest of its history, Andros has been the square peg in a round archipelago. After the Athenian victory at Salamis, Themistocles fined Andros for supporting Xerxes. The Andrians refused to pay up, and Themistocles besieged the island, but was unsuccessful and had to return home empty-handed. Although the islanders later assisted the Greeks at Plataea, Athens continued to hold a grudge against Andros, and in 448 BC Pericles divided the island between Athenian colonists, who taxed the inhabitants heavily. In response, the Andrians supported Athens' enemies whenever they could: when the Peloponnesian War broke out, they withdrew from the Delian league and sided with Sparta, supporting the neurotic reactionaries throughout the war, in spite of another

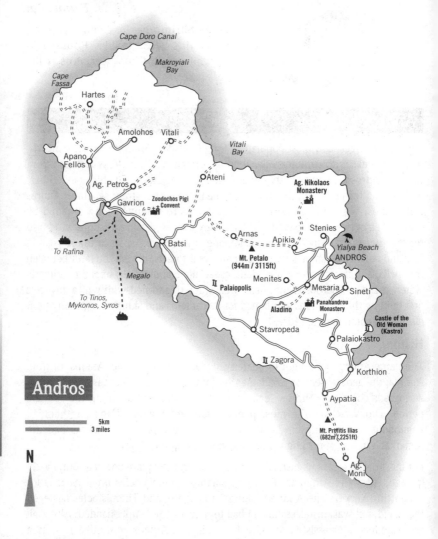

Cape Doro Canal

Makroyiali Bay

Cape Fassa

Hartes

Amolohos
Vitali

Vitali Bay

Apano Fellos

Ag. Petros

Ateni

Gavrion

Zoodochos Pigi Convent

Ag. Nikolaos Monastery

Batsi

Stenies

To Rafina

Arnas
Apikia

Yialya Beach
ANDROS

Mt. Petalo (944m / 3115ft)

Megalo

Menites

Mesaria
Sineti

To Tinos, Mykonos, Syros

II Palaiopolis

Aladino

Panahandrou Monastery

Castle of the Old Woman (Kastro)

Stavropeda

Palaiokastro

Andros

5km
3 miles

II Zagora

Korthion

N

Aypatia

Mt. Profitis Ilias (682m / 2251ft)

Ag. Moni

Athenian siege led by Alcibiades and Konon. Spartan oppression, however, proved just as awful as Athenian oppression, and things were no better during the succession of Hellenistic rulers, although a magnificent statue of Hermes, the Conductor of the Dead, dating from the 1st or 2nd century BC and found at Palaiopolis, suggests that at least art survived the constant change of bosses.

For resisting their inevitable conquest, the Romans banished the entire population of Andros to Boetia, and gave the island to Attalos I, King of Pergamon. When permitted to return, the inhabitants found their homes sacked and pillaged. Byzantium proved a blessing compared with the past, despite Saracen pirate raids. In the subsequent Venetian free-for-all, another nephew of Doge Enrico Dandolo, Marino Dandolo, took Andros, and allied himself with his cousin Marco Sanudo, the Duke of Naxos. Most of the surviving fortifications were constructed under the Dandoli.

In 1566 the Turks took the island. Apart from collecting taxes, they left it more or less to its own devices, and many Albanians from nearby Karystos (Evia) settled on Andros. In 1821 Andros' famous son, the philosopher Theophilos Kairis, declared the revolution at the cathedral of Andros, and the island contributed large sums of money and weapons to the struggle. In 1943 the Germans bombed the island for two days when the Italians stationed there refused to surrender.

Connections

Daily with Rafina, Tinos and Mykonos, less often with Syros, three times a week with Paros, Naxos, Kos and Rhodes, once a week with Astypalaia, Kalymnos, and Amorgos.

Tourist Police

See regular police, Gavrion, ✆ (0282) 71 220 or Chora, ✆ 22 300.

The Capital (Chora/Andros)

The capital, alternatively known as Chora or **Andros**, is built on a long, narrow tongue of land, decorated with the grand neo-Classical mansions of the island's ship-owners. At the edge of the town a bridge leads to the Venetian castle, **Kato Kastro**, built by Marino Dandolo and damaged in the 1943 bombardment, now watched over by a statue of the Unknown Sailor. **Plateia Riva**, the square before the arch, has a small **museum** dedicated to Andros' seafaring history, but you may have to ask around for the key. Below, at a spot called **Kamara**, the locals dive into the sea—there are sandy beaches on either side of town, but they're often windswept.

The pedestrian-only main street, paved with marble slabs and scented with cheese and custard pies made at the local bakery, is lined with old mansions converted into public offices; post and telephone offices and banks are in the centre of town, and the bus station is just a few steps away. Chora's inadequate port, **Emborios** has given up sheltering large boats (the ferry calls at Gavrion) to become a popular beach; a small church, **Ag. Thalassini** guards one end of the harbour from a throne of rock. The cathedral **Ag. Georgios**, is built on the ruins of a 17th-century church.

The following legend is told about a third church, **Theoskepasti**, built in 1555. When the wood for the church's roof arrived in Andros from Piraeus, the priest found that he couldn't afford the price demanded by the captain of the ship. Angrily, the captain set sail again only to run into a fierce, boiling tempest. The sailors prayed to the Virgin, promising to bring the wood back to Andros should she save their lives. Instantly the sea grew calm again, and Theoskepasti, or Sheltered by God, was completed without further difficulty. It was dedicated to the Virgin Mary, who apparently is on a hotline to the miracle-working icon inside the church.

Two other museums in Chora are gifts from the Goulandris shipping family: the 1981 **Archaeology Museum**, where the 'Hermes of Andros'—the real McCoy—is on display, along with material found on the island, architectural illustrations and pottery collections; and the **Museum of Modern Art**, in Plateia Kairis, which houses exhibitions of international modern artists, together with sculptures by Michael Tombros.

The Villages outside Chora

From Chora frequent buses leave for the island's many villages, with extra journeys to Gavrion when a ship is coming in (check the timetable at the bus station). Nearby attractions include **Stenies** with its lovely beach, Yialya. **Apikia** bottles Sariza mineral water and owns the 16th-century monastery Ag. Nikolaos to the north. The main road to the west coast passes through the fertile Mesaria Valley with its numerous farming villages, winding stone walls and dovecots. One old custom may still be heard: in the evening after a hard day's work, the patriarch will pipe the family home from the fields.

Up in the mountains **Menites** is a well-watered village and its church **Panayias tis Koumulous** may have been the site of Dionysos' miraculous temple. Nearby **Mesaria** has a Byzantine church of the Taxiarchos built in 1158 by the Emperor Manuel Comnenus. Mesaria was the home of an 18th-century nun, a faith healer who made an icon of Ag. Nikolaos from her own hair, which you can still see in the church of the saint (1732). From Mesaria an hour's walk takes you to the most important monastery on Andros, **Panahrandou**, founded shortly after Nikephoros Phokas' liberation of Crete in 961, and supposedly visited by the emperor himself. South-west of Mesaria, at **Aladino**, a stalactite cave called Chaos may be visited—bring a light—the villagers know its location as Lasthinou.

Other buses go to the Bay of Korthion in the southeast, with a beach, hotel and rooms. The fishing here is excellent, but if they're not biting you can always eat in one of the seafood tavernas along the waterfront. To the north of the bay is the ruined **Castle of the Old Woman**, named after a gritty old lady who abhorred the Venetians. She tricked them into letting her inside the fort, and later secretly opened the door to the Turks. Appalled at the subsequent slaughter of the Venetians, the old woman leapt from the castle and landed on a rock now known as 'Tis Grias to Pidema' or Old Lady's Leap.

Just to the north of Korthion is **Palaiokastro**, another fortification built by Dandolo and now in ruins. Ruined **Zagora** on the west coast was inhabited until the 8th century BC, when it boasted a population of 4000; it was heavily defended, sheer cliffs surrounded it on three sides, while the fourth was a solid wall. Within, inhabitants lived in small, flat-roofed houses (some remains still exist) and cultivated the fields outside the wall. Excavated by Australians in the 1960s, finds from Zagora are now in the island's museum.

Palaiopolis, further up the coast, was the original capital of Andros, inhabited until around AD 1000 when the people moved to Mesaria. An earthquake in the 4th century AD destroyed part of it, and over the years pirates finished the job. Walls and part of the acropolis are preserved, along with the ruins of buildings and temples, although the site has yet to be thoroughly explored.

Batsi, to the north, is Andros' most popular tourist resort, and is very popular with UK package tour companies; it featured in the BBC TV series *Greek Language and People*, which put it on the map for UK holidaymakers. There are some small pensions with rooms, but it's not really a big centre for independent travellers. Occasionally the steamer calls here, as well as at the superficially grim Gavrion. From Batsi you can visit the convent **Zoodochos Pigi**, built in the 14th century and containing icons from that century onwards. The nuns run a weaving factory. Shady well-watered **Arnas**, on the northern slopes of Andros' highest peak, Mt Petalo, is the garden of Andros, and it doesn't take long for a visitor to the Cyclades to appreciate how important fresh water and greenery are to the inhabitants.

The main port, **Gavrion**, lies further up the coast, with many facilities and a beach, although with little charm to distinguish itself. From here it's a 40-minute or so walk up to **Ag. Petros**, the best-preserved ancient monument on Andros. Dating from the Hellenistic era, the tower stands some 20m high—the upper storeys were reached by ladder—and its inner hall is still crowned by a corbelled dome. The landscape around here abounds with stone walls that resemble huge, arched caterpillars.

Further north, **Amolohos** is an isolated mountain village locally famous for its beauty. Another ancient tower is located further north at Zorkos Bay.

The whole of the island is good for walkers, as it's lush inland with plenty of village paths.

Festivals

15 August, at Korthinon; Theoskepasti, 15 days before Easter, and 19 June (approx, date varies); Analipsis, both at Andros; 23 August, at Menites.

© *(0282–)*   ### Where to Stay

Like Kea, Andros is an island whose tourism infrastructure is geared to long-term stays. The Athenians who don't own villas fill up the hotels and it may well be difficult, especially in the capital, to find a hotel or pension that will let you stay for only a few nights.

expensive

In Batsi, **St George's Apartments** (A), *©* (41591, overlooks the bay; in Apikia, **Pghi Sarisa** (B), *©* 41226, is a holiday complex with pool and its own mini-bus for transfers. The most elegant place in the capital is the **Paradissos Hotel** (B), *©* 22 187, in a graceful, neo-Classical confection near the centre of town. The **Xenia** has rooms at about the same price, *©* 22 270. In Gavrion, on the beach, the mini-complex **Andros Holiday** has a pool, tennis, sauna and gym, *©* 71 443.

moderate

Most visitors end up staying in Gavrion or Batsi, both of which have small hotels and numerous rooms to rent. The latter is much nicer and of its pensions the **Chryssi Akti**, *©* 41 236, with 60 rooms, is pleasant and just on the beach. The smaller **Skouna**, *©* 41 240, is also by the water, and costs about the same. **Aneroussa Beach Hotel**, *©* 41 444, overlooks Delavoyos Beach, which is popular with nudists. In Gavrion, **Hotel Galaxy**, *©* 71 228, is handy for the ferry.

cheap

In Batsi **Avra**, *©* 41 216, is the cheapest pension; facilities are shared. Otherwise there are simple rooms (except at the peak period) to be had in Batsi, Gavrion and Chora. Apikia, just north of the capital, also has rooms.

Waves of foreign tourists always hike up prices, but this hasn't happened yet in Andros. The best restaurants are in Andros town, **Platanos** and **Delfinia**, where a full meal runs to around 2000 dr. In Gavrion you can get standard Greek fare at **Petros** for the same price. In Batsi, the taverna opposite the Dolphin Hellas agency is excellent, and is famous for its lamb parcels.

Delos

Delos, holy island of the ancient Greeks, centre of the great maritime alliance of the Athenian golden age, a major free port in Hellenistic and Roman times that controlled much of the east–west trade in the Mediterranean, is today completely deserted except for the lonely guardian of the ruins. Even though the ancients allowed no burials on Delos, the islet is haunted by memories of the 'splendour that was Greece'; the Delians themselves have been reincarnated as little lizards, darting among the poppies and broken marble.

Mythology

The most ancient name of Delos was Ortygia, derived from one of Zeus' love affairs, this time with a maiden named Asteria. Asteria fled the lusty king of the gods in the form of a quail, and Zeus turned himself into an eagle the better to pursue her. The pursuit proved so hot that Asteria turned into a rock and fell into the sea. This rock was known as Ortygia ('quail') or Adelos, the invisible one, as it floated all over Greece like a submarine just below the surface of the sea. Some time later Zeus fell in love with Asteria's sister Leto, and despite the previous failure of the bird motif, succeeded in making love to her in the form of a swan—the subject of some of the most erotic fancies produced by Michelangelo and other artists in the Renaissance.

But Zeus' humourless, jealous, Thurberesque wife Hera soon got wind of the affair and begged Mother Earth not to allow Leto to give birth anywhere under the sun. All over the world wandered poor, suffering, overripe Leto, unable to find a rock to stand on, as all feared the wrath of Hera. Finally in pity Zeus turned to his brother Poseidon and asked him to lend a hand.

Poseidon thereupon ordered Ortygia to halt, and anchored the islet with four columns of diamond. Thus Adelos the Invisible, not under the sun but under the sea, became Delos, the Visible. Delos, however, was still reluctant to have Leto, fearing her divine offspring would give her a resounding kick back into the sea. But Leto promised the islet that no such thing would happen; indeed her son would make Delos the richest sanctuary in Greece. The island conceded, and Leto gave birth first to Artemis, goddess of the hunt and virginity, and then nine days later to Apollo, the god of truth and light.

History

In the 3rd millennium BC Delos was settled by people from Karia. By 1000 BC the Ionians had made it their religious capital, centred around the cult of Apollo whom they believed to be the father of the founder of their race, Ion—a cult first mentioned in a Homeric hymn of the 7th century BC. Games and pilgrimages took place, and Delos was probably the centre of the Amphictyonic maritime league of the Ionians. In 550 BC Polycrates, the Tyrant of Samos, conquered the Cyclades but respected the sanctity of Delos, putting the islet Rheneia under its control, and symbolically binding it to Delos with a chain.

With the rise of Athens, notably under Pisistratos, began the greatest glory and greatest difficulties of Delos. What was once sacred began to take on a political significance, and the Athenians invented stories to connect themselves to the islet—did not Erechtheus, the King of Athens, lead the first delegation to Delos? After slaying the Minotaur on Crete did not Theseus stop at Delos and dance around the altar of Apollo? In 543 BC the Athenians even managed to trick the oracle at Delphi into ordering the purification of the island, which meant removing the old tombs, a manoeuvre designed to alienate the Delians from their past and diminish the island's importance in comparison to Athens' rising status.

In 490 BC the population of Delos fled to Tinos before the Persian king of kings Darius, who, according to Herodotos, not only respected the sacred site and sacrificed 300 talents' worth of incense to Apollo but allowed the Delians to return home in safety. The Persians lost the war, and after the Battle of Salamis the Athenians, to prevent further invasions, organized a new Amphictyonic league, centred at Delos. Only the Athenian fleet could guarantee protection to the island allies, who in return were required to contribute a yearly sum and ships to support the navy. Athenian archons administered the funds.

The Delian alliance was effective, despite resentment among islanders who disliked being lorded over by the Athenians. No one was fooled in 454 BC when Pericles, in order better to 'protect' the league's treasury, removed it to Athens' acropolis; some of the money went to repair damage incurred during the previous

Persian invasion, and some to beautify Athens generally. Shortly afterwards, divine retribution hit Athens in the form of a terrible plague, and as it was determined to have been caused by the wrath of Apollo, a second purification of Delos (not Athens, mind) was called for in 426 BC. This time not only did the Athenians remove all the old tombs, but they forbade both births and death on Delos, forcing the pregnant and the dying to go to Rheneia. Thus the alienation of the Delians was complete. When the people turned to Sparta for aid during the Peloponnesian War, the Spartans remained unmoved: since the inhabitants couldn't be born or die on the island, they reasoned that Delos wasn't really their homeland, and why should they help a group of foreigners? In 422 BC Athens punished Delos for courting Sparta by exiling the entire population (for being 'unpure') to Asia Minor, where all the leaders were slain by cunning. Athenian settlers moved in to take the Delians' place, but Athens herself was punished by the gods for her greed and suffered many setbacks against Sparta. After a year, hoping to regain divine favour, Athens allowed the Delians to return home. From 403 to 394 BC Delos had a breath of freedom when the Spartans defeated Athens. Then Athens formed its second Delian alliance, although it was far less forceful, and 50 years later the Delians had plucked up the courage to ask the league to oust the bossy Athenians altogether. But the head of the league at the time, Philip II of Macedon, refused the request, wishing to stay in the good graces of the city that hated him most.

In the confusion following the death of Philip's son, Alexander the Great, Delos became free and prosperous, supported by the pious Macedonian general-kings. New buildings and shrines were constructed and by 250 BC Delos was a flourishing cosmopolitan, commercial port, inhabited by merchants from all over the Mediterranean. When the Romans defeated the Macedonians in 166 BC they returned the island to Athens, which once again exiled the Delians. But by 146 BC and the fall of Corinth, Delos was the centre of all east–west trade, and declared a free port by the Romans in order to undermine the competition at Rhodes. People from all over the world settled on Delos and set up their own cults in complete tolerance. Roman trade guilds, each with its own *lares*, centred on the Italian Agora. New quays and piers were constructed to deal with the heavy flow of vessels. Markets thrived.

In the battle of the Romans against Mithridates of Pontus in 88 BC, Delos was robbed of many of her treasures; 20,000 people were killed, and the women and children carried off as slaves. This was the beginning of the end of Delos. Sulla regained the island, but 19 years later Delos was again destroyed by pirates allied to Mithradates, and the population was again dragged off to the slave markets. General Triarius retook the island and fortified it with walls, and Hadrian attempted in vain to revive the waning cult of Apollo with new festivities.

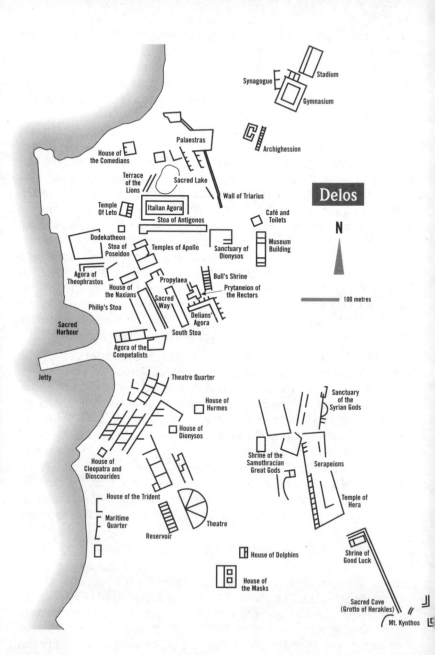

Synagogue

Stadium

Gymnasium

Archighession

Palaestras

House of
the Comedians

Terrace
of the
Lions

Sacred Lake

Wall of Triarius

Temple
Of Leto

Italian Agora

Café and
Toilets

Stoa of Antigonos

Museum
Building

Dodekatheon

Stoa of
Poseidon

Temples of Apollo

Sanctuary of
Dionysos

Agora of
Theophrastos

House
of the Naxians

Propylaea

Bull's Shrine

Prytaneion of
the Rectors

Philip's Stoa

Sacred
Way

Delians'
Agora

Sacred
Harbour

South Stoa

Agora of the
Competalists

Jetty

Theatre Quarter

House of
Hermes

Sanctuary
of the
Syrian Gods

House of
Dionysos

House of
Cleopatra and
Dioscourides

Shrine of the
Samothracian
Great Gods

Serapeions

House of the Trident

Temple of
Hera

Maritime
Quarter

Reservoir

Theatre

House of Dolphins

Shrine of
Good Luck

House of
the Masks

Sacred Cave
(Grotto of Herakles)

Mt. Kynthos

Delos

N

100 metres

Wretched Delos went into such a decline that when Athens tried to sell the islet, no one offered to buy it. In AD 363, Roman Emperor Julian the Apostate tried to renew paganism on Delos until the oracles solemnly warned: 'Delos shall become Adelos'. Later Theodosius the Great banned heathen ceremonies altogether. A small Christian community survived on Delos until the 6th century, when it was given over to the rule of pirates. House builders on Tinos and Mykonos used Delos for a marble quarry, and its once busy markets became a pasture.

After the War of Independence, Delos and Rheneia were placed in the municipality of Mykonos. Major archaeological excavations were begun in 1872 by the French School of Archaeology in Athens under Dr Lebeque, and work continues to this day.

Connections

Tourist boat from Mykonos 9am daily (except Mon), returning 12.30pm, or 10.15am, returning 1.30pm, with a guide (cost 4000 dr.), or hire a private boat at the main harbour. There's an admission fee (1000 dr.) to the island, which is a 3.5sq km outdoor archaeology museum.

The Excavations

A trip to **Delos** *begins as one clambers out of the caique and pays the entrance fee. The quality of 'official' guides varies, and you have to fit in with their timetables. Major sites are labelled, badly translated guidebooks are on sale (1000dr.), and everything of interest can be seen in hours. Be warned, the site is overrun with tourists.*

To your left from the landing stage is the **Agora of the Competalists**. *Compita* were Roman citizens or freed slaves who worshipped the Lares Competales, or crossroads gods. These Lares gods were the patrons of Roman trade guilds, while others came under the protection of Hermes, Apollo or Zeus. Many of the remains in the Agora are votive offerings to these gods. A road, once lined with statues, leads from here to the sanctuary of Apollo. To the left of the road stood a tall and splendid Doric colonnade called **Philip's Stoa**, built by Philip V of Macedon in 210 BC, and now marked only by its foundations; it once held a votive statue dedicated by Sulla for his victory over Mithridates. The kings of Pergamon built the **Southern Stoa** in the 3rd century BC, and you can also make out the remains of the **Delians' Agora**, the local marketplace in the area.

The **Sanctuary of Apollo** is announced by the **Propylaea**, a gateway built of white marble in the 2nd century BC. Little remains of the sanctuary itself, once crowded with temples, votive offerings and statues. Next door is the **House of the Naxians** (6th century BC). A huge kouros, or statue of Apollo as a young man, originally stood there, of which only the pedestal remains. According to Plutarch the kouros was crushed when a nearby bronze palm donated by Athens (symbolic of the tree clutched by Leto in giving birth) toppled over in the wind.

Next are the **three temples of Apollo**. The first and largest was begun by the Delians in 476 BC. The second was an Athenian construction of Pentelic marble, built during the Second Purification, and the third, of porous stone, was made by the 6th-century Athenian tyrant Pisistratos. Dimitrios the Besieger contributed the **Bull's Shrine**. This originally held a trireme in honour of the sacred delegation ship of Athens—the one Theseus sailed in on his return to Athens after slaying the Minotaur, and whose departure put off executions (most famously that of Socrates) until its return to Athens. Other buildings in the area were of an official nature—the **Prytaneion of the Rectors** and the **Councillor's house**. Towards the museum is the **sanctuary of Dionysos** (4th century BC), flanked by lucky marble phalli. The **Stoa of Antigonos** was built by a Macedonian king of that name in the 3rd century BC. Outside is the **Tomb of the Hyperborean Virgins**, who came to help Leto give birth to Apollo and Artemis, a sacred tomb and thus the only one to stay put during the two purifications.

On the opposite side of the Stoa stood the **Abaton**, the holy of holies, where only the priests could enter. The **Minoan fountain** nearby is from the 6th century BC. Through the **Italian Agora** one comes to the **Temple of Leto** (6th century) and the **Dodekatheon**, dedicated to the twelve gods of Olympos in the 3rd century BC. Beyond, where the **Sacred Lake** has dried up, is the famous **Terrace of the Lions**, ex-votos made from Naxian marble in the 7th century BC. The lake, called sacred for having witnessed the birth of Apollo, was surrounded by a small wall which still exists. When Delos' torrent Inopos stopped flowing, the water evaporated. Along the shore are two **Palaestras** (for exercises and lessons) along with the foundation of the **Archighession**, or temple to the first mythical settler on Delos, worshipped only on that island. Besides the **Gymnasium** and **Stadium** are remains of a few houses and a **synagogue** built by the Phoenician Jews in the 2nd century BC.

A dirt path leads from the tourist pavilion to Mt Kythnos (110m). Along the way stand the ruins of the **Sanctuary of the Syrian Gods** of 100BC with a small religious theatre within. The first of **three Serapeions** follows, dedicated to the Egyptian god Serapis and all built in the 2nd century BC. Between the first and second Serapeions is the **shrine to the Samothracian Great Gods**, the Cabiri or underworld deities. Next is the third Serapeion, perhaps the main sanctuary, with temples to both Serapis and Isis, with half a statue remaining. In the region are houses with mosaic floors, and a **temple to Hera** from 500 BC. The **Sacred Cave** is on the way to the top of Mt Kythnos, where Apollo ran one of his many oracles. Later it was dedicated to Heracles. On the mountain itself is the **Shrine of Good Luck**, built by Arsinoe Philadelphos, wife of her brother, the King of Egypt. On the summit of Kythnos signs of a settlement dating back to 3000 BC have been discovered, but better yet is the view, encompassing nearly all the Cyclades.

The **Theatre Quarter** consists of private houses surrounding the 2nd-century BC **Theatre of Delos**, with a capacity for 5500; beside it is a lovely eight-arched **reservoir**. The houses of this quarter date from the Hellenistic and Roman ages and many have mosaics, some beautifully preserved, such as in the **House of the Dolphins** and the **House of the Masks**. All of these residences have a cistern beneath the floor, spaces for oil lamps and sewage systems. Some are built in the peristyle 'style of Rhodes' with a high-ceilinged guest room; colonnades surround the central courts which are open to the sun. Seek out the **House of the Trident** and the **House of Dionysos**, both with mosaics, and the **House of Cleopatra and Dioscourides**, where the statues stand a headless guard over the once-great town.

Surrounding Delos are the islets **Ag. Georgios** (named after its monastery), **Karavonissi, Mikro** and **Megalo Rematiaris**, the last consecrated to Hecate, the Queen of the Night. **Rheneia,** also known as Greater Delos, lies just west of Delos and is just as uninhabited. Here came the pregnant or dying Delians—a large number of little rooms were excavated in the rock to receive them, before they moved into the realm of tombs and sepulchral altars. A necropolis near the shore was the repository of the coffins which the Athenians exhumed in the second purification. On the other side of Rheneia are the ruins of a lazaretto, once used by Syros-bound ships sent into quarantine.

Where to Stay

It is illegal to stay the night on Delos. Permission may be granted to archaeologists by the relevant authorities in Athens or Mykonos.

Eating Out

Near the museum building is a café for the tourists. There are no seats, delays are long, the staff are surly and the snacks are overpriced. Don't be caught out; bring food and water with you.

Folegandros

Folegandros is a small dry island of 650 inhabitants, one of the smallest in Greece with a permanent population. It has become a popular place for escapists, whose peace and quiet is only interrupted by an occasional load of day-trippers from Ios. Its name Folegandros comes from the Phoenician 'Phlegundum' meaning 'rocky island', which fits it to a tee.

Connections

Daily excursion boats from Ios, ferry 4–5 times a week with Piraeus, Ios, Santorini, less frequently with Sikinos, Milos, Sifnos, Serifos and Kythnos, roughly once a week with Kimolos, Crete, Kassos, Karpathos, Halki, Naxos, Paros, Symi and Rhodes. Catamaran once a week to Ios, Naxos, Paros, Mykonos, Tinos, Syros and Piraeus.

Around Folegandros

Boats to Folegandros land at **Karavostassis**, the tiny harbour, where you'll find restaurants and rooms to rent. It lies within walking distance of shady **Livadi** beach, from where a rough path continues inland to remote **Evangelistra monastery** dominating the rocky southern shores of the island. An easier path leads back to Chora from here, although if you're considering any long walks in the summer, a sun hat and a bottle of water are essential.

A bus runs from the port to medieval **Chora**, the capital, perched on the pirate-proof cliffs some 300m above the sea. It is a pretty village with shady squares. It becomes packed out in summer with trendy young Italians; there are lots of tasteful craft shops, bars and restaurants. The squares are lively at night, and one taverna even has a blackboard for backpacker messages.

The sparse remains of an ancient city are located on a high plateau above Chora, where in the 13th century Marco Sanudo built his fortress, or **Kastro**; the walls are formed by the solid square of tall, inward-looking houses themselves.

The church **Assumption** stands high up on a commanding headland; beyond it, a large grotto, **Chrisispilio** (the Golden Cave) has stalactites and stalagmites, but access is difficult; ask in Chora for someone to guide you.

Ano Mera, 5km west, is the only other village on Folegandros, and has two tavernas and a limited number of rooms to rent; from here on a clear day you can see Crete. Trails weave down to seldom-visited beaches at **Vigla**, **Livadaki** and

Vathi. From the road between Ano Mera and Chora a path descends to the beach of **Agali**, as away from it as you can get, with simple tavernas and rooms for rent, but no electricity. Next door is the quiet Ag. Nikolaos beach with a basic canteen. Both of these beaches can be reached by the boat which leaves Karavostassis at 11.15am, returning at 5pm.

Festivals

15 August at Panayia; and Easter, when an icon is paraded and trips are made in boats around the island.

© (0286–)

Where to Stay

moderate

Folegandros now has several small hotels, and the number grows year by year. **Hotel Danassis**, © 41 230, in Chora, is a lovely 500-year-old house with rooms that look down the sheer cliffs to the sea. It has been done up, but still retains character. **Kalimera Rooms**, © 41 389, is on the plateia near the bus stop, over a café. **Anemomilos Apartments**, © 41 309, is newly built, but in the traditional style, with balconies overhanging the sea. **Folegandros Apartments** (C), © 41 239, was built in 1990 in Cycladic style around a courtyard; **Hotel Odysseus**, © 41 224, is owned by the same family, on the cliffs in Chora. The once-popular old mansion **Fani-Venis**, © 41 237, seems run-down in comparison these days. Down in Karavostassis the **Aeolos**, © 41 205, is on the beach.

cheap

The old and established **Pavlo's Rooms**, © 41 232, is on the road to Chora. It has very basic chalet-style accommodation set in a lovely garden. There are rooms to let in private homes in Chora. The beach at Livadi has a **campsite**, with taverna, bar and laundry facilities. However, there are always more visitors than available space in the summer, so be prepared to sleep out, and, if it comes to that, be sure to find shelter from the strong, nagging winds.

Eating Out

In Karovostassi, **I Kalia Kardia** is ideal for fish; in Chora, **O Nikolaos** on the first plateia is an institution, a baggage store as well as a taverna, while

Pounta is very trendy. Also in Chora the taverna **O Kritikos** (the owner is Cretan) has delicious chicken on the spit; it's not a tourist place, it's a local, very Greek hang-out. Other possibilities are **I Piatsa** and **Kalimera Café**. In Ano Mera, **Taverna Iliovasilema** has local specialities and you can watch the sun set over Milos.

Ios

Although desperately trying to change its image as the Torremolinos or Benidorm of the Aegean, Ios remains the Mecca for throngs of young people who spend their days lounging on the best beach in the Cyclades and their evenings sauntering from one watering hole to another. To discourage raucous parties and late-night revellers sleeping out on the beach, four lovely campgrounds have been provided. The seasonal Irish invasion is so great that the island's name has been re-interpreted as the acronym for 'Irish Over Seas'. If it's the easy life you're seeking, Ios is the place. Otherwise, despite the loveliness of Ios and its beach, you may well feel disenchanted by the crowds, the lager louts, and the all-night loud parties. There are people who go back to Ios every summer, and people who definitely won't be returning; theft is depressingly common during the main tourist season.

Connections

Ios is very well connected. There are daily ferries to all the major Cyclades and Piraeus, five times a week to Crete, once a week to Thessaloniki; daily excursion boats to Santorini, Mykonos, Paros, Naxos, Sikinos and Folegandros; catamaran to Santorini, Sikinos, Folegandros and Piraeus.

Tourist Information

Information office in the port of Gialos, © (0286) 91 028. Also *see* regular police in Chora, © (0286) 91 222.

Gialos and Ios Town

The island's name (also rendered Nios) comes from the Ionians who built cities on the sites of Gialos and Ios town, when the island was famous for its luxuriant oak forests. Over the century, the oaks became ships and Ios became the arid rockpile

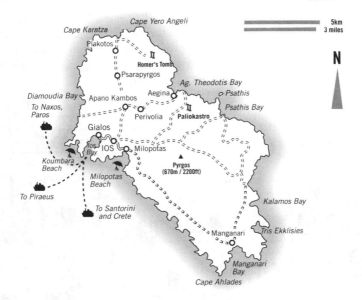

it is today; after the earthquake of 1951, when all the water was sucked out of Ios Bay and rushed back to flood and damage Gialos, the island may well have been abandoned had not the first tourists begun to trickle in.

Gialos, the port, has the island's best fish tavernas and quietest lodgings; it has a beach in the bay, but it tends to be very windy. From the port beach a rough track leads to **Koumbara** beach, a pretty sandy cove that is usually less crowded, and offers a couple of convenient tavernas for lunch. From Gialos frequent buses go up to Ios town and Milopotas Beach, or you can brave the 15-minute climb up the steps.

Ios town, 'The Village', one of the finest in the Cyclades, is increasingly hard to find behind the discos, bars and tourist shops. Traces of the ancient walls are preserved, and only bits more survive of the fortress built in 1400 by the Venetian Lord of Ios, Marco Crispi. A local story shows how remote the inhabitants of small islands were to the big political events in Greek history: when Otho of Bavaria, the first modern King of Greece, paid a visit to Ios, he greeted the villagers in the café, treated them to a round of drinks and promised he would pay to have the village cleaned up for them. The grateful Niotes, scarcely knowing what majesty

Otho pretended to, toasted him warmly: 'To the health of the King, Ios' new rubbish collector!'

Of the 18 original windmills behind the town, 12 remain, along with three olive oil presses. Two very old churches, out of the 400 or so chapels on the island, stand half-ruined on the hill above the town, where supposedly an underground tunnel leads to Plakotos, used as a hiding place during pirate raids. All the main facilities—police, telephone, post office, the bus stop—are at one end of the town, by a square; once there was a swing on this square, where Niotes courted their fair ladies and where ghosts now dance when no one's looking.

Beaches around Ios

Milopotas with its superb sandy beach has several tavernas and two campsites, although most people just bed down where they can find room. Don't count on getting much shut-eye wherever you end up: Ios' all night beach parties are infamous, and have unfortunately ended in several deaths caused by overdoses of drugs and alcohol. Excursion boats leave Gialos every day for **Manganari Bay**, where there is a smart German-built bungalow resort, and **Psathis Bay**, where a church dedicated to the Virgin fell into the sea; at **Ag. Ioannis Kalamos**, a huge *paniyeri* takes place on 29 August.

More remote (but now accessible by bus) is the fine beach at **Ag. Theodotis Bay**, near the ancient Ionian city of Aegina and overlooked by the ruined **Paliokastro**, a fortress built in the Middle Ages. On one occasion attacking pirates managed to bore a hole in the fortress gate, big enough to allow one man in at a time—only to be scalded to death one by one in burning oil poured on them by the besieged men and women. In Ag. Theodotis monastery the door the pirates broke through on the way to their doom is on display, and on 8 September a big celebration there commemorates the event with food and dance. In **Perivolia**, a small settlement in the middle of the island, are clustered Ios' fresh-water springs and trees; its valley church **Ag. Barbara**, has a *paniyiri* on 26 July. **Apano Kambos**, once inhabited by a hundred families but today reduced to three or four, is another pretty place. Nearby, at a place called **Hellinika**, are huge monoliths of mysterious origin.

Plakotos and Homer

Tradition has it that the mother of Homer came from Ios, and it was here that the great poet returned at the end of his life. Some say it was a riddle told by the fishermen of Ios that killed Homer in a fit of perplexity: to wit, 'What we catch we throw away; what we don't catch, we keep' (not wanting any readers to meet a similar fate, the answer's just below). Homer's supposed tomb is at **Plakotos** on the mountain, although earthquakes have left only the rock on which it was built. On 15 May each year, the *Omiria*, or Homer festival, takes place in town, with much merriment and many sporting events, and a flame is carried from the port to his grave. Plakotos itself was an ancient Ionian town which once had a temple to Apollo as well, but it slid down the cliff. You can look down and see the ruined houses; only one tower, Psarapyrgos, remains intact to mark the town.

© (0286–)   ***Where to Stay***

Ios, the paradise of the footloose and fancy free, can be reasonable, though we know of people who've paid 6000 dr. for a cramped and dirty room in peak season. You would get more peace and quiet staying in the port, but it's not much fun, and there are hundreds of rooms to let and several small hotels up in Chora.

luxury

Dionyssos Hotel (B), *©* (010) 30 286 21215, in Mylopotas is built in traditional style and has a pool. Down at Manganari Bay, the **Manganari Bungalow complex** offers luxury rooms and suites, with a restaurant and nightclub for those who like their entertainment sane and close to home, *©* 91 200/215. Accessible only by boat from Gialos.

On Milopotas beach the **Ios Palace** is designed and decorated in the old island style, and has good views of the bay, © 91 224. A few minutes from the beach at Milopotas, the appropriately-named **Far Out Hotel**, © 91446, is in cubist style with far out views; the rooms are extremely comfortable.

moderate

At Gialos, **Hotel Flisvos** (C), © 91315, is pleasant. The **Afroditi Hotel**, © 91 546, a bit outside of the tumultuous town centre is one of the best values you'll find. **Homer's Inn** in the town is also good value, but in high season you must book ahead, © 91 365. On Milopotas Beach, **Markos Beach**, © 91 571 has standard rooms at lower rates in this category, and rooms come with private shower. In town, or just on the fringe of town near the 'Dubliner Disco', **Markos Pension**, © 91 059, is for the younger crowd. It has a friendly little bar, and doesn't suffer from its proximity to the nightclub.

cheap

Petradi's, © 91510, has sea-view balconies; **The Wind**, © 91139, is large and friendly. The cheapest pension in Ios is **Violetta**, © 91 044, with basic, simple rooms. There are hundreds of rooms for rent in private homes, and 3 **campsites** on Milopotas beach. If you want to sleep out, remember that the police are cracking down, but in high season you may well have no other choice.

Eating Out

The **Ios Club**, on the footpath up from the harbour, has long been renowned for views of the sunset, good drinks and Classical music (programme posted daily). At night it turns into a discotheque; it now has a restaurant as well with good food, some Greek and some more exotic dishes (3000 dr. a meal). The **Pithari**, near the church, is one of the best places on the island, serving excellent Greek food and barrelled wine (2500–3000 dr.). In the heart of Ios town **Saini** has inexpensive Greek dishes; try the *dolmades* and stuffed squid (1500 dr.). The **Calypso** maintains its high reputation; the good music and civilized atmosphere is matched by the food (2500 dr). **The Nest** (I Folia) continues to be good and popular, especially for its prices—you can eat well for 1200 dr. One thing you wouldn't expect on Ios is an excellent *ouzeri*; **Ouzeri Manolis** has a fine spread of *meze*, and good wine if you're not up to tippling anis fire water. Opposite the Dubliner Disco there's English grub on offer at the **Captain's Table**, plus 'Fair dinkum Aussie Hamburgers'. Down in Gialos the **Afroditi** is worth a look-in; choose well and a fine Greek meal is yours for 2000 dr. On Koumbara beach, a 15-minute walk from the port, try the **Polydoros** for good dishes, seafood and vegetarian dishes (you can also ask here about rooms). Fish 'n chips and hot dogs can be found everywhere, but drinking takes priority over eating, and many of the little houses in the charming town have been turned into bars. Draught Guinness is on sale all over. One of the best places to sit and have a drink and gawk is **Frankie's**. The big discotheques, **The Dubliner**, **Sweet Irish Dream** and the **Red Lion** are all a short stagger apart.

local speciality

Ios' speciality, *meyifra*—a hard white cheese similar to Parmesan, mixed with perfume and fermented in a goatskin—is hard to find these days (all the better, some might add). It's not to be confused with *mezithra*, the soft sheep's-milk cheese. But meyifra cheese is not the answer to Homer's riddle: what the fishermen caught was lice.

Kea (Tsia)

Closest of all the Cyclades to Athens, Kea has for many years been a favourite place to build a summer villa—timed correctly, the island can be reached from the metropolis in less than 4 hours. It feels very different from most of the other Cyclades: well watered, Kea has been famed since antiquity for its fertility, its delicious red wine, lemons, honey and almonds. Its traditional architecture, while interesting, lacks the pristine white cubism of its sister isles. Its beaches are lovely, but hardly empty in the summer. Most weekends it is brimming with Athenians, so if you are planning a short stay, try and time it for mid-week. If you want to enjoy Kea's unhurried pace and atmosphere, do it now, before the entrepreneurs and tour operators develop her unexploited charms; regrettably, more and more hotels materialize each year, with people to fill them.

History

Traces of a Neolithic fishing settlement dating back to 3000 BC were discovered at Kefala on Kea's north coast. These first settlers were certainly no pushovers; when the mighty Minoan thalassocrats founded a colony *c.* 1650 BC at modern-day Ag. Irene, they were forced to build defences to protect themselves from attacks, not by sea but by land. The discovery (1960) of the colony by John L. Caskey of the University of Cincinnati is one of the more intriguing in recent years. Built on a small peninsula, it coincides nicely with the myth that Minos himself visited Kea and begat the Kean race of a native lady named Dexithea; it also reveals a fascinating chronicle of trade and diplomacy between the Minoans and the older Cycladic culture, and later, after the fall of Crete, with the Mycenaeans.

In the Classical era, Kea was divided into four towns: Ioulis, near modern Chora, Karthaea, Poiessa and Korissia. The 5th-century BC Lyric poets, Simonides and Bacchylides, the philosopher Ariston and the physician Erasistratos were all sons of Kea. During the Middle Ages, the Venetian Domenico Michelli used Ioulis' temple of Apollo to build a castle; in the 1860s the Greek government dismantled the cannibalized Classical bits to put in a museum.

Kea's name cropped up again in 1916, when the hospital ship *Britannic*, sister-ship to the *Titanic*, sank 3 miles off shore after an explosion. Of the more than a thousand people aboard, only 21 lost their lives when their lifeboat capsized. Speculation at the time produced two theories: one, that the ship had secretly been carrying munitions, which had accidentally exploded in the hold, or that the British had scuttled the ship themselves, hoping to pressure Athens to forbid enemy craft from navigating freely in Greek waters.

Connections

Daily with Lavrion, weekly with Kythnos. Daily hydrofoil in summer from Piraeus (Zea) and Anavissos on the southwest Attica coast, a 2-hour drive from central Athens.

Tourist Police

On the quay, © (0288) 31 300.
Tourist police, © (0288) 21 100.

Korissia and Ag. Irene

Kea's port **Korissia** has recently expanded beyond its purely functional role, anxious to become a resort like Kea's other coastal villages. Korissia, of course, recalls

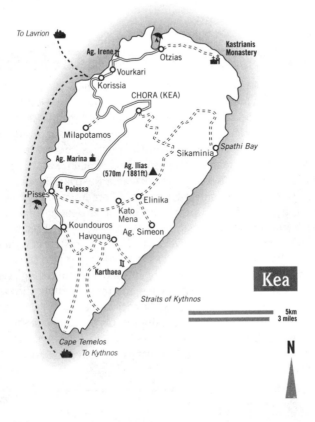

the ancient town that once stood on the site; most locals, however, still call it Livadi, as they continue to call their island Tsia instead of the official Kea. Just north is the small sandy beach of **Yialiskari** with a taverna, and a kilometre further north, on attractive Ag. Nikolaou Bay, **Vourkari** is a pretty fishing village and resort. North of Vourkari, on the peninsula of Ag. Irene (named after a small church) are the excavations of the **Bronze Age–Minoan–Mycenaean settlement**. It's not hard to make out the temple, originally constructed in the Bronze Age, a late Minoan palace-type hall, walls and a street. Among the artefacts found at Ag. Irene are inscriptions in the Minoan script Linear A.

From here the coastal road continues to the delightful but popular beach resort at **Otzias**, its bay ringed with a lacy mass of almond blossom in early spring, and to **Panayia Kastriani**, with an 18th-century monastery dedicated to the Virgin, and panoramic views down the coast.

Chora

Buses connect Korissia port with **Chora**, the island capital, hidden inland like so many Cycladic towns from the view of sea-going predators. The **Kastro** quarter of town occupies the site of ancient Ioulis' acropolis and medieval walls; all that remains are the stone blocks from the original temple of Apollo. A small museum in town contains other pieces of it, as well as artefacts from ancient Kea's four cities. A few Venetian mansions remain intact around Kastro, and several churches date back to the Byzantine era: **Panayia Kastriani** is noted for a miracle-working icon. A 10-minute walk east of Chora leads to the town's most curious attraction—a powerful **petrified Lion**, an ancient guardian some 3 m high and 6m long, gazing bemusedly out of the chiselled rock. Equally majestic is the renovated, square Hellenistic tower at the ruined monastery of **Ayia Marina**, southwest of Chora. One of the finest of such towers in Greece, its masonry has withstood time better than the monastery built around it. From Ag. Marina the road cuts across to the west coast beaches and resort communities at **Pisses** (which perhaps should consider reviving the ancient spelling of its name, Poiessa, of which a few traces remain) and **Koundouros**. On the southeast shore at Poles Bay is **ancient Karthaea**, where Simonides had his school of poetry. Inside its walls you can see the remains of a Doric temple dedicated to Apollo and several other buildings.

Festivals

17 July, Ag. Marina; 10 February, Ag. Charalambos, patron of Kea, at Chora; 15 August, Panayia, at Chora; 7 September, Ag. Soustas, at Otzias.

© (0288–)

Where to Stay

expensive

Nearly all the places to stay are along the coast. In Korissia you can sleep in something you don't find every day on a Greek island—a motel, the **I Tzia Mas**, © 31 303, a clean and friendly place, but book well in advance for the summer. The same warning holds for the **Kea Beach**, ℂ 31 230, a hotel and bungalow complex at Koundouros, with restaurant, nightclub, pool, tennis and watersports; bungalows here accommodate up to 4 persons. **Pension Ioulis**, ℂ 22 177, in Chora and **Pension Korissia** (A), 21 484, in Korissia, are both very comfortable.

moderate

There are only two places that fall into this category, the C class **Carthea**, ℂ 21 204, in Korissia, and **Filoxenia**, ℂ 22 057, in Chora.

cheap

There's not a wealth of places to stay on the cheap. Rooms are to be found in private homes in Korissia, some in Chora, Koundouros and Pisses, where there's a **campsite**. There are two pensions in Ioulidhas.

Eating Out

Although foreign visitors have begun trickling in, Kea is still very Greek and the tavernas serve up unadultered Greek fare at fairly reasonable prices. On the front in Korissia, as you get off the ferry, are a line of eating places, where you can spend a pleasant evening over a grilled fish at **Faros** or **Kostas** (3000 dr.), or have lunch on traditional Greek food further along at **Nostimies**, although in the evening the emphasis switches to continental and Cypriot specialities (2500 dr.) Good fish dinners await at any of the beachside tavernas, particularly at **Aristos** in Vourkari, popular with yachtsmen who can moor their boats a few feet from where they eat. Good Greek cooking and, if the wind has been blowing the right way and there's been a good haul of fish, a delicious *kakavia* (Greek *bouillabaisse)* will be on the menu (2500 dr.). At Pisses, two respected fish tavernas are **O Simitis** and **Kabi**.

Kimolos

Once known as Echinousa, or sea urchin, the island's modern name is thought to be derived from its first inhabitant. But Kimolia also means chalk in Greek, and whether the name comes from the producer (chalk was once a main export of Kimolos) or vice versa, no one is quite sure. Another ancient export was fuller's earth, used in the dying of cloth. At one time Kimolos was attached to Milos, but the isthmus linking the two islands sank into the sea, leaving a channel only a kilometre wide. An ancient town went under the waves as well, but its necropolis survives on Kimolos at a site called Elliniko.

Kimolos is a quiet island, a perfect place to relax and do absolutely nothing. Most of it is rocky and barren (the Venetians chopped down the once-plentiful olive groves and nothing has grown there since). The largest building on the island is a retirement home built by a local philanthropist, where Kimolos' elderly live free of charge. Apart from the one town, there are several shady beaches, but the only chalk you'll find these days is in the local school.

Connections

Three times a week with Piraeus, Milos, Kythnos, Serifos and Sifnos, once a week with Folegandros, Sikinos, Ios and Santorini, water taxi three times a day to Milos.

Chora and Around

At the little port, **Psathi**, caiques relay passengers to shore, and from here it's a 15-minute walk up to the typically white capital village **Chora**. On the way up you'll pass the retirement home, where a small museum in the basement takes in whatever potsherds and ancient bric-à-brac the locals happen to dig up. Chora has a few small cafés and tavernas, and a main church, **Evangelistra**, built in 1614. From here you can walk up to the ruined Venetian castle built by Marco Sanudo at **Paliokastro**, at Kimolos' highest point (355m). Within its forbidding walls is the island's oldest church, Christos. Another walk, taking in the Elliniko cemetery and its graves from the Mycenaean period (2500 BC) to the early centuries AD, follows the mule path to the west coast, near **Ag. Andreas**. You can finish up with a swim at the beach at **Kambana**.

A small hamlet near Psathi has the odd nickname of **Oupa**; Oupa has the most abundant fish in the Aegean these days, and here, supposedly, people used to scoop them out by the basketful. It's a very pretty little place, with a good beach untouched by tavernas or snack bars. **Prassa**, 6km to the north, has another good beach and an undeveloped radioactive spring. Goats are the only inhabitants of **Poliegos**, the large islet facing Psathi.

Festivals

27 August, Ag. Fanouris; 27 July, Ag. Panteleimonos; 21 November, Panayias; 20 July, Profitis Elias; 4 August, Ag. Theothoso.

Not many people stay overnight on Kimolos, and if you want to you'll have to ask around in the bars and tavernas to see who has a vacant room. Camping is usually 'no problem' as the Greeks say—you could try Klima and Aliki beaches.

Up in Chora are three tavernas, all serving standard Greek fare at low prices: **Ramfos, Panorama** and **Boxoris**, which also has rooms. If Kimolos' charms are wearing thin, you can sit under the umbrellas at the port snack bar and ogle the new arrivals off the ferry.

Kythnos

Time your visit right and you can have this island to yourself, avoiding the Athenian invasion of July and August. Like its neighbours, Kea and Serifos, Kythnos receives relatively few foreigners, and even the majority of Greek arrivals are not tourists, but folks full of aches and pains who come to soak in the thermal spa. But it does its best by them; since the closure of Kythnos' iron ore mines in 1940, islanders who closed their ears to the siren song of emigration have had to get by as best they can by fishing, farming (mostly figs and vines) and basket weaving. Perhaps because of their frugal, hard lives Kythniotes tend to celebrate *paniyiria* and special days with great gusto, donning their traditional costumes; carnival is a big event here. Best of all, it's the kind of island where the old men still offer to take you fishing—and the fishing off Kythnos is good indeed.

History

In Classical times the tale was told that Kythnos was uninhabited because of its wild beasts and snakes and Ofiohousa ('snaky') was one of the island's ancient names. Recently, however, archaeologists have uncovered a Mesolithic settlement (7500–6000 BC) just north of the port of Loutra that not only spits in the eye of tradition, but currently holds the honour of being the oldest settlement yet discovered in the Cyclades.

Much later the Minoans held the island, followed by the Driopes, a semi-mythical tribe who were chased out of their home on the slopes of Mt Parnassos by

Heracles and scattered to Evia, Cyprus and Kythnos; their king Kythnos gave his name to the island and their capital to this day is known as Dryopis. During the Hellenistic period Kythnos was dominated by Rhodes. Two great painters came from the island, Kydian and Timatheus (416–376 BC), the latter famous in antiquity for his portrait of Iphegenia. In 198 BC all Kythnos was pillaged, except for Vyrokastro, which proved impregnable. Marco Sanudo took the island for Venice, and for 200 years it was under the rule of the Cozzadini family who still live in Bologna today. In order to maintain their authority the Cozzadini paid taxes both to the Venetians and to the Turks.

Connections

Daily with Piraeus, Serifos, Sifnos and Milos, 2–3 times a week with Lavrion, Kimolos, Folegandros, Sikinos, Ios and Santorini. Kythnos has two ports; all ships these days put in at **Merihas** on the west coast, though when the winds are strong they'll come in to **Loutra** in the northeast.

Tourist Police

Chora, ✆ (0281) 31 201.

Hot Springs, Icons and Beaches

Merihas is a typical Greek fishing harbour, with a small beach, Martinakia. Just to the north are the meagre Hellenistic ruins of the once impregnable **Vyrokastro**, and another beach.

Buses make the 7-km trip from Merihas to the capital **Chora**, also known as Messaria. Although as Cycladic towns go it's on the dull side, it does have a pretty church, **Ag. Savas**, founded in 1613 by the island's Venetian masters, the Cozzadini, who decorated it with their coat-of-arms. Other churches in Chora claim to have icons by the Cretan-Venetian master Skordilis. The buses continue to **Loutra**, the most important thermal spa in the Cyclades. The iron once mined on Kythnos impregnates the water, leaving a characteristic reddish deposit. Since ancient times Loutra's two springs have been used for bathing and as a cure for gout, rheumatism, eczema and other complaints. Loutra has a beach as well, and the aforementioned Mesolithic settlement was found on the promontory just to the north. On the northernmost tip of Kythnos, Cape Kefalos, stands the **medieval citadel** (known variously as Paliokastro or Kastro tou katakefalou). About an hour's walk from Loutra, you can poke around its derelict towers,

Cape Kefalos

Kalakefala

Kastro ⚔

ᶲAderas

Loutra ᶲ   ᶲAg. Irene

To Kea

To Piraeus

⚔ **Vryokastro**

Apokrissi   CHORA

Episkopi ᶲ

**Mt. Profitis Ilias
(326m / 1076ft)** ▲

Ag. Stefanos

Merihas ᶲ

Dhriopidha

⚔

Kalo
Livadiᶲ

Flambouria ᶲ

To Serifos

Kanala ᶲ

Kythnos

5km
3 miles

Mavri
Punda

ᶲ Ag. Dimitri

N

houses and churches (one, **Our Lady of Compassion**, still has some frescoes), all abandoned around the middle of the 17th century.

A paved road leads from Merihas up to **Dhriopidha** (also known as Dryopis), the only other inland village and departure point for **Katafiki cave**, the most accessible of several Kythnos' grottoes, where the people of Dhryiopidha hid during pirate raids. From Dhryiopidha you can also walk down to the beaches at **Ag. Stefanos** and **Ag. Dimitri** or take a four-wheel drive down to the one at **Kanala**. Overlooking the bay, the monastery **Panayia tin Kanala** houses the island's most venerated icon, supposedly painted by St Luke himself. Other beaches on the island, attainable only by foot or boat, include Fikiado, Lefkas and Episkopi.

15 August and 8 September, at Kanala; 2 November, Ag. Akindinos, at Merihas. On Sundays you can often hear the island's music at Dhriopidha.

© *(0281)* **Where to Stay**

expensive

Merihas is the most convenient place to stay on Kythnos and there are quite a few rooms to rent as well as the large, modern class C **Possidonion Hotel**, © 31 224. The most luxurious place to stay on the island is the **Kythnos Bay Hotel**, © 31 218 in Loutra. **Meltemi Apartments** (C), © 31 271 have fully equipped flats at Loutra.

moderate–cheap

In Loutra the **Xenia Anagenissis** overlooks the beach, © 31 217. There are also rooms to rent in Loutra, and pensions catering primarily to spa customers. You can also find rooms in Chora, and in Merihas there are many pensions near to where the ferry docks.

Eating Out

There's an average restaurant in Chora and several good tavernas in Merihas and Loutra. In Merihas **Kissos** has a good name, and **Yalos**, with tables right by the water, whips up a few facsimiles of international specialities (stroganoff, schnitzel) to complement the Greek staples and fish. When you eat out, ask for the locally made cheese, which is excellent.

Milos

Like Santorini, Milos is a volcanic island, but where the former is a glamorous beauty associated with misty tales of Atlantis, Milos is a sturdy fellow who has made his fiery origins work for a living. Although the island lacks drama, it certainly has a catalogue of geological eccentricities: hot springs bubble up here and there amid its low rolling hills, the rocks startle with their Fauvist colours, and the landscape is gashed with obsidian, sulphur, kaolin, barium, alum, bensonite and perlite quarries begun in the Mesolithic era and exploited to this day. Walks through the gently undulating countryside will bring you down to tiny whitewashed chapels at the water's edge, or unique little settlements that sit on the water, with boat garages beneath their balconies. Milos also has one of the finest natural harbours in the whole of the Mediterranean. It seems an odd trick of Mother Nature to so endow such an out-of-the-way island. In spite of all its strange and wonderful rocks, Milos still mourns for the one which it lost—the renowned Venus, now in the Louvre.

History

At the dawn of the Neolithic era people braved the Aegean to mine Milos's uniquely rich sources of obsidian, that hard black, volcanic glass, prized for the manufacture of tools before the discovery of copper. Until the recent discovery of the Mesolithic settlement in Kythnos, Milos laid claim to the oldest town in the Cyclades, at Phylokope, settled by either Phoenicians or Cypriots; under Minoan and later Mycenaean rule the island became rich from trading obsidian all over the Mediterranean.

As the inhabitants of Milos in later years were predominately Dorian, they sided with their fellow Dorians from Sparta in the Peloponnesian War. When the Athenians made war in the east, the Milians again refused to fight with them. Athens sent envoys to Milos to change their minds. Their discussion, 'The Milian dialogue', included in the fifth chapter of Thucydides, is one of the most moving passages in Classical history. When Milos still refused to cooperate, the Athenians besieged the island, and when the Milians unconditionally surrendered, they massacred all men of fighting age, enslaved all the women and children, and resettled the island with colonists from Athens.

Christianity came early to Milos in the 1st century, and the faithful built a great series of catacombs—the only ones in Greece. Marco and his brother Angelo Sanudo captured Milos, and later placed it under the Crispi dynasty. The Turks laid claim to the island in 1580, even though Milos was infested with pirates. One of them, John Kapsis, declared himself King of Milos, a claim which Venice recognized for three years, until the Turks tricked Kapsis into coming to Istanbul, where he was slain. In 1680 a party of colonists from Milos emigrated to London, where James, Duke of York, granted them land to build a Greek church—the origin of Greek Street in Soho.

In 1820, farmer George Kentrotis (or Betonis) found a cave while planting his corn and discovered within a sensuous statue of the goddess Aphrodite. What happened next is uncertain; either the Turkish authorities seized it, or George's friends warned him that they would do so, and advised him to sell it to (or give it into the safekeeping of) the French consul in Istanbul. Whatever happened, the statue lost her arms and pedestal in transit. It was presented to Louis XVIII, who put it on display in the Louvre, where it remains to this day.

In 1836 Cretan war refugees from Sfakia fled to Milos and founded the village Adamas, the present port. During the Crimean War the French navy docked at the great harbour of Milos and left many monuments, as they did during the First World War; at Korfos you can see the bases of the anti-aircraft batteries installed during the German occupation in the Second World War.

Connections

Daily by air from Athens; ferry six times a week from Piraeus, six times a week to Sifnos, Serifos and Kythnos, two or three times a week with Crete. Three times a week with Folegandros and Santorini, twice a week with the Dodecanese. Daily taxi boat from Kimolos to Pollonia.

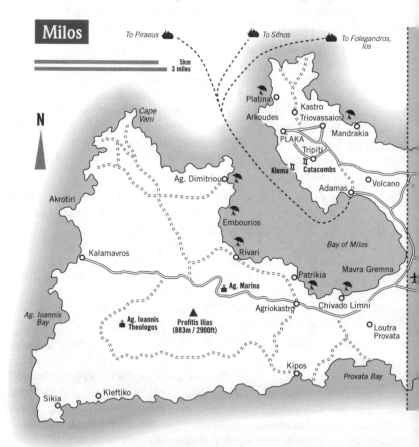

Tourist information booth, on the quay, © (0287) 22 290.
Tourist police, *see* regular police, Plaka, © (0287) 21 204.

Adamas, Plaka and its Plaster Venus

Even before you reach the port Adamas, you can see a sample of Milos' eccentric rocks: a formation called the **Arkoudes**, or bears, who guard the vast Bay of Milos (to the left as you sail into the harbour). The Cretans who founded **Adamas** brought their holy icons, now displayed in the churches of **Ag. Triada** and **Ag. Charalambos**: in the latter, one ex-voto, dating from 1576, portrays a boat attacked by a raging fish; the captain prayed to the Virgin, who resolved the struggle by snipping off the fish's nose. West of town a monument commemorates the French who died here during the Crimean War.

Adamas has most of Milos's available rooms and hotels; several shops hire out bicycles, and it's the main departure point for the island's buses. Above the village a site known locally as 'the Volcano' is actually a steaming fissure in the ground.

Buses leaves frequently for Plaka, the pleasant but modern capital. Next to the bus stop is the **Archaeology Museum** (*9–3, closed Mon*), its entrance marked by a queue of broken statues. Inside are finds dating back to the Neolithic era; in a back room is a plaster cast of the Venus which Milos lost, a thoughtful consolation prize from Paris. Signs point the way to the **Folklore and Laographic Museum** (*10–1 and 6–8, closed Mon*), especially fun if you can find someone to tell you the stories behind the exhibits, which include everything—and a kitchen sink to boot. The Frankish castle on top of **Plaka Kastro** affords good views of the island. Within its ruined walls is the 13th-century church **Thalassitrias**, its unusual name evoking Milos' seafaring past.

Ancient Melos and its Catacombs

Archaeologists believe that **Plaka** is built over the acropolis of ancient **Melos**, the town destroyed by the Athenians and resettled by the Romans. In the 1890s the British school excavated the site at **Klima**, a short walk below Plaka (if you take the bus, ask to be let off at Tripiti). Here you can see the **Catacombs** (*daily except Wed and Sun, 8.45–3*), dating from the 1st century and one of the best-preserved Early Christian monuments in Greece: carved into the rock are long corridors of arched tomb niches, each with a little light before it that you can move about in order to examine a tomb more closely. When first discovered, the catacombs were full of bones, but contact with the fresh air turned them to dust. Some niches held five or six bodies; others were buried in the floor. On some, inscriptions in red still remain (writing in black is later graffiti).

The habit of building underground necropoli (besides the many at Rome, there are catacombs in Naples, Syracuse and Malta) coincides with the presence of soft, easily worked volcanic tufa more than with romantic notions of Christian persecution and secret underground rites; burying the dead underground saved valuable space and answered to the desire of early Christians to stick as close as possible to the holiest members of their congregations, as if hoping to grab onto their boot-straps when their souls ascended on Judgement Day. Curiously, the modern cemetery of Milos near Plaka resembles a row of catacombs above ground.

A path from the Catacombs leads to the place where the Venus of Milos was discovered (there is a marker by the fig tree) and past the ancient walls to the well-preserved **Roman Theatre**, where spectators looked out over the sea. Part of the stage remains, although three tiers of seats have been left unexcavated, they say, as evidence of the Milians' indifference to tourism. However a theatre company from Athens sometimes performs in the theatre in August. Remains of a **temple** are on the path back to the main road.

Around Plaka

Most of the population of Milos is concentrated in the villages around Plaka. On the north coast, paths lead down to a wide selection of beaches, some adorned with wonderfully-coloured rocks. Two of most popular swimming holes are

Platina near the Arkoudes and the best place on Milos to watch the sun set, and **Mandrakia** on the opposite side of the peninsula, where you can drink the purgative **waters of Tsillorneri** if too much ouzo hasn't already done the trick.

Pollonia and Phylokope

From Adamas or Plaka buses depart for **Pollonia**, with its many trees, tavernas, rooms and places to camp out, as well as the caiques to Kimolos. Pollonia is within walking distance of **Phylokope** (or Filokopi), one of the great centres of Cycladic civilization, excavated by the British in the 1890s. The dig yielded three successive levels of habitation: the early Cycladic (3500 BC), the Middle Cycladic (to around 1600 BC) and Late Cycladic/Mycenaean.

Even in Early Cycladic days Milos traded obsidian far and wide—pottery found in the lowest levels at Phylokope shows an Early Minoan influence. Great urban improvements were made in Phylokope during the Middle Cycladic period: a wall was built around the more spacious and elegant houses, some with frescoes—one depicts a flying fish, that in the absence of Venus has become the artistic symbol of Milos. A Minoan-style palace was built; fine vases and Minoan ware were imported from Knossos; the obsidian trade reached the coasts of Asia Minor. Late in this period Phylokope, like the rest of the Cyclades, may have come under the direct rule of the Minoans, suggested by a tablet found on the site written in a script similar to Linear A. The top, or Late Cycladic level revealed a Mycenaean wall around the palace, a shrine, and Mycenaean pottery and figurines. Phylokope survived to see the decline of Milos' importance, as the use of metals began to replace the need for obsidian. Unfortunately, for all that, there's not very much to see at the site itself, and what can be seen—walls, mostly—are quite overgrown and inexplicable to the layman.

A Geological Mystery Tour of Milos

From Adamas excursion boats putter across the bay to the beach at **Embourios**, which also has rooms to rent and a taverna, or to visit the curious **Glaronisia**, four cave-pocked basalt islets north of Milos, the largest of which is shaped like a massive pipe organ. Near **Ag. Konstantinos**, off the road to Pollonia, steps lead down to **Papafragas**, where a pool of brilliant azure water is enclosed by a circular rock formation, once used by trading boats as a hiding place from pirates. More remote, on the southwest coast, is **Kleftiko**, another set of fantastic rock formations, accessible only from the sea. You can also sail near **Andimilos** to the northwest, home to a rare variety of chamois goat.

No buses—and therefore few tourists—visit the rest of Milos, but there are many rewards for anyone willing to don their walking shoes. South of Pollonia, at **Komia**, are ruined Byzantine churches and nearby at **Demenayaki** are some of Milos' obsidian mines. **Zefyria** further inland is also called Chora, for it served as the capital of Milos from the Middle Ages to the 18th century. Panayia Portiani was the principal church of the village; a story recounts that its priest was accused of fornication by the inhabitants, and although he steadfastly denied it, the villagers refused to believe him. With that the priest angrily cursed the people, a plague fell on the town, and everyone moved down to Plaka. Today Zefyria is a very quiet village of old crumbling houses, surrounded by olive trees. Alyki on the bay is a good beach near the **Mavra Gremna**, or the black cliffs, with more fantastical rock formations. At several places out in the bay the sea bubbles from the hot springs released below.

At **Loutra Provata** you can examine remains of Roman mosaics, followed by a natural sauna. The waters are famous for relieving rheumatism; Hippocrates wrote of the healing properties of Milos' waters. Local legend has it that the generous **Alikis** spring near the airport is a sure bet against sterility in women.

South and West Milos

Kipos, towards the south coast, has two churches: one, the 5th-century Panayia tou Kipou, is the oldest in Milos. The old monastery Chalaka is at **Ag. Marina**, and from here you can climb to the top of **Profitis Ilias**, with a gods' eye view over Milos and neighbouring islands. There are beaches at **Patrikia** and further north at **Ag. Dimitriou**, although the latter is often battered by winds. If you hire a boat, the small coves carved in the south coast make ideal stopovers for a skinny dip.

Ag. Ioannis Theologos, in the southwestern corner of Milos, has a celebrated *paniyiri* on 7 May. Ag. Ioannis is known here as the Iron Saint—during one festival the party-goers were attacked by pirates, and in response to the people's prayers, the saint saved them by turning the door of the church into iron (one can still see a scrap of a dress caught in the door as the last woman entered). The pirates could not break in, and when one of them tried to shoot someone through a hole in the church dome, Ag. Ioannis made his hand fall off.

Festivals

17 July, Ag. Marina; 19 July, Profitis Ilias on the mountain; 20 June and 31 October, Ag. Anargyroi (Byzantine church); 7 May and 24 September, Ag. Ioannes Theologos at Chalaka; 14 August at Zefyria; 28 August, Ag. Ioannis

Prodromou; 5 August, Sotiris at Paraskopou; 26 July, Ag. Panteleimonos at Zefyria; and 25 July, Ag. Paraskevi at Pollonia.

© (0287–)   **Where to Stay**

Except for a few scattered rooms to let in Plaka and near the more popular beaches, most of the accommodation is at Adamas.

expensive

Kapetan Tassos (A), © 41 287, in Pollonia is pretty smart. In Adamas **Venus Village** is a large hotel and bungalow complex on the beach, © 22 030, that dwarfs the local competition.

moderate

Pension Popi (B), © 21988, and Pension Adamas, © 41844, are two of the smarter hotels in Admamas. Prettiest among the less expensive hotels is the D class Semiramis, © 22 118, each room with private bath. The large, casual and slightly tatty hotel Corali is a walk up the hill from the waterfront, but fairly convenient all the same, © 22 204. In Klima the Panorama , © 21 623, has rooms with private bath.

cheap

The Georgantas, © 41 636, in Adamas is cheap. Rooms in private houses on the island go for around 3500–4000 dr. If you want to sleep out, do so with caution—the local police can be sticky and do levy big fines.

Eating Out

Again, nearly everything is in Adamas, and if you come in an off-season month, look for oysters from Ahivadolimni. On Adamas' waterfront the friendly Flisvos has the usual fish and ready food offerings, and you can eat well for 2000 dr. Next door **O Kynigos** serves similar fare in unpretentious but pleasant surroundings (2000 dr.). After contemplating the bay in Adamas over an evening ouzo, a short stroll (past the taxi and bus stop) will take you to an excellent pair of tavernas, where the food is of the highest quality, the wine good and the prices low: **Trapatselis** and **Navyio**. In town head for **O Kinigos**, where they take extra care in the preparation of seafood and standard Greek dishes (2–3000 dr.). Local favourites in Pollonia and Plaka are the **Petrakis** and **Karamitsos**, respectively.

Mykonos

This dry, barren island frequently plagued by high winds, but graced with excellent beaches and a beautiful, colourful, cosmopolitan town has the most exciting and sophisticated nightlife in Greece. This, and its proximity to Delos, has earned it the reputation as the most popular island in the Cyclades. If the surge in tourism in recent years caught the other islands unawares, Mykonos, at least, didn't bat an eyelid, having made the transformation long ago—relatively speaking—from a traditional economy to one dedicated to the whims of the international set. If you seek the simple, the unadorned, the distinctly Greek—avoid Mykonos, but the party will go on without you; Mykonos' streets are jammed with some of the zaniest, wildest, raunchiest and most beautiful people in Greece. It also has the distinction of being one of the most expensive islands, and the first officially to sanction nudism on some of its beaches; it is now the Mediterranean's leading gay holiday resort, though it's popular with a mixed crowd of people with money to spend.

To Tinos

To Syros

Rheneia

Kounelonisi

Megalo
Rematiaris

Delos

To Naxos, Paros
and Santorini

History

The Ionians built three cities on Mykonos: one on the isthmus south of Chora, the second at Dimastos, dating back to 2000 BC, and the third at Panormos near Paliokastro. During the war between the Romans and Mithridates of Pontus, all three were destroyed. Chora was rebuilt during the Byzantine period, and the Venetians surrounded it with a wall that no longer exists; however, at Paliokastro a fort built by the Gizzi rulers still remains.

In myth Mykonos is best known as a graveyard, site of the rock tombs of the last giant slain by the hero Heracles and that of Ajax of Oileus, one of the Achaean heroes of the Trojan War. This Ajax was known as Little Ajax to differentiate him from Big Ajax, who committed suicide when the weapons of the dead Achilles were not given to him but to Odysseus. After the capture of Troy, Little Ajax proved himself just as pathetic a hero when he raped Priam's daughter Cassandra who had sought protection in a temple of Athena. Athena avenged this blasphemy by wrecking Ajax's ship off the coast of Mykonos. Poseidon saved him in a sea storm but, as horrid as ever, Ajax declared that he would have been perfectly able to save himself without the god's assistance. Poseidon's avenging trident finished Ajax then and there, and his Mycenaean tomb can still be seen at Linos.

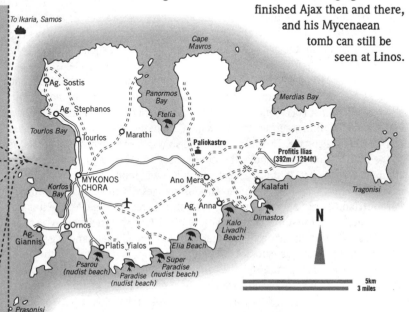

Connections

By air: daily connections with Athens, several times a week with Santorini, Rhodes, Herakleon, Crete. Less frequently with Chios, Mytilini, Samos.

By ship: daily with Piraeus, Rafina, Andros, Tinos, Syros, Paros, Naxos, Ios and Santorini; several times a week with Samos, Herakleon (Crete), Amorgos, Astypalaia, Kos, Rhodes, Koufonissia, Shinoussa and Heraklia. Twice a week with Sikinos, Folegandros, Skiathos and Thessaloniki, once a week with Kalymnos, Sifnos, Serifos, Nissyros, Tilos and Ikaria; hydrofoil daily to Rafina and other Cyclades; catamaran and hydrofoil daily to Piraeus, Tinos, Paros, Naxos, Andros and Syros. Daily to Delos at 9am, or at 10.15am with a guide (4500 dr.), returning at 1.30pm.

Tourist Police

On the quay, ✆ (0289) 22 482.

Prosperity has kept the homes of **Chora**, the island's picture-postcard capital and port well maintained, gleaming and whitewashed, with brightly painted wooden trims. In the main square a bust of Mando Mavroyenous (the heroine from Mykonos who fought in the War of Independence) once served as the island's guardian of left luggage; now dire little notices keep the backpacks away. The square also maintains the taxi stand and several tacky but inexpensive snack bars. Further up the waterfront is the departure quay for the boats to Delos. The pelican mascot of Mykonos, the successor of the original Petros, may often be found preening himself in the shadow of the small church here. This side of the harbour also has the Tourist Police office, and on the hill overlooking the harbour are several windmills. Until recently one of them still ground wheat; another has been converted into a cottage. They are a favourite subject for the many local artists, as is 'the little Venice of Mykonos', the houses of Alefkandra, tall and picturesque and built directly beside the sea, just below the windmills. Mykonos claims to have 400 churches, and the most famous of these is the unusual **Panayia Paraportiani**, an asymmetrical masterpiece of folk architecture. Next to it is the island's **Folklore Museum**, a collection of bric-à-brac salvaged from Mykonos' past. Upstairs you can visit a re-created bedroom and kitchen, and a gallery of 19th-century prints of sensuous Greek odalisques gazing dreamily into space; downstairs is an exhibition, 'Mykonos and the Sea' (*7–9pm*). The **Archaeology Museum**, on the far side of the harbour near the Leto Hotel, highlights artefacts from the islet of Rheneia, excavated by the Greek archaeologist Stavropoulos; after the Athenian purifications, Rheneia served as the necropolis of Delos. Other exhibits include a *pithois* (storage pot) carved with scenes from the Trojan War, discovered on Mykonos itself (*8.45–3, Sun 9.30–2.30, closed Tues*). The **Nautical Museum**, at the end of the main street Matogianni, consists of four rooms containing ships' models from ancient times and a collection of paintings, prints and old coins. The attractive garden has become the last resting place of old anchors, ships' wheels, cannons, compasses and huge fans from a lighthouse operated by an oil lamp (*11–1 and 6–9*).

Around Mykonos

In ancient times Mykonos had the dubious distinction of being famous for the baldness of its men and even today the old fishermen of the island never take off their distinctive caps. Despite all the changes they've seen, they have kept their sense of humour, and if you speak a little Greek they'll regale you with stories of the good old days—before all the tourist girls (and boys) began chasing them around. The only other town on Mykonos is **Ano Mera**, where the **Tourliani Monastery** with its 15th-century carved steeple is the main attraction (open mornings only). Sandy **Panormos Bay** to the north was the site of one of Mykonos' three ancient cities. The second ancient city, **Dimastos**, is believed to have been on top of Mt Ayios, Mykonos' highest point. At Linos are the remains of a Hellenistic tower and walls; at **Portes** you can spit on the tomb of Ajax the troublemaker. The greenest spot on the island is the **Garden of Rapaki**, east of Chora (a good half-hour walk).

Dragonisi, the islet off the east coast of Mykonos, has numerous caves, and if you're very lucky you may see a rare monk seal in one of them. Boats for the excursion or a private trip to Delos may be hired at **Platis Yialos**. **Paradise** and gay **Super Paradise** are the main nudist beaches on the island; there are so many others scattered along the island's coasts that you could spend an entire holiday visiting them all. Particularly popular are **Psarou**, just before Platis Yialos, and **Ornos**. Both have a selection of tavernas serving fresh fish. One of the more pleasant and less crowded beaches is **Elia**, which has the added advantage of being accessible by local bus, on the road past the Hard Rock Café.

© (0289–)   ***Where to Stay***

There's certainly no lack of places to stay on Mykonos, although prices tend to be higher than almost anywhere else in Greece. Sleek new hotels, many incorporating elements of the local architecture, occupy every feasible spot on the coast, especially along the road to Platis Yialos. When you arrive off the ferry you'll be inundated with people offering rooms; many of these are up the hill above Chora, in a barren, isolated and ugly area of holiday apartments. If you want a more attractive location, hunt around in Kalogera Street, a pretty cobbled walkway in the heart of town; the area's very popular, but you might get lucky if you get there in the morning before 11am.

luxury

Princess of Mykonos (A), © 23 031, at Ag. Stephanos, isn't in the heart of the action, but it's only a taxi-ride away. On the beach, within walking distance of town is the cubist beauty **Cavo Tagoo**, © 23 692, with a sea water pool, beautiful view of Mykonos, and the chance to rub shoulders with the occasional Greek celebrity or politician. Smaller and in an equally pretty location is **Petinos Beach** at Platis Yialos, © 24 310, again with its own pool, and watersports.

expensive

If you want to be in the centre of the action (extremely difficult to do without reservations from June onwards), **Carbonaki**, 27 Panahrandou, © 22 461, is a good choice, with rooms arranged in cubist blocks, and it has a pool. **Hotel Aegean**, Tagoo (B), © 22 869, is well-appointed but still family-run and friendly. **Leto**, © 22 207, has a wonderful view over the harbour and town, and has for many years been the classiest place to stay on the island, but again the high season price reflects this. Off season, prices drop by around 20% or more. Adjacent to the apron of sand that forms the town beach is the small, 7-roomed **Delos**, © 22 312. **Manto**, 1 Evangelistrias, © 22 330, is convenient for connoisseurs of the night scene, while **Apollon** is a comfortable, friendly hotel, perfectly situated in the middle of the windy seafront, © 22 223. Two km outside town, **Rhenia** offers tranquil bungalows overlooking Chora and Delos, © 22 300. Small but stylish is the **Sunset Hotel**, Toulos Beach, © 23 010; the **Ornos Bay Pension**, © 23 961, is on the beach at Ornos Bay.

moderate

Even if you arrive in the middle of summer without a reservation, you may well be greeted by a convoy of hotel vans and people with rooms to let in town or along Ag. Stefanos beach, where the C class **Artemis**, © 22 345, or the smaller D class **Mina**, © 23 024, both have perfectly acceptable rooms with bath. For a little more you can make reservations at the delightful **Hotel Philippi**, located in the heart of Chora at 32 Kaloyera St, © 22 295. The rooms are spotless and scented by the hotel's lovely garden. Just out of town at Vrissi, the **Sourmeli**, © 22 905, has a pleasant garden, and equally pleasant rates.

cheap

It would be naïve optimism to expect any hotels or pensions in this category on Mykonos. Rooms in private houses are at least 4000 dr; ask at the Hellenic Travel Centre at the Fabrica bus stop, © 23 904. All campers are referred to the large campground at Paradise Beach and next door Paranga Beach (continuous boat service from Platis Yialos).

Again, no lack of opportunities here, especially if you have deep pockets. Within a few blocks you can sample a genuine American doughnut, top that off with a seafood pizza, and wash it down with a pint from the Irish Bar. If you take the complimentary bus out of Chora, there's even a (real) **Hard Rock Café** where you can eat expensive fast food and lounge by a pool. In contrast, there are numerous snack bars and bakeries with cheese pies, etc. if you're counting pennies. You can eat swordfish kebabs and squid and not pay an arm and a leg for it at the large restaurant connected to the motel on Platis Yialos Beach (dinner for 2000 dr.); **Philippi's** restaurant (connected to the Hotel Philippi) has the best reputation in town for international and Greek cuisine, served in the lovely garden—count on 6000 dr. Close by and in the same price range (the wine is more expensive) is the **Edem**, also offering a varied international menu in a garden setting. Centrally placed **Katrin's**, again fairly expensive, has many French specialities. If, in the wave of international food and music, you need to be reminded that you're in Greece, head for **Niko's Taverna**, behind the town hall, or **Maky's**, just around the corner, with good dinners in the 2000 dr. range. Eat at least once at **Spiro's**, below the windmills, with a view of waves rolling up to the foot of the houses of 'little Venice'; seafood specialities in the medium price bracket. A notable exception to the rule that the backstreets hide the best, secret tavernas is **Antonini's**, slap in the middle of the activity on taxi square; genuine Greek food at fair prices: varied and excellent *meze*, shrimp salad and very tasty veal or lamb casserole (2000 dr.). For fish, dine out at **Kounelas**, at the end of the waterfront, where the owner, a colourful character, promises consistently fresh seafood (4000 dr.). At Tourlos Bay, north of town before Ag. Stefanos, **Mathew** is well patronized, and at Ag. Anna, at the end of the road that crosses the island, **Nikolas** is the place to eat.

Nightlife

The international and gay set still bop the night away in a number of spots ranging from the cosy to the crazy. The **Veranda Bar** has a pleasant view of the windmills; **Bolero**, in the centre of town, has good music and cocktails; **Kastro's** in Little Venice will be forever famous for its sunset views; live music and snazzy cocktails can be had at the **Piano Bar** above taxi square, but get there early for a seat; **Thalami**, below the city hall, has Greek music and dancing, as does the perennial favourite, the **Mykonos Dancing Bar**; **Pierro's** remains the most frenzied of the lot, where hordes of people, from the young to the not-so-young, dance to the loud, lively music and spill out into the square. Prices, it almost goes without saying, are exorbitant in Mykonos; more than you might pay in London or New York. A small bottle of lager will cost upwards of 600dr. in one of the late-night bars of Chora.

Naxos

Naxos, 448 sq km in area, is the largest of the Cyclades and the most mountainous, its highest point, Mt Zas (or Zeus), crowning the archipelago at 1004m. It can also claim to be the most fertile, its cultivated valleys a refreshing green even in the height of the dry, sun-browned Cycladic summer. Lemons, and Kitron, a liqueur distilled from them, are Naxian specialities. Souvenirs of the island's ancient, Byzantine and Venetian past abound, and the entire west coast is almost one uninterrupted beach. It's not surprising, then, that this once little-known island attracts more visitors every year. The new airport will accelerate the island's tourist industry; until now it has served mostly as a retreat for people overwhelmed by the summer hordes on Mykonos and Paros.

History

Naxos was one of the major centres of the distinct Cycladic culture. Around 3000 BC, as now, the main settlements appear to have been near Chora, on the hill of the Kastro, and at Grotta, where the sea-eroded remains of the Cycladic town can still be seen in the clear water. Tradition has it that the island was later colonized by a party from Karia, led by a son of Apollo named Naxos.

Although these Naxians were Ionians, their most troublesome enemy was Miletus in Ionia proper, where some Naxian refugees, eager to take back the island for themselves, helped stir up trouble. According to Plutarch, many battles were fought between the two rivals at the fort called Delion, of which a few vestiges remain near Naxos town. The Naxian heroine Polykrite sought refuge here when her island was besieged by Miletus, only to find the gate of the fortress closed against her. One of the Miletian leaders found her there and fell so much in love with her that he agreed to help and informed Polykrite of all the movements of his armies. His information enabled the Naxians to make a sudden and vicious attack on the Miletians. However, in the confusion of the battle, Polykrite's lover, turned traitor for her sake, also perished, and the girl died in sorrow the next day, despite being acclaimed as the saviour of Naxos.

Naxos was one of the first islands to work in marble, and in the Archaic period produced the lions of Delos and kouroi statues of incredible size. Indeed, for a period, huge was beautiful on Naxos; in 523 BC the tyrant Lugdamis declared he would make the buildings on the island the highest and most glorious in all Greece. All that remains today of Lugdamis' ambition is the massive lintel from the gate of the Temple of Apollo on the islet of Palatia. An ancient mole still links Palatia to the mainland, attesting to the glory of Naxos when the island was the leader of the Ionic Amphictyonic league. As with most of the islands, Naxos declined in importance in the Classical age. In Hellenistic times it was governed by Ptolemy of Egypt who fortified Apano Kastro and Chimaru. The Byzantines continued to build defences on this rich and strategic island: and at their Castle T'apaliru, Marco Sanudo besieged them for two months in 1207.

With the taking of T'apaliru, Marco Sanudo became the self-proclaimed Duke of Naxos and held sway over all the Venetians who had grabbed Aegean Islands after the conquest of Constantinople in 1204. When Venice refused to grant Sanudo the independent status he desired, he broke away in 1210 and went over to the Latin Emperor, becoming the Duke of the Archipelago. The word archipelago, 'the chief sea', was the Byzantine name for the Aegean; under Sanudo and his successors, it took on its modern meaning, 'a group of islands', in this case the Cyclades, which the Venetians ruled as a fief for 300 years. They built a palace and a Catholic cathedral on the top of Chora, and a second residence at Apano Kastro, used in defence against both outsiders and rebellious islanders. Even after the Turkish conquest in 1564 the Dukes of Naxos remained in nominal control of the Cyclades, although answerable to the Sultan.

A latter-day Naxian, Petros Protopapadakis, planned the Corinth canal and gave many public works to the island. He was the Minister of Economics during the 1920–22 misadventure in Asia Minor, and was executed with other members of that sad government by the subsequent regime. His statue now stands by the port.

Mythology

After slaying the Minotaur, the Athenian hero Theseus and the Cretan princess Ariadne stopped to rest at Naxos on their way to Athens. Yet the next morning, while Ariadne slept, Theseus set sail and abandoned her. This, even in the eyes of the Athenians, was dishonourable, especially since Theseus had promised to marry Ariadne in return for the vital assistance she had rendered him in negotiating the Labyrinth. Various explanations for Theseus'

ungallant behaviour have sprung up over the centuries. Did he simply forget about her, did he find a new mistress, or did the god Dionysos, who later found her and married her, desire her from the moment she set foot on Naxos, and warn Theseus away? Historically, some believe the myth demonstrates the rise of a late Cycladic civilization after the fall of Crete; some say that Ariadne, as a priestess of Crete, would have forfeited her rights and authority if she had gone to Athens. Common, however, are the accounts that it was the jilted bride's curse on Theseus that made him forget to change his black sails to white, inadvertently causing his father's death. In all events, Ariadne lived happily ever after with Dionysos, who taught the Naxians how to make their excellent wine and set Ariadne's crown, the Corona Borealis, amongst the stars; the Celts called it Ariansrod, where their heroes went after death. The story of Theseus and Ariadne inspired many later artists, including Richard Strauss, who composed the opera *Ariadne auf Naxos*.

Connections

Daily by air from Athens. Daily ferry to Paros, Syros, Ios, Santorini, Mykonos, Tinos, Andros and Piraeus; daily boat to Amorgos via Koufonissia, Heraklia and Shinoussa, connections three times a week with Herakleon (Crete), Sifnos, Serifos, Samos, Ikaria and Rafina, twice a week with Sikinos and Folegandros; catamaran or hydrofoil daily to other Cyclades and Piraeus.

Tourist Police

See regular police, Naxos town, © (0285) 22 100.

Naxos Town and its Venetian Citadel

Naxos, or Chora, the island's port and capital, is a fine Cycladic town, although some people find its twisting streets so narrow as to be almost claustrophobic and bewildering, which is just as the natives intended them to be, to confuse invading marauders. The old town, up on the hill, is divided into two neighbourhoods: **Bourgos** where the Greeks lived, and **Kastro** above, residence of the Venetian–Catholic nobility. In the former, the Orthodox cathedral, the **Metropolis of Zoodochos Pigi**, was created in the 18th century out of an old temple and older churches; its iconostasis was painted by Dimitrios Valvis of the Cretan school. Archaeologists have made some interesting discoveries near the

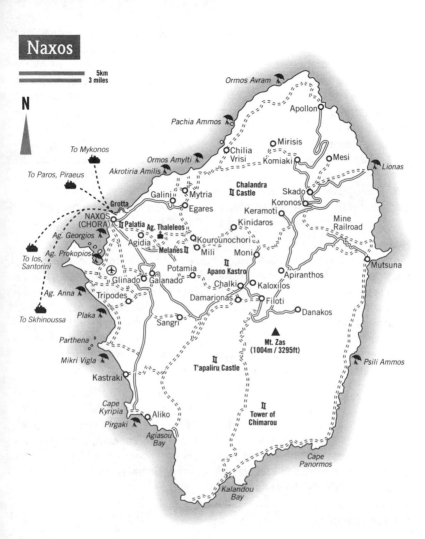

Naxos

5km
3 miles

N

To Mykonos

To Paros, Piraeus

To Ios, Santorini

To Skhinoussa

Ormos Avram

Apollon

Pachia Ammos

Mirisis

Chilia Vrisi

Komiaki

Mesi

Lionas

Ormos Amylti

Akrotiria Amilis

Chalandra Castle

Galini

Mytria

Egares

Skado

Koronos

Keramoti

Grotta

NAXOS (CHORA)

Palatia

Ag. Thaleleos

Kinidaros

Mine Railroad

Ag. Georgios

Agidia

Kourounochori

Ag. Prokopios

Melanes

Mili

Moni

Mutsuna

Potamia

Apano Kastro

Apiranthos

Glinado

Galanado

Chalki

Kaloxilos

Ag. Anna

Tripodes

Damarionas

Filoti

Danakos

Plaka

Sangri

Parthena

Mikri Vigla

▲
**Mt. Zas
(1004m / 3295ft)**

Psili Ammos

Kastraki

T'apaliru Castle

Cape Kyripia

Aliko

Pirgaki

Tower of Chimarou

Agiasou Bay

Cape Panormos

Kalandou Bay

Metropolis and would gladly knock it down for a slam bang dig if only the bishop would let them.

Although the city walls have all but disappeared, the inner walls of the Kastro remain. Inside, some 19 Venetian houses still bear their coats-of-arms—something you'll almost never see in Venice proper, where displays of pride were frowned upon, if not forbidden. Most of the Kastro's current residents claim descent from the Venetians, and many of their grandparents' tombstones in the 13th-century **Catholic Cathedral** boast grand titles. The cathedral was founded by Marco Sanudo, whose own palace, or what remains of it, can be seen directly across the square. Only one of the seven original towers of Kastro survives, locally known as **Pirgos**, guarding one of the three entrances to the enceinte. During the Turkish occupation Naxos had a reputation for its schools. In the Kastro there was the School of Commerce, and a school run by Catholic friars, attended for two years by the young Nikos Kazantzakis. One of the school's buildings, not far from the cathedral, is now an **Archaeology Museum** (*8.45–3, Sun and holidays 9.30–2.30, closed Tues*), with improved lighting to display its collection of Cycladic figurines, Mycenaean pottery, a Roman mosaic of Europa, pieces of Archaic kouroi and a statuette of a pig about to be sick in a sack.

North of the port, the ancient causeway stretches out to the islet of Palatia and the unfinished **Temple of Apollo**, begun in 522 BC. The massive lintel on the temple platform, a lone gateway to nowhere, is now used as a dramatic frame for sunset photos. A small sandy beach curves around the causeway, protected by the ancient **harbour mole**, rebuilt by Marco Sanudo. **Grotta**, so named for its numerous caves, occupies the north shore of Chora, and it is here that you can see remains of the Cycladic buildings underwater. In one place a few steps are discernible; the locals claim that in ancient times a tunnel went from Grotta to Palatia. It is near the site of the ancient **Fort Delion**.

The busy waterfront has filled up with tourist establishments; in early August the main square, near the ferry port and bus station, is the site of the Dionysia, a festival of folk music and dance, wine and souvlaki. To the south, above the Agrarian Bank, is the 11th-century **Church of Panayia Pantansassa**, once part of a Byzantine monastery and famous for its very early icon of the Virgin. Further south numerous hotels and a whole new suburb of Chora, Nea Chora, has sprung up around popular **Ag. Georgios beach**.

Naxian Beaches

The busiest beach on the sandstrewn west coast of Naxos is **Ag. Anna**, linked by public bus and caique from Chora; well sheltered from the notorious meltemi, this beach and the neighbouring ones of **Ag. Prokopios** to the north, and **Plaka** to the south, offer a variety of watersports for experts and beginners alike; Ag. Prokopios even has jet skis to rent. Plaka has a camping site and beach, considered the best in Naxos, and a favourite of a new crop of young hippies; it's also nudist once you get away from the settlements.

Further south stretch the vast strands of **Mikri Vigla** and **Kastraki**. The sea here is brilliantly clear, the beaches are of pure white sand. Mikri Vigla is in fact a cape; to the north, **Parthena** beach is excellent for surfing and swimming, and to the south, **Sahara** is well equipped for sea sports. Further south, Sahara extends into **Kastraki**, again with sparkling clean sea and white sands, ideal for swimming, sunbathing and letting the kids run wild. Kastraki derives its name from the ruined Mycenaean fortress, built over the remains of a Cycladic acropolis. From here you can walk up to **T'apaliru**, the Byzantine castle high on its rock that defied Marco Sanudo and his mercenaries for two months. If the above beaches are too busy for your taste, there's a more remote strip of sand beyond Kastraki at **Pirgaki**.

Marble Quarries, Venetian Towers and Olive Groves

The main asphalted road south of Chora leads through the fertile and flat **Livadi Valley**. After a couple of kilometres the road splits, the left branch leading towards **Melanes** and the ancient marble quarries in the heart of Naxos; at the one called Flerio, 3km east, lie two 7th-century BC **kouroi**, each 18-ft high. *Kouros* means 'young man', and in the Archaic period such statues—highly stylized, stiff figures, their arms hugging their sides, one foot stepping forward—were probably inspired by Egyptian art; the young men they portray are believed to have been Zeus' ancient guardians (the Cretan Curetes) or perhaps the Ionian god Apollo. At **Kourounochori** near Melanes stand ruins of a Venetian castle; **Ag. Thaleleos** in the same area has a monastery with a fine 13th-century church.

Back at the crossroads, the right branch of the main road from Naxos town leads to **Galanado**, site of the ruined Venetian tower called **Belonia** and the twin Venetian church of St John, with a Catholic chapel on one side and an Orthodox church on the other. The recently restored **Ag. Mamas**, dating from the 8th century and Naxos' original cathedral, is a short walk from the road en route to **Sangri**. Sangri's name is the Hellenized version of Sainte Croix, in turn the French name for the 16th-century Monastery Timious Stavrou. Sangri actually consists of three small villages spread out over the plateau, with many Byzantine and medieval towers and churches in the area; one of these, **Ag. Ioannis Gyroulas** in Ano Sangri, is built over a temple of Demeter.

The Valley of Tragea and Slopes of Mt Zas

From Sangri the road descends into the beautiful Valley of Tragea, flanked on either side by Naxos' highest mountains. Olives are the main product of the numerous small villages in the valley, including **Chalki**, where both the

Byzantines and Venetians built towers: the Byzantine **Francopoulo**, in the centre, and up a steep path the **Apano Kastro**, last repaired by the Venetians and used, it is believed, as Marco Sanudo's summer home. He was not, however, the first to enjoy the splendid panorama of forests, olive groves and mountains from the summit; the fortress sits on Cyclopean foundations, and Mycenaean tombs have been discovered in the immediate area. In Chalki itself there are two fine churches with frescoes: 12th-century **Panayia Protothronis** and 9th-century **Ag. Diasoritis**.

From Chalki a paved road leads up to **Moni**, home of the most unusual church on Naxos, **Panayia Drossiani**, crowned with ancient corbelled domes of field stones. The main road through the Tragea valley continues on to **Filoti**, on the slopes of Mt Zas, the largest village in the region, with splendid views, and the chance to eavesdrop on everyday life in a traditional Naxian village. There are many good walking paths in the region, one leading up the slopes of **Mt Zas**. Dedicated to the goddess Za or to Zeus, the father of the gods, there's a cave near the summit once used as a religious sanctuary. A 3-hour path from Filoti follows the west flanks of the mountain to the excellently preserved Hellenistic **Tower of Chimarou**, built by Ptolemy, its isolation the main reason for its survival over the centuries. In Filoti itself there's the Venetian stronghold of the De Lasti family, and the church **Koimisis tis Theotokou** with a fine carved marble iconostasis, and another church, **Panayia Filotissa** with a marble steeple.

From Filoti the road skirts the slopes of Mt Zas on its way to **Apiranthos**, where the Venetian families Crispi and Sommaripa built towers. Many contemporary families, however, claim Cretan blood, descended from migrants who came during the Turkish occupation to work in the emery mines. Apiranthos is one of Naxos' more traditional villages, where some women still weave on looms; it's also the site of a small **museum**, devoted to mostly Neolithic finds. A road from here descends to the port of **Mutsuna**, where the emery used to be brought down from the mountains near Koronos by a rope funicular (more successful than the disastrous one used in *Zorba the Greek*) and loaded onto ships. Mutsuna has a fine beach; from here a dirt road follows the east coast south to the remote beach of **Psili Ammos**. Another beach, **Lionas**, is linked by paved road to **Koronos**.

Beyond Koronos the road turns into a winding, hairpin serpent leading to pretty **Komiaki**, highest of the island's villages, with stunning views over terraced vineyards. The road leads back down to **Apollon**, a dreary little town with a (very) public beach, several tavernas heavily patronized by tourist buses, and some mid-range pensions. Ancient marble quarries are carved out of the slopes of the mountain, and steps lead up to a colossal unfinished **kouros**, abandoned in the

7th century BC. Because Apollon was sacred to Apollo, the kouros is believed to represent the god; even more intriguingly, the long-vanished temple that stood here is part of the equilateral triangle formed by the temples of Apollo on Delos and Paros. Apollon is as far as the bus goes; by car you can chance the unpaved road along the north coast back to Naxos town, passing the isolated beaches of **Ormos Abram** and **Pachia Ammos**, near the **monastery of Faneromeni** dating from 1606. There are lovely beaches in this northwest corner of the island, although when the *meltemi* roars they are far from pleasant. **Galini**, where the road improves, has the Byzantine fortified monastery **Ipsiloteras**. From here it's 6km back to Chora.

Festivals

Like the Cretans, the Naxians sometimes improvise verses at their *paniyiria*, a custom dating back to ancient times. Some of the many celebrations are: 20 May, Ag. Thaleleos; 17 July, at Koronos; 15 August, Panayia at Filoti; 1 July, Ag. Anargyroi at Sangri; 23 August, at Tripodes; 14 July, Ag. Nikodimos at Naxos; 29 August, Ag. Ioannis at Apollon and Apiranthos; 23 April, Ag. Georgios at Kinidaros. The first week of August sees the Dionysia festival in Naxos town, with folkdancing in local costume; free food in the central square.

© (0285–)   Where to Stay

Naxos is still one of the least expensive of the popular islands in this group, and even in August there still seem to be plenty of private rooms available, especially in the unlovely but nearby suburb of Nea Chora (New Town). If you take one, however, make sure you can find it again. This new addition to the capital is as bewildering as the old with its anonymous streets and countless skeletons of future buildings.

expensive

One of the most genteel places to stay is in the capital, at the traditionally-styled **Château Zevgoli**, in the backstreets up towards Kastro, © 22 993, with 10 rooms in rustic antique decor; but expect to pay around 15000 dr.. In Ag. Anna there's a new development, **Iria Beach Hotel Apartments**, © 24 178, at around 5000 dr. to 7000 dr. per night; UK-based Sunvil Holidays also uses these apartments for package trips. At **Mikri Vigla**, the new Mikri Vigla is a low rise mini-resort hotel in the Cyclades style, on the beach with a pool, surfing centre and restaurant, © 75 240.

Five minutes from the Chora centre, **Hotel Anatoli**, ✆ 24 426, has a pool and views of the town and sea. Of the small hotels in Bourgos, just outside Kastro's walls, **Panorama** on Amphitris Street is the loveliest, with a marvellous sea view, ✆ 22 330. In Ag. Georgios there's a fairly wide selection of moderately priced hotels, including the family-run **Aeolis Hotel**, ✆ 22 321, and the smaller **St. George Pension** on the beach, ✆ 23 162.

cheap

Rooms in Nea Chora are cheap—around 3500 dr. Cheapest of all is the dormitory at the **Dionysos**, up near the Kastro, ✆ 22 331, where beds go for 1000 dr. a night. You can find rooms in most of the seaside villages, but the pickings are on the slim side, and rooms at Chalki, Filoti and Apollon. There are campgrounds at Ag. Georgios, Ag. Anna and Plaka. Outside the capital in **Ag. Anna** is a good C class hotel of the same name, from 3500 dr.; ✆ 23 870/24 20. Ag. Anna is a good compromise between the quiet beach of Plaka and the nighlife of Chora, easily accessible by bus.

Eating Out

There's a restaurant or taverna to suit all tastes and wallets in Naxos, and you don't have to depend on the numerous fast food joints around the harbour if you're on a budget. On the waterfront, seek out **Popi's Grill**, which cooks superb chicken grills at very reasonable prices in basic surroundings, but with an authentically Greek atmosphere. If you walk through the square towards the new town, you'll see **Papagalos**. This is run by Americans and serves 'international' cuisine, but don't let this discourage you; the food is well-prepared, there are plenty of vegetarian dishes, the prices are very reasonable, and the staff are pleasant and eager to please. If you want to splash out, **Oniro** in the Kastro has candle-lit tables in a courtyard; be warned that the cobbled streets around the Kastro have scores of expensive tourist restaurants serving overpriced schnitzel. At Ag. Anna, **Gorgona**, just by the bus stop, serves a very competent evening spread and sells *hima* wine by the half-litre.

You can try the liqueur Kitron in the local tourist bars, or buy a bottle or two as souvenirs in the Promponas shop on the waterfront; you can have a free trial tasting (or three) first.

Paros

Despite the thousands of tourists who descend on Paros each summer, the peculiar Cycladic style of houses, the narrow alleys, little bridges and balconies overflowing with potted plants seem to dilute their presence, and the Parians have approached the inevitable increase in tourism with less fervour than their neighbours on Mykonos, managing, against overwhelming odds, to maintain a Greek island atmosphere. The inhabitants have, for the most part, remained fun-loving and hospitable and, if you can find a place to stay, it's a fine spot to while away a few days on golden beaches and charming villages, whose main building material comes from Paros' gentle mountain, Profitis Ilias (771m)—some of the finest, most translucent marble in the world, prized by Classical sculptors and architects. Paros is one of the larger and more fertile Cyclades, with vineyards, wheat and barley fields, citrus and olive groves, and—an unusual sight in the archipelago—pastures of grazing cattle and sheep. Apart from its beaches, the island has several other attractions, including a famous Byzantine cathedral and a valley filled with butterflies in the summer.

History

With the trade in Parian marble, the island of Paros prospered early on. Its thriving Early Cycladic town was connected with Knossos and later with the Mycenaeans in the Late Cycladic period (1100 BC). In the 8th century BC Ionians moved in and brought about a second wave of prosperity. The 7th-century BC poet Archilochos, inventor of Iambic verse, and the sculptor Ariston were famous sons of ancient Paros. During the Persian Wars, Paros supported the Persians at both Marathon and Salamis; when Athens' proud General Miltiades came to punish them after Marathon, they withstood his month-long siege, leaving Miltiades to retire with a broken leg that developed into the gangrene that killed him. During the Peloponnesian Wars Paros remained neutral until forced to join the second Delian league in 378 BC. The island produced the great sculptor Skopas in the Hellenistic period and did well until Roman times, exporting marble to make the Temple of Solomon, the Venus de Milo, the temples on Delos and, much later, part of Napoleon's tomb. When the Romans took over Paros, their main concern was to take over the marble business.

Later invasions and destructions left the island practically deserted, and after 1207 the Venetian Sanudos ruled Paros from Naxos. Barbarossa captured the island in 1536, and from then on the Turks ruled by way of their proxy Duke of

Naxos, although his control was often shaky, especially in the 1670s, when Paros was the base of Hugues Chevaliers, the original of Byron's *Corsair*. In 1770, the Parians had to put up with more unlikely visitors when the Russian fleet wintered on the island. During the War of Independence Mando Mavroyenous, whose parents were from Paros and Mykonos, led guerrilla attacks against the Turks throughout Greece; after the war the heroine returned to Paros and died there.

Connections

By air: five flights daily (eight in the summer) from Athens.

By sea: daily ferry connections to Syros and Piraeus, Naxos, Mykonos, Ios, Santorini, Herakleon (Crete), Antiparos and Sifnos, three–four times a week with Rafina, Samos, Ikaria, Karpathos, Rhodes, Koufonissia and Amorgos, less frequently with the lesser Cyclades, Tinos, Skiathos and Thessaloniki; once a week in summer to Corfu and Ancona in Italy; frequent boats to Antiparos from Paroikia and Pounta; summer hydrofoil and catamaran connections with Naxos, Mykonos, Ios, Santorini, Tinos, Syros, Amorgos and Piraeus.

Tourist Information

Plateia Mando Mavroyenous, ℡ (0284) 21 673. There is also an information centre in the Windmill on the quay.

Paroikia

Paroikia, the island's chief town and main port, doesn't seem much at first glance. But this initial impression is belied by the immaculate streets, white houses and tidy blue domes within Paroikia itself: a Cycladic beauty traversed by a long, winding main street that invites leisurely exploration, without having to trudge up hundreds of stairs.

It is the home of the Aegean School of Fine Arts, founded by Brett Taylor in 1966 and attended chiefly by American art students. The most striking monument in the heart of town is a narrow 13th-century wall, a survivor of the Venetian castle, built out of the temples of Apollo and Demeter, forming an attractive collage of columns and pediments that now serve as the walls of neighbouring houses.

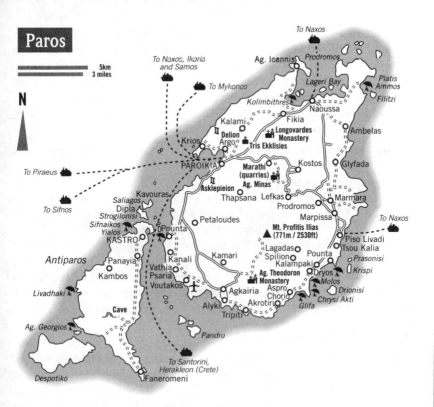

Paros

5km
3 miles

N

To Naxos, Ikaria and Samos

To Naxos

To Mykonos

To Piraeus

To Sifnos

Ag. Ioannis
Prodromos
Lageri Bay
Platis Ammos
Filitzi
Kolimbithres
Naoussa
Kalami
Fikia
Longovardes Monastery
Ambelas
Krios
Delion
Argo
Tris Ekklisies
PAROIKIA
Marathi (quarries)
Kostos
Glyfada
Asklepieion
Ag. Minas
Kavouras
Saliagos
Dipla
Thapsana
Lefkas
Prodromos
Marmara
Strogilonisi
Sifnaikos
Yialos
Petaloudes
Marpissa
To Naxos
Pounta
KASTRO
Mt. Profitis Ilias (771m / 2530ft)
Lagadas
Spilion
Pounta
Piso Livadi
Tsou Kalia
Antiparos
Panayia
Kanali
Kamari
Kalampaki
Prasonisi
Krispi
Kambos
Vathia
Psaria
Voutakos
Ag. Theodoron Monastery
Dryos
Molos
Drionisi
Livadhaki
Agkairia
Aspro Chorio
Chrysi Akti
Cave
Alyki
Akrotiri
Glifa
Ag. Georgios
Tripiti
Pandro
Despotiko
To Santorini, Herakleon (Crete)
Faneromeni

The Church of a Hundred Doors

On the west side of town, beyond a pine grove, stands Paros' chief monument, the cathedral **Ekatontapyliani** or 'church of a hundred doors'. According to tradition, it was founded by St Helen, mother of the Emperor Constantine, whose ship put into port at Paros during a storm, although actual construction of the church wasn't begun until the 6th century by Justinian. He hired an architect named Ignatius, an apprentice of the master builder of Ag. Sofia in Constantinople, and the story goes that when the master came to view his pupil's work, he was consumed by jealousy and pushed Ignatius off the roof—but not before Ignatius had seized his foot and dragged him down to his death as well—a story told by the frieze in the north corner of the walled courtyard in front of the church. Another story accounts for its name: in reality only 99 doors have ever been found but when the 100th is discovered, it is a sign that Constantinople will return to the Greeks.

Since the 6th century, earthquakes have forced several alterations and rebuildings, and in the 1960s an attempt was made—although not entirely successfully—to remove the Venetian Baroque trappings from the façade to restore its early Byzantine appearance. Yet in the interior, reshaped in the 10th century to form a Greek cross with a dome on pendentives, the atmosphere is shadowy, jewel-like and Byzantine. Many stones are recycled from earlier Byzantine and pagan structures. Roman tombs and a well lie beneath the church floor.

On the carved wooden iconostasis is an icon of the Virgin, worshipped for its healing virtues; the church also contains the mortal remains of the Parian saint, Ag. Theoktisti. After being captured by pirates, she managed to flee into the forests of Paros. For 30 years Theoktisti lived a pious existence alone in the wilderness. A hunter finally found her, and when he brought her the communion bread she requested, she lay down and died. Unable to resist a free saintly relic, the hunter cut off her hand (now on display in a box) and made to sail away, but he was unable to depart until he had returned it to the saint's body. Beneath a wooden pallet is Theoktisti's footprint: the Greeks take off their shoes and fit their feet into it for good luck. Behind the iconostasis are frescoes and a carved marble Holy Table. The Baptistry to the right of the church has a sunken font.

Archaeology Museum

Near the church, a new building houses the **Archaeology Museum** (*closed Tues*), containing a section of the renowned 'Parian Chronicles'—a history of Greece, emphasizing the arts, from Kerkops (*c.* 1500 BC) to Diognetos (264 BC). The chronicle, carved in marble tablets, was discovered in the 17th century and to read the rest of it you'll have to visit the Ashmolean Museum in Oxford. The Paros museum also has finds from the local temple of Apollo, a 5th-century BC Winged Victory, and a short biography and frieze about Antilochos, a Parian who took part in the colonization of Thassos before he turned to lyric poetry.

Nearby is the small church of **Ag. Nikolaos**, built at the same time as the Ekatontapyliani. Just outside Paroikia, by a spring, are the ruins of a Classical-era **Asklepieion** (dedicated to the god of healing). Originally a temple to Pythian Apollo stood nearby.

Naoussa

Frequent buses connect Paroikia with the island's second port, the lovely **Naoussa**. Near the harbour stand the half-submerged ruins of the Venetian castle, as colourful fishing boats bob below. On the night of 23 August a hundred of these craft don torches and 'storm' the harbour in memory of the islanders' battle against Barbarossa, and all ends in merriment, music and dance. Naoussa has a **Byzantine Museum** with good icons, and there are others in the church Ag. Nikolaos Mostratos.

Between Naoussa and Paroikia, the 7th-century basilica **Tris Ekklisies** was built over the site of a 4th-century BC heröon, or tomb-shrine of a hero or notable, in this case of the poet Archilochos. Northeast of Paroikia the marble foundation and altar of the **temple of Delian Apollo** still remain. Curiously, together with temples to Apollo on Delos and Naxos, it forms part of a perfect equilateral triangle. One of the triangle's altitudes extends to Mycenae and Rhodes town, site of the Colossus—the biggest of all the statues of Apollo. Another heads up to Mt Athos.

Beaches are within walking distance of Naoussa, or you can make sea excursions to others, notably **Kolimbithres**, with its bizarre, wind-sculpted rocks; other sands nearby are at **Lageri**; take the caique from Naoussa harbour, then walk to the right for about ten minutes. Lageri is nudist, a relaxed mix of gay and straight. **Santa Maria** is even further around the coast, as is the fishing village of **Ambelas**, with a taverna and a quiet hotel.

The winds on Paros can be strong, especially the meltemi. As a result it's become a mecca for serious windsurfers, especially **Chrysi Akti** on the opposite side of the island to Paroikia; in 1993 the World Windsurfing Championships were held here. Beautiful people flock to **Pounta** (the one on the far side of the island, not the ferry port for Antiparos) by motorbike, as there's a happening music bar on the beach, and this has become the hip place for Athenians and trendy foreigners to wind down and make new friends.

Into the Land of Marble

From Paroikia, the main road east leads to Paros' ancient marble quarries at **Marathi**, not far from the fortified but abandoned monastery of Ag. Minas. The quarries too are abandoned, for economic reasons (they were last used for Napoleon's tomb), but it's fun to poke around, especially if you bring a light—the longest tunnel stretches 90m underground. It produced an almost translucent stone called 'Lychnites' by the ancients, or 'candlelit marble', for its wonderful ability to absorb light. One of the quarries still has an ancient inscription.

The road continues to Paros' attractive medieval capital **Lefkas**, where farming, textiles and ceramics are the major industries. East of Lefkas **Prodromos** is an old farming village; **Marmara**, another village, lives up to its name ('marble')—even some of the streets are paved with it. Prettiest of the three, though, is **Marpissa**.

Above its windmills are the ruins of a 15th-century Venetian fortress and the 16th-century **monastery of Ag. Antonios**, constructed out of Classical materials and containing lovely marbles and paintings (note the 17th-century fresco of the Second Coming). The ancient city of Paros is believed to have been in this area.

Down on the east coast **Piso Livadi** historically served as the port for these villages and the marble quarries. Now it's the centre of Paros' beach colonies: **Molos, Dryos**, and the island's best beach, the golden **Chrysi Akti**, stretching 700m, and a favourite with surfers. Luxurious villas line the bay at Dryos where the Turkish fleet used to put in on its annual tax-collecting tour of the Aegean.

Southwest of Paroikia

Beyond the ruins of the Asklepieion, the road south of Paroikia continues to **Petaloudes** (or Psychopiani), where swarms of tiger moths set up housekeeping in July and August and fly up in clouds as you walk by. Petaloudes/Psychopiani has the ruins of a Venetian tower, while just outside the village stands the convent of Paros' second patron saint, **Ag. Arsenios**, the schoolteacher, abbot and prophet who was canonized in 1967. The saint is buried in the convent, but this time men are not allowed in. At **Pounta** there is a beach, and from here the small boat crosses to Antiparos (*see* p. 160). There's another beach at **Alyki** which has some facilities—and Paros' airport.

Festivals

15 August, Ekatontapyliani at Paroikia; 23 April, Ag. Georgios at Agkairia; 21 May, Ag. Konstantinos at Paroikia; 40 days after Orthodox Easter, Analypsis at Piso Livadi; in July, Fish and Wine Festival, Paroikia; 29 August, Ag. Ioannis at Lefkas; 18 August, Petaloudes.

© (0284–)

Where to Stay

Paros is packed in the summer, and it's very hard to find a place if you just drop in. Nearly everyone stays in Paroikia, Naoussa or Piso Livadi. Mid-range prices are higher than in most of the other Greek islands, in many cases double what you might expect; 6–8000dr. in the high season for a pleasant but basic mid-range room.

expensive

Paros' best hotel is on the beach in Pounta, the **Holiday Sun**, © 91 284, with all mod cons. The B class **Xenia** above Paroikia has a lovely view over the village in its green amphitheatre, and there's a bar and good restaurant, ℂ 21 394.

moderate

In the town of Paroikia, **Dina**, ℂ 21 325, with its garden is the most charming, with the highish prices (6000 dr.) typical of Paros. The **Argonauta**, just back from the waterfront, is a pleasant family-run place, ℂ 21 440. An alternative in the interior, the stone-walled **Xenia Hotel** up in Lefkas, is a mere 10-minute bus ride from the beaches at Piso Livadi, ℂ 41 646. In Naoussa prices tend to be about the same. Try the **Hotel Aliprantis**, with balconies overlooking the square, ℂ 51 571; it's just above the outdoor tables where everyone congregates, and is far preferable to the new developments on the edges of the town. In Piso Livadi the class B pension **Marpissa**, ℂ 41 288, has slightly lower prices and an attractive view, although rooms are without bath; alternatively **Hotel Lonos**, ℂ 41 218, is also basic, but is okay. In Marpissa, **Afendakis Apartments**, ℂ 41 141 are nicely done out. There are plenty of Cycladic rooms in Dryos.

cheap

Private rooms exist in Paroikia, Naoussa, Piso Livadi, and some principal beaches, and go for 3–4000 dr. There are several campsites—**Naoussa Camping** between Naoussa and Paroikia may well intercept you at the ports, **Koula** and **Parasporos** near Paroikia, **Capt. Kafkis Camping** near Piso Livadi, **Surfing Beach Paros** at Alyki (the biggest, and best organized) and **Krios** at Krios, the beach opposite the port.

Eating Out

The best food in Paroikia, or on all of Paros for that matter, is at **To Tamarisko**, where you can dine delectably in a garden for around 3000–4000 dr. **Levantis**, back from the harbour to the right of the Venetian castle walls, has Greek, Lebanese and French dishes (3500 dr.). Near Ekatontapyliani church is the **Lobster House** with the obvious speciality. Take a full wallet. For a simple, inexpensive taverna try **Nissiotissa**, behind the hospital; everything's good, especially the fresh fish. If you're fond of oriental cuisine, **May Tey**, tucked away in the backstreets and a bit hard to find, has a limited but high quality choice of Chinese, Vietnamese, and other Southeast Asian dishes (3000 dr.). For sunset views over a cocktail, the popular **Pebbles Bar** along from the port will provide, with classical music till sunset, thereafter jazz, occasionally live.

Naoussa is one of the most picturesque places to eat in all Greece; tavernas huddle by the water's edge in the little port, and cars can neither be seen nor heard. These harbourside tavernas are inevitably dearer than others further up the hill, and the bars can be a rip-off, so choose carefully. If you want something inexpensive, **Diamante** just up the hill serves good food at good prices, serves hima wine in copper vessels, and may even have a few unusual Greek offal dishes of the day if you're lucky. At the other end of the price scale, **Lalula** is the place for a splurge in elegant surroundings. For snacks and breakfast, the café below **Hotel Aliprantis** takes some beating. There's also a good taverna on the beach at Dryos, and laid-back garden bars **The Lake** and **Golden Garden** at Dryos and Golden Beach.

There are two excellent and authentic tavernas in the centre of Pios Livadi, where the favoured watering holes are the **Remezzo**, **Anchorage** and **Flotilla** bars. Paros is the Cyclades' main producer of quality dry red wines, made from indigenous Greek grapes; the Boutari version is one of the better ones.

Antiparos

Little Antiparos ('before' Paros) was anciently known as Oliaros, and was connected to its larger neighbour by a causeway. In the time of Alexander the Great a large, deep cave full of stalactites was discovered on Antiparos, and for the past 2000 years it has been a must stop for every traveller in the region. Many who find Paros too tourist-ridden end up on a quiet Antiparian beach (there are good ones at Kastro, at Sifnaikos Yialos in the north, and Ag. Georgios in the south). Fish is plentiful, even in the restaurants, and there are many rooms to rent and three hotels.

Connections

Hourly every day by caique from Paroikia, Paros and hourly car ferry from Pounta, Paros.

See regular police in town, © (0284) 61 202.

Kastro and the Cave

Lacking any defences, Antiparos was uninhabited after the fall of Rome until the Venetians, under Leonardo Lorentani, built a small castle. There are also two 17th-century churches, the cathedral **Ag. Nikolaos** and **Evangelismos**.

The **cave** remains Antiparos' star attraction, despite centuries of tourists whacking off free souvenir stalactites. In the summer excursion boats run not only from Kastro, but also from Paroikia and Pounta. From the boat landing stage it's a half-hour walk up by foot and less by donkey, and then a 70m descent by steps into the fantastic, spooky chamber. The cave is really about twice as deep, but the rest has been closed as too dangerous for visits. Perhaps to make up for breaking off the stalactites, famous visitors of the past have smoked and carved their names on the walls, including Lord Byron and King Otho of Greece (1840). One stalagmite attests in Latin to a Christmas mass celebrated in the cavern by Count Nouantelle in 1673, attended by 500 (paid) locals. Unfortunately, a famous older inscription has been lost; its several authors declared that they were hiding in the cave from Alexander the Great, who had accused them of plotting an assassination attempt. The church by the entrance of the cave, **Ag. Ioannis**, was built in 1774. If you come in the winter, you'll have to pick up the key to the cave's entrance in Kastro.

Of the islets off Antiparos, **Strogilonisi** and **Despotiko** are rabbit-hunting reserves. On **Saliagos**, a fishing village from the 5th millennium BC has been excavated by John Evans and Colin Renfrew, the first Neolithic site discovered in the Cyclades.

Festivals

23 April, Ag. Georgios; 21 May, Ag. Konstantinos at Glyfa; and 8 May, Ag. Ioannis Theologos, by the cave.

© (0284–)

Where to Stay

moderate–cheap

Many people who can't find a place to stay in Paros come to Antiparos, though prices are only marginally lower here. Little **Chryssi Akti** on the beach is an elegant class C hotel, © 61 220. Slightly less expensive, the 36-room **Mantalena** on the waterfront offers nice views of the harbour and Paros, © 61 206. There are also quite a few pensions (**Korali** seems to be about the cheapest, © 61 236), and rooms to let, and although there's an organized **campsite**, © 61 221, freelancers are winked at if they distance themselves from town.

Eating Out

Unfortunately, demand has also jacked up the price of food here, and eating out is no cheaper than in Paros. In the port a number of self-service and fast food places have sprouted up, among them Anargiros, with a decent selection of ready food. In town the locals head for **Klimataria** for good food at (reasonably) low prices, or the slightly more expensive **Makis**. **Giorgios Taverna**, open at night, is known for well-prepared fish dinners.

Santorini (Thira)

As most people's favourite Greek island, the pressure is on Santorini to come up with the goods; it does, though the awesome mixture of towering, sinister multi-coloured volcanic cliffs, dappled with the 'chic'-est, most brilliant-white, trendiest bars and restaurants in the country, gives the island a peculiar split personality. Usually bathed in glorious sunshine, but occasionally lashed by high winds and rain, everything seems more intense here, especially daily life. Some call it Devil's Island, and find a stay here both exhilarating and disturbing—with such a concentration of visitors, something out of the ordinary is guaranteed to happen every day.

As your fragile ship sails into the volcano's rim, the black islands on your right indeed look demonic. Volcanically fertile Santorini has, literally, had its ups and downs: throughout history parts of the island and its circular archipelago have seismatically appeared and disappeared under the waves. Human endeavours on the island have fared similarly: you can visit no fewer than three former 'capitals'—the Minoan centre of Akrotiri, a favourite candidate for Metropolis, the capital of the legendary Atlantis; the Classical capital Thira at Mesa Vouna; and the medieval Skaros, as well as the picturesque modern town of Fira, perched on the edge of Santorini's cliffs. But this, too, was flattened by an earthquake in 1956 (though lovingly rebuilt). Although the island is now one of the most popular destinations in the Aegean and a must on the itinerary of most cruise ships, older inhabitants can remember when Santorini hosted more political prisoners than tourists, and nights were filled with the rumour of vampires rather than the chatter of café society sipping Bloody Marys, watching the sun go down in one of the world's most enchanting settings.

History

The history of Santorini, or Thira, is closely related to its geology. In the long distant past the island was created from volcanic debris, circular in shape, with a crater called Strogyle in the centre. Its regular eruptions created a rich, volcanic soil, which attracted inhabitants early on—from Karia originally, until they were chased away by the Cretans. They built their colony at Akrotiri at the height of the Minoan civilization and in approximately 1450 BC, the volcano erupted again, destroying not only Akrotiri, but causing irreparable damage to the mighty Minoan civilization in Crete as well.

This relatively recent theory was proposed by the Greek archaeologist Spirydon Marinatos. In 1939 he decided that the destruction of Amnisos, the port of Knossos on Crete, could only have been caused by a massive natural disaster, such as a tidal wave from the north. What, he wondered, could have caused such a catastrophe? Marinatos put together the following clues: southeast of Santorini

oceanographers had discovered volcanic ash from Strogyle on the sea bed, covering an area of 900km by 300km; on nearby Anafi and Eastern Crete itself there's a layer of volcanic tephra 3–20mm thick. This would be sufficient to destroy plant growth and ruin farming for a generation.

A Classical clue came from the Athenian reformer Solon, who in 600 BC wrote of his journey to Egypt, where the scribes told him of the disappearance of Kreftia (Crete?) 9000 years before, a figure Solon might have mistaken for a more correct 900. The Egyptians, who had maintained steady trade links with Crete and Santorini, supposedly described to Solon the lost land of Atlantis, made of red, white and black volcanic rock (like Santorini today) and spoke of a city vanishing in 24 hours. In his *Critias*, Plato described Atlantis as being composed of one round island and one long island, connected by one culture and rule (Santorini and Crete, under Minos?); a sweet land of art, flowers and fruit—as portrayed on the frescoes discovered at Akrotiri. In the 19th century French archaeologists had discovered Minoan pots at Akrotiri, and it was there that Marinatos began to dig in 1967, bringing to light from under its deep tephra tomb a well-preserved Minoan town.

Whether or not Santorini was in fact the Atlantis of the ancients, the theory of the ruin of Minoan life by a series of earthquakes, volcanic explosions and subsequent tidal wave has support in the similar explosion of Krakatoa in 1883, of such force that it could be heard 3000 miles away in Western Australia. When the island blew up, it created a caldera (a crater left by volcanic explosion) of 8.3sq km. As the sea rushed in to fill the caldera, it created a tidal wave more than 200m high that destroyed everything in a 150km path. Consider that the caldera left by Strogyle, that is the present bay of Santorini, is 22 sq km. The fact that no bodies were found at Akrotiri lead archaeologists to suppose that earthquakes and other omens warned the inhabitants to flee in time. The islets of Therasia and Aspronisi mark the edges of the caldera.

In the 8th century BC the Dorians moved into Santorini, building their capital at Mesa Vouna, which survived until the early decades after Christ. Thira was the island's Doric name, and legends have it that the Thirians founded the city of Cyrene in Libya. In Hellenistic times, Ptolemy of Egypt fortified the island and dedicated temples to Dionysos and to his own family.

Like the Ptolemies, the Byzantines also considered the island to be of strategic importance and fortified it, but most of their citadels have been toppled by earthquakes. Skaros near Imerovigli became the Venetian capital, when it was ruled by the Crispi, who preferred to call their fief after its patron saint Irene, elided over the years into Santorini.

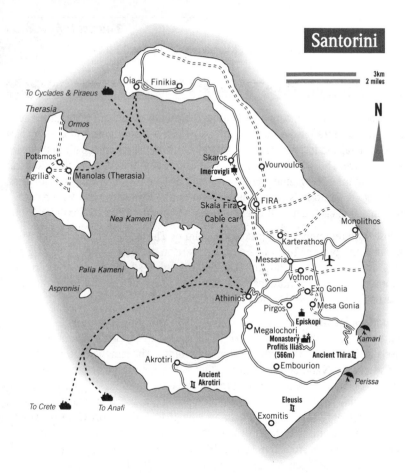

Santorini

3km
2 miles

N

To Cyclades & Piraeus

Therasia

Oia   Finikia

Ormos

Potamos

Agrilia   Manolas (Therasia)

Nea Kameni

Palia Kameni

Aspronisi

Skaros
Imerovigli

Vourvoulos

Skala Fira
Cable car

FIRA

Monolithos

Karterathos

Messaria

Vothon

Exo Gonia

Athinios

Pirgos

Mesa Gonia

Megalochori

Episkopi

Kamari

Monastery
Profitis Ilias
(566m)

Ancient Thira

Akrotiri

Embourion

Ancient
Akrotiri

Perissa

To Crete   To Anafi

Eleusis

Exomitis

Connections

By air: daily flights from Athens; daily flights from Mykonos, Herakleon
(Crete) and Rhodes.

By sea: daily ferry connections with Piraeus, Ios, Paros, Naxos, Mykonos
and Herakleon (Crete). Frequently with other Cyclades, two–three times
a week with the Dodecanese, Skiathos and Thessaloniki. Ferries call at
Athinios, from where there is a road up to the capital; there are also frequent catamaran services to other Cycladic islands and Piraeus.

Santorini (Thira)   165

See regular police, 25 tou Martiou St, ✆ (0286) 22 649.

Fira

Most passengers disembark at **Athinios**; those who disembark beneath the towering cliffs at **Fira** (cruise ships, mostly), can take a motor launch to the tiny port of Skala Fira, and from there hire a donkey to travel the winding path to the town 270m above. Those in more of a hurry can glide up on the Austrian-built cable car in two minutes. It ws donated to the island by ship-owner Evangelos Nomikos; profits go to Santorini's communities—and to the donkey drivers, who receive a percentage of each ticket. It operates every 15 minutes from 6.45am to 8.15pm.

Those who remember **Fira** (also spelt Thira or Thera), the capital, before 1956 say that the present town bears no comparison architecturally to its original, although it's pleasant enough—Cycladically white, built on several terraces, adorned with pretty churches. The cliff is hung with cafés and restaurants, all boasting one of the world's most magnificent views.

Santorini's **museum** (*8.45–3, Sun 9.30–2.30, closed Tues*) is near the cable car on the north side of town. It houses finds from Akrotiri, Mesa Vouna and Early Cycladic figurines found in the local pumice mines. The famous Santorini frescoes are still in the National Museum in Athens, although there are rumours that a new museum will be built in Fira to house them on the island. As well as the museum one can also visit the handicraft workshop founded by Queen Frederika, where women weave large carpets on looms. The **Megaron Gyzi museum**, located in a beautiful 17th-century mansion, houses exhibits on the island's history—manuscripts from the 16th–19th centuries, costumes, old maps of the Cyclades, and some photographs of Santorini before the 1956 earthquake (*10.30–1.30 and 5–8*).

Akrotiri

Buses from Fira make several trips daily to **Akrotiri** (*daily, 8–7*), the Minoan town discovered in 1967 by Marinatos. Excavations here are infinitely laborious due to the thick layer of tephra, or volcanic ash that buried Akrotiri; fittingly, tephra is quarried to make cement for tombstones. The ancient city revealed beneath it is wonderful and strange, made even more unreal by the huge modern roof that protects the excavations from the elements. A carpet of volcanic dust silences all footsteps as you walk amid houses up to three storeys high, many still containing their huge *pithoi*, or storage pots. In one of the houses is the grave of Marinatos, who died 20 years ago after a fall on the site; his earlier request to be buried by his life's work was granted. The huge filing cabinets hold pottery sherds yet to be pieced together. For more details, pick up the locally available *Art and Religion in Thira: Reconstructing a Bronze Age Society*, by Dr Nanno Marinatos, son of the archaeologist. Below the excavation site is a black rock beach and taverna; there are also some coffee shops and rooms in the vineyard-surrounded villages above.

Exomitis to Ancient Thira and Profitis Ilias

East of Akrotiri, **Exomitis** has one of the best-preserved Byzantine fortresses of the Cyclades; submerged nearby are the ruins of the ancient town of Eleusis. The island's best beach, **Perissa**, is around to the east, linked by road to the attractive old village of **Embourion**; like the other beaches of Santorini, the sand here is volcanic and black and warms quickly in the sun. Perissa has good restaurants, tavernas and a campsite. A modern church stands on the site of the Byzantine Saint Irene, for whom the island is named.

Up on the rocky headland of Mesa Vouna (a track leads up from Perissa) is **Ancient Thira**, its extensive ruins built on great terraces. Excavated by the German archaeologist Hiller von Gortringen in the late 19th century, the site produced the fine 'Santorini vases' in the museum. Most of what you see today dates from the Ptolemies, who used the city as a base for their enterprises further north and adorned it with temples to the Egyptian gods, Dionysos, Apollo, to their semi-divine selves and to the mythical founding father Thira. There are impressive remains of the agora and theatre, with a dizzying view down to the sea; also several cemeteries and a gymnasium. Numerous houses still have mosaics; graffiti dating from 800 BC may be seen on the Terrace of Celebrations, recording the names of competitors and dancers of the *gymnopedies*. Note the unusual Cyclopean walls nearby.

North of Ancient Thira stretches another black beach, **Kamari**, with tavernas, while inland, up the slope from Mesa Vouna, is the **Monastery Profitis Ilias**, built in 1712 on Santorini's highest point (566m). On a clear day you can see Crete from here, and on an exceptionally clear day, it is said, even Rhodes hovers faintly on the horizon. The locals, never forgetting the terrifying earthquake of 1956, say the monastery is the only place that will protrude above sea level when the rest of Santorini sinks into the sea to join its other half. At the foot of Profitis Ilias, by the village of Mesa Gonia, is the 11th-century **Panayia Episkopi** or Kimisis Theotokou, converted by the Venetians to the Catholic rite when they conquered Santorini, but under the Turks the Orthodox recovered their own. Inside are Byzantine icons, and on 15 August it holds the biggest *paniyiri* on the island.

Pirgos, near the centre of Santorini, shares with Embourion the title of the oldest surviving village on the island, with interesting old houses, Byzantine walls, and a Venetian fort. **Athinios**, the port below, has a small beach, bars and restaurants.

North of Fira

Skaros, on the road to Oia, was the medieval capital of Santorini, but it has been much damaged by earthquakes. Its Ag. Stephanos is the oldest church on the island, and you can also see the crumbling ruins of a Catholic convent of Santa Katerina, built after a young girl's vision in 1596. The nuns lived a life of extreme hardship until 1818 when they moved to Fira, and now the desolate convent is about to tumble down. In **Imerovigli** stands a convent, built in 1674 and still inhabited, dedicated to Ag. Nikolaos.

At the end of the road, that mouthful of vowels called **Oia**, or Ia, is the third port of Santorini, though these days only tourist caiques to Therasia call here. Half-ruined by the earthquake, its white houses are piled on top of one another up the steep slope. Although it's a long hard walk up from the beach, you can fill your pockets with pumice-stone souvenirs for friends at home.

Around the Caldera

Santorini's caldera is 10km wide and 380m deep. Curving around the north-western rim, the islet **Therasia** was part of Santorini until another eruption-earthquake in 236 BC blasted them apart. Pumice mined here went into the building of the Suez Canal. In one of the quarries a Middle Cycladic settlement was discovered, pre-dating Akrotiri, though there are no traces of it now. There are three villages on Therasia; the largest, **Manolas**, has tavernas and rooms to rent. Excursion boats also make trips out to the 'burnt isles', **Palia and Nea Kameni**, both still volcanically active, especially the Metaxa crater on Nea Kameni. However, even though a local brochure refers to Nea Kameni as 'the strange volcano which cause you greatness', be forewarned that half the people who visit it come away disappointed. The tourist trail up the mountain is rubbish-strewn and there's no sign of recent volcanic activity, though there's plenty of black ash. There are also tourist excursion boats taking people to swim in the 'healthy' sulphurous mud nearby, which, if nothing else, makes an unusual chat-up line in the bars of Fira.

Festivals

19 and 20 July, at Profitis Ilias; 20 October, Ag. Artemiou in Fira; 26 October, Ag. Dimitriou in Karterathos; 15 August, at Mesa Gonia and Fira.

✆ *(0286–)*   ### Where to Stay

There's nothing like staying in Fira with a view over the great caldera, but do book in advance. Expect to pay through the nose.

luxury

Still at the top of the list for luxury and the view is the **Hotel Atlantis**, ✆ 22 232, fax 22821, a class A establishment near the heart of town. In Oia, the **Katikies** are a set of beautifully decorated apartments with views of the sea and neighbouring islands, ✆ 71 401.

expensive

With the classic view, facing the volcano, the **Porto Carra**, ✆ 22 979, is typical of the many C class hotels in Fira. In the central square, the **Pelican**, ✆ 23 113, is another. Should either of these be full, try the larger **Kallisti Thira**, another pleasant option, with 33 rooms, ✆ 22 317. If you are travelling in company, consider staying at **Dana Villas**, with self-contained apartments for 2–6 people, fully furnished in traditional island style, with fabulous views and sunsets, ✆ 22 566.

The NTOG has restored 30 traditional homes to let out to visitors at reasonable prices, furnished with native embroideries and handcarved furniture. Each house accommodates 2–7 people; for reservations and current prices, contact the NTOG or Paradosiakos at Ikismos Oias, Oia, ✆ 71 234. Among these places are the **Perivolas** (A) in Oia with a pool, ✆ 71308, fax 71309; **Nano** (A), Venetian-style houses near Kamares ✆ 31001; the old **Sea Captain's House** at Finikia, ✆ 31095; and the Oia village Cycladic settlement (A) ✆ 71114.

moderate

When Fira is full, you can almost always find a room elsewhere on the island, and as bus connections are good it's not all that hard getting about.

Kamari has many modest-sized hotels and pensions, although the prices tend to be rather bold—the C class **Matina** has doubles starting at 6500 dr., © 31 491. Another place in Kamari which (just) fits into this category is **Hotel Sunshine**, next to the sea, © 31 394. In Oia there are a number of moderately-priced rooms and pensions. It is just possible to get a place overlooking the caldera for a moderate price; **Hotel Loukas** (B) in Fira, © 22 480. In Kamares, near the beach, **Hotel Hermes**, © 31664, is a good, family-run place; **Akis**, © 31 670, is in the village centre.

cheap

There are **youth hostels** in Fira, © 22 722, and Oia, © 71 465, open April–Oct, card not required. In town the **Kamares Hostel** is near the cable car. The island's campsites are at Fira, Kamari and Perissa. If you land in Athinios, the owners of rooms (mostly in Messaria, Embourion and Karterathos) will meet you in their vans and whisk you away. Expect to pay at least 4000 dr. in season.

Eating Out

Be prepared for high prices. For international cuisine and reputedly the best food on Santorini, **Castro** near the cable car will set you back a good 5000 dr. or more for one of its lavish spreads. **Nikolaos Taverna**, situated right in the heart of Fira, is a reassuring real Greek taverna in this island of excess; you'll recognize it by the people waiting at the door to get in (so get there early). On the main street near the port police, try and squeeze in at **The Roosters**, a fun little restaurant with tasty Greek dishes, where the owner will know all about you within 5 minutes of your arrival. It would be worth the price to eat at **Meridiana** for the view alone, but the food is good, too, and the atmosphere elegant, with a piano bar; dinner here costs around 4000 dr., with decent Santorini wine.

In Oia there are two excellent choices—**Kyklos**, built into the caves and romantically atmospheric, with main courses starting at 1500 dr., and **Mama Africa** with an exotic menu that includes Thai and Indian dishes. In Kamari, **Kamari** has good, inexpensive dining in a family-run taverna, serving the island speciality *fava* (a purée of yellow peas, oil, lemon and onion). Next to the sea, **Irinis** is another local favourite. More expensive, and offering some international dishes, **Camille Stefani** is at the end of the main road on Kamari beach. Perissa has the **Retsina**, a simple, popular taverna.

Santorini is one of Greece's great white wine producing islands. Moribund for many years, churning out high alcohol, low-quality wine, Santorini has recently had a shot in the arm from one forward-thinking winemaker working for Boutari. A sweet wine called Vissanto is also made here, by sun-drying the grapes before pressing. Some places serve local wines by the glass. You can see the terraced vineyards on the road from Fira to Oia. There are two wineries which offer wine tasting; the **Boutari** one, at Megalochori, towards Akrotiri, and **Kutsoyanopoulos**, on the road to Kamari. While connoisseurs are most welcome, they still insist you have a good time.

Cafés and Nightlife

Café and bar life takes up as much time as eating in Santorini. Many people like to be seen at **Bonjour** in the main square, while **Bebis** is the watering hole for a pleasantly loony young crowd. **Kirathira** appeals to all types and age groups, while **Alexandria** is more sedate and attracts an older set (by Santorini's standards, anyway). **Franco's** is still *the* place to go for sunset, even if the price of a coffee there is sky high. In Kamari the **Sail Inn** has loud music, fun evenings and glamorous bar girls, and **Valentino's** always has a large crowd. Drop in at the **Yellow Donkey** discotheque in the early hours and dance till dawn—there's very little point in trying to get an early night on this fun-loving island anyway.

Serifos

Where its neighbour Sifnos welcomes the visitor with green terraces and dovecots, Serifos, 'the barren one' tends to intimidate with its stark rocks. The island owed much of its prosperity in antiquity to its iron and copper mines, among the richest in Greece. However, when other sources were discovered in Africa that could be exploited more economically, the mines on Serifos were abandoned, and the population drastically decreased. Historically, the fate of Serifos follows that of the other Cyclades; Chora, high above the sea, was once fortified with a Byzantine-Venetian castle and walls, and here and there on the island are odd remains left by other conquerors.

The appealing, if dishevelled port, Livadi, with a little line of friendly tavernas and bars straggling along an unpaved dirt road, provides an informal foreground to the imposing view of Chora behind, seemingly inaccessible as it climbs impressively up the steep slopes. After the gleaming, spotless artificial waterfronts of some more popular islands, Serifos' unkempt air is a refreshing reminder that you are in Greece after all, where the *kafeneíons* buzz with village gossip, and walking about means side-stepping fishing boats being repainted in the backstreets. If you can put up with water shortages in August, Serifos offers not only island authenticity but also some of the most serene beaches in the Cyclades.

Mythology

What Serifos may lack in history is more than compensated for by its mythology, for it was here that Danaë, set adrift in a box with her infant son Perseus, washed up on shore. This cruel deed was done by Danaë's own father, Acrisius, King of Argos, for it had been prophesied that a son of Danaë would slay him. In order to foil the oracle Acrisius had locked his daughter in a tower, but even there her beauty did not fail to attract the amorous attentions of Zeus, who came to her in a shower of golden rain and fathered Perseus.

Enraged but unable to put his daughter or grandson to death, Acrisius decided to leave the issue to fate and set them adrift in the box. Zeus guided them to Serifos, where a fisherman discovered them and brought them to Polydectes, the king of the island. Struck by her beauty, Polydectes wanted to marry Danaë but she refused him, and as Perseus grew older he defended his mother's decision. Polydectes pretended to lose interest in Danaë, while he plotted to remove Perseus from the scene by asking him to do a favour: fetch the head of the gorgon Medusa, the only mortal of the three horrible Gorgon sisters, who had hair made of living snakes, whose eyes bulged and whose teeth were fangs. The sisters were so ugly that a mere glance at one of them turned a human to stone.

Despite Danaë's horror at this treachery of Polydectes, Perseus accepted and accomplished the task, assisted by the goddess Athena, who helped him procure a mirror-like shield, winged shoes, a cloak of invisibility and other essential tools. With Medusa's awful head in his pouch Perseus returned to Serifos (saving Andromeda from a sea monster on the way), to find his mother hiding from the forceful Polydectes in the hut of the fisherman who had saved them so long ago. Angrily Perseus went up to the palace, where he found a very surprised Polydectes at a great banquet. Perseus told him that he had succeeded in his quest and held up the prize as proof, instantly turning everyone in the room into stone.

The kind fisherman was declared King of Serifos by Perseus, and the hero and his mother went home to Argos. Still fearing the old prophecy, Danaë's father fled before them. But fate caught up with the old King in another town, where Perseus was competing in an athletic contest and accidentally killed his grandfather with a javelin in the foot.

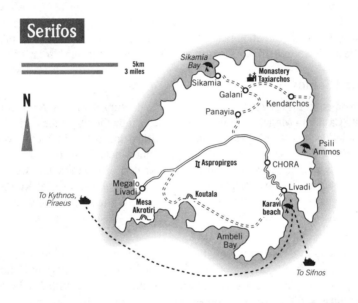

Connections

Daily with Piraeus, Sifnos, Milos and Kythnos, four times a week with Kimolos, three times a week with Santorini and Folegandros, twice a week with Sikinos and Ios, once a week to Syros.

Tourist Information

Livadi, © (0281) 51 300.

Livadi and Chora

Most people who visit Serifos stay in **Livadi**, the port, where there's a beach and many rooms to rent. There are two other beaches within easy walking distance from Livadi, towards the south; the second has become the unofficial campsite on the island.

Serifos, or **Chora**, the main town, is linked to the port by an hourly bus service. Buses also go to the villages once a day in the summer. Chora is a pretty town, with houses here and there made from pieces salvaged from the old fortress while others date back to the Middle Ages; its old windmills still stand, and in the spring you may find a rare carnation that grows only on Serifos. From Chora a 20-minute walk leads down to **Psili Ammos**, an excellent beach on the east coast.

Around Serifos

The road continues beyond Chora past the 6th-century Byzantine **Aspropirgos** (White Castle) to **Megalo Chorio**, believed to occupy the site of the ancient capital of Serifos; below, **Megalo Livadi**, now visited for its beach, once served as the loading dock for the iron and copper mined near Megalo Chorio. From Megalo Livadi you can walk around **Mesa Akrotiri** where there are two caves: the cave of the Cyclops Polyphemus with stalactites and another at **Koutalas**, where signs of prehistoric settlement were found. Both caves are now off limits but Koutalas offers a beach by way of compensation, and a track from here follows the south coast back to Livadi.

Sikamia Bay in the north is a good place to get away from it all, not only for its beach but also for the rare bit of shade and fresh water. The village of **Galani** is half an hour on foot from Sikamia, and from here you can visit **Taxiarchos Monastery**, built in 1500 and containing a precious old table, 18th-century frescoes by Skordilis, and Byzantine manuscripts in the library. The oldest church on Serifos is from the 10th century, at **Panayia**. **Kalitsos**, not far from Galani, is another pleasantly green place, with two restaurants.

Other beaches on Serifos are Karavi, Lia, Ag. Sostis, Platys Yialos, Halara and Ganima. Most of these are remote but can be reached by motorcycle. Karavi, south of Livadi, is one of the most popular.

Festivals

Fava beans are the big speciality at these celebrations: 5 May, Ag. Irene at Koutalas; 27 July, Ag. Panteleimonos at Mt Oros; 7 September, Ag. Sosoudos at Livadi; 6 August,

Sotiros a Kalobelli; 15–17 August, Panayia near the Monastery and at a different village each day.

Where to Stay

Serifos is well-known enough for its hotels and rooms to fill up in the summer–more often than not, with German visitors. The following are all near the sea, most of them in Livadi.

moderate

All the hotels are in Livadi, and all are on the beach. As a general rule, the further along the beach you go, the cheaper the accomodation. **Hotel Albatross**, © 51 148, is good, and the owner meets the ferry with a mini-bus. The **Serifos Beach Hotel** is the island's biggest, © 51 209, with a nice taverna downstairs, or for the same price you can stay at the **Areti**, a B class pension with a garden and view over the water, © 51 479. More expensive is the **Maistrali**, © 51 381, while the smaller **Pension Perseus**, © 51 273, is an old standby. Not far from the Serifos Beach there are excellent rooms with balcony for 5500 dr. above the Cavo d'Oro supermarket.

cheap

If you can put up with no lock on the communal bathroom door, erratic showers even by Greek standards, and the odd pane of glass missing, **Corali's** dilapidated charms may suit your budget—it's well situated a few metres from the harbour above the bakery. Otherwise there are rooms in Livadi and 20 or so up in Chora. There's a campsite in Livadakia, with good facilities.

Eating Out

The sea is clean and the fish is especially good in Serifos' seaside tavernas. Like the accommodation, the tavernas get cheaper the further along Livadi's beach you walk. Popular with locals and tourists alike, **Teli's**, on the waterfront, offers excellent and inexpensive food and friendly service. For a pleasantly zany atmosphere, with good, wholesome food (spaghetti, chicken curries) apart from the usual Greek fare, try **Benny's Tavern-Mokkas** at the end of the port where the locals, yachties, tourists, various children and an assortment of cats and dogs mingle happily together, though we've heard of variable standards. Whenever you come across that endangered species, the *ouzeri*, treasure it; the **Meltemi** will give you a *carafaki* (enough for three or four good drinks) and plenty of tasty nibbles (hot cheese pies, etc) for less than 800 dr. Round the bay, wiggle your toes in the sand at **Stamatis Taverna**, and enjoy his excellent ready food or grilled meats (2000 dr.). A few metres away, in the restaurant of the hotel Cyclades, you can savour spaghetti with shrimps, mussels and clams, or an excellent shrimp casserole with *feta* cheese and tomatoes (2500 dr.).

Up in Chora, **Stavros** is traditional and okay; **Maroulis** is in the lovely piazza by the town hall (climb up the steps where the bus stops), and serves *meze* with a difference, a definite relief if your relationship with Greek salads is wearing thin; try the sun-dried tomatoes, sautéed in butter, fennel done the same way, Serifot specialities such as *keftedes*, *spetsofai* and chick-peas from the wood oven, all washed down with the family's own wine (2500 dr.). Also in Serifos, open in mid-summer only, the **Petros** is a long-time favourite with the usual Greek food, but cooked just that bit better.

Sifnos

Sifnos in recent years has become the most popular island in the western Cyclades, with good reason—it's the prettiest, with its peaceful green hills and terraces, charming villages, and one long sandy beach. Here and there the landscape is dotted with Venetian dovecotes, windmills, some 40 ruined Classical towers and over 300 miniature chapels. It is an exceptionally pleasant island for walks. Among the Greeks Sifnos is famous for its pottery and its cooks, both of which have been in such demand elsewhere that few remain on Sifnos, although the legacy of good cooking remains. The island's olives are said to produce the best oil in the Cyclades, but sadly agriculture on the island is in decline (as is often the case, in direct correlation with the rise in tourism), and once-fertile Sifnos now has to import almost all of its foodstuffs.

History

The Phoenicians, one of the first groups of people to settle on Sifnos, named the island Meropia according to Pliny, and began to mine its gold. They were followed by the Cretans, who founded Minoa near Apollonia, and who were in turn replaced by Ionians who lived near Ag. Andreas and elsewhere. Meropia, meanwhile, had become famous for its gold; at one time, it is said, there was so much of the precious stuff that the Sifniotes simply divided it among themselves each year, with enough left over in the 6th century to pave their main square with the most costly Parian marble. In the same century Apollo at Delphi demanded that the wealthy Sifniotes contribute a tithe of gold in the form of a solid egg to his sanctuary every year. In 530 BC they constructed a magnificent treasury at Delphi to house the gold and adorned it with a fine frieze and pediment which can still be seen, and for many years Sifnos could boast the richest of all the oracle's treasures. But one year the Sifniotes, who began to have a reputation for greed and cunning, decided they needed the gold more than Apollo, and sent the god a gilded rock. Apollo soon discovered he had been duped and cursed the island. This gave Polycrates, the Tyrant of Samos, a good excuse to extract a huge fine from Sifnos; 40 triremes plundered and ransomed most of the island's gold, and the curse supposedly caused the mines to sink and give out. Thus the island became empty, or *sifnos* in Greek. Nowadays most of the ancient mines are underwater, at Ag. Mina, Kapsalos and Ag. Suzon.

After shooting itself in the foot with its twopenny fraud, Sifnos went into decline and the inhabitants moved up to Kastro, where a Roman cemetery has been discovered. In 1307 the Da Koronia family ruled the island for Venice; in 1456 Kozadinos, the Lord of Kythnos, married into the family and his descendants ruled Sifnos until the Turks took the island in 1617. Towards the end of the 17th century the Ottomans made an attempt to re-open the ancient mines, or at least got as far as sending out experts from Istanbul to examine them. Supposedly, when they got wind of these plans, the islanders hired a band of French pirates to sink the Sultan's ship. The experts, in turn, heard of the deal with the pirates, and simply went home. Later the French themselves exploited the local deposits of iron ore and lead; mining ended in 1914.

Sifnos has also made an important contribution to Greek letters. At the end of the 17th century the 'School of the

Holy Tomb' was founded on the island to keep alive the ancient Greek language and classics during the Turkish occupation, attracting students from all over Greece. Nikolaos Chrysoyelos, the most famous headmaster, led a contingent of Sifniotes in the War of Independence, and went on to become modern Greece's first Minister of Education. Another islander, the 19th-century poet-satirist Cleanthis Triandafilos, who wrote under the name Rabagas, was a thorn in the side of the monarchy until he was imprisoned and committed suicide. Ioannis Gyparis (d. 1942) was another Sifniote of note; along with Cadafy, he was one of the first poets to espouse the use of the demotic language (as opposed to the formal *katharevousa*) in literature.

Connections

Daily with Piraeus, Kythnos, Serifos and Milos; four times a week with Kimolos, two–three times a week with Ios, Santorini, Folegandros and Sikinos, once a week with Paros, Crete, Rhodes, Karpathos, Kassos, Halki and Symi.

Tourist Information

Kamares, © (0284) 31 977.
Tourist police, *see* regular police, Apollonia,
© (0284) 31 210.

From Kamares to Apollonia and Artemon

The island's port, shady **Kamares**, has become in recent years a typical waterside jumble of tourist facilities. Situated between two steep, barren cliffs that belie the fertility inland, Kamares has some good places to camp, tavernas, and other services useful to the traveller. Only two of the many pottery workshops that once lined the north side of the harbour still survive. Sifnos' single bus route begins from Kamares: a dramatic climb up to the capital **Apollonia**, then on to Artemon, Chrissopigi, the resort Platys Gialos, Faros and Kastro.

Apollonia is a Cycladic idyll, spread out across the hills, a circle of white from the distance. Its name comes from a 7th-century BC temple of Apollo, superseded in the 18th century by the church **Panayia Ouranoforia** in the highest part of town. Fragments of the temple can still be seen, and there's a marble relief of St George over the door. Another church, **Ag. Athanasios** (next to the pretty square dedicated to Cleanthis Triandafilos), has frescoes and a carved wooden iconostasis. In the bus stop square the **Museum of Popular Arts and Folklore**

5km
3 miles

N

To Serifos

Ormos Ag. Georgiou

Herortissos

Ag. Marina

Kamares

Artemonas

Kastro

Kato Petali

APOLLONIA

Exambela

Ormos
Seralia

Profitis Ilias
(678m / 2237ft)

Katavati

Faros

Ag. Andreas

Vathi

Platys Gialos

Chrissopigi
Monastery

To Milos

Kitriani
Islet

To Paros

houses a fine ethnographic collection of Sifniot pottery, embroideries and costumes (*open by arrangement; ask for the key*). There are numerous dovecots in the region with triangular designs which are repeated in the architecture of some of the houses. Local music, played on the violin and *laouto*, can frequently be heard in the cafés on Sundays.

Artemis is Apollo's twin sister; similarly **Artemonas** is Apollonia's twin village and the second largest on Sifnos. Beneath its windmills are the island's most ambitious residences and churches. The church of **Kochi**, with its cluster of domes, occupies the site of a temple of Artemis; also in Artemon as little 17th-century **Ag. Georgios tou Afendi** contains several fine icons from the period, and **Panayia ta Gournia**, near the bridge, has a beautiful interior (keys next door). Between Apollonia and Platys Yialos the monastery of **Ag. Andreas**, sitting on a hill, has some ruins of the double walls that once encircled the ancient citadel, and a little further north, but not accessible by road, is the monastery of **Profitis Ilias**, with a small network of catacombs and cells. Check that these are open before setting out.

Kastro and Panayia Chrissopigi

Kastro, overlooking the east coast, is a 3km walk from Artemonas. This was the Classical and medieval capital of Sifnos, a charming village overlooking the sea, surrounded by Byzantine-style walls made from the backs of the houses; some of the older residences still bear their Venetian coats-of-arms. Ruins of the Classical acropolis and walls remain, and there are many churches with attractive floors, among them the two of the Panayia, Eleoussa (1653) and Koimmissi (1593), and Ag. Aekaterini (1665). The old Catholic church, St Antonio, may soon be converted into a museum of local antiquities. The site of the School of the Holy Tomb, closed in 1834, is now Kastro's cemetery. At Kastro there's plenty of deep blue sea to dive into from the rocks, and many people dispense with costumes. If you prefer sand, paths from Kastro lead down to **Seralia** and **Poulati** and their lovely beaches.

Just south of Artemonas the bus passes through **Exambela**, a quiet village in the middle of one of Sifnos' most fertile areas. A monastery near Exambela called **Vrissi** (1612) contains many old manuscripts and objects of religious art.

Further south, by the seaside village and beach at **Faros** is the island's most famous church, **Panayia Chrissopigi**, built in 1650 on a holy rock. Long ago two women fled to the monastery from a band of approaching pirates. Desperately they prayed to the Virgin and she answered their pleas by splitting the cape right in the pirates' path, creating a gap 18m wide, which in these pirate-free days is spanned by a bridge. The icon of the Virgin in the church was discovered in the sea by fishermen attracted by the light it radiated. To visit the church ask the bus driver to let you off at Chrissopigi and walk down the mule path; there's also a road for cars. Near Faros is the beach of **Fasolou**, popular with nudists.

Platys Gialos and Around

Platys Gialos with its broad sandy beach is the island's busiest resort, though you can escape its worldly concerns by lodging in the serene convent of **Panayia tou Vounou** up on the cliff, affording a gorgeous view over the bay below. The last nuns left nearly a century ago, but the church with its ancient Doric columns is still used for island *paneyeria*. Two other seaside hamlets, **Vathi** and **Heronissos** are best accessible by boat from Kamares (although they can be reached by jeep, and Vathi is a 1-hour hike from Platys Gialos). **Vathi**, surrounded by high hills, has several tavernas on the beach and rooms—some available in the 16th-century monastery of Taxiarchis. Heronissos is simpler, and has no electricity.

Festivals

1 September, Ag. Simeon near Kamares; 20 July, Profitis Ilias near Kamares; 29 August, Ag. Ioannes in Vathi; 25 March and 21 November, Panayia tou Vounou; 15 August, Panayia ta Gournia; 14 September, Stavros, at Faros; Ascension (Analypsis) at Chrissopigi.

© (0284–)

Where to Stay

Most of the island's accommodation is in Kamares and Apollonia.

expensive

Platys Gialos offers two places with all the comforts of home, although their rates (around 17,000 dr.) are very high considering the facilities: **Platys Gialos**, on the beach, © 31 324, where all rooms are air conditioned and come with a fridge to raid, and the **Alexandros Sifnos Beach** two minutes from the water, © 32 333, with a rather redundant pool.

moderate

In Kamares **Boulis** is on the beach, and good value, © 32 122. The C class **Hotel Stavros** has rooms with baths, © 31 641, or, for the same price, you can stay at the B class **Kamari**, 300m from the beach, © 31 710. In Chrissopigi the small, family-run **Flora** pension has rooms with private bath for under 6000 dr., © 31 778.

cheap

Up in Apollonia is one of the real bargains on the island: the charming class B **Pension Apollonia**, © 31 490, with 9 rooms going for under 4000 dr. There are also rooms in Kastro, Artemonas , Faros and Vathi.

The restaurant fare on Sifnos was once better than on the other islands, but with the influx of tourists, overall standards have plummeted.

You can still get superb food though. Taverna **O Manganas** in Artemonas is one of the best eating places in the Cyclades, and probably the whole of Greece. The local speciality is *rivithia*—oven-baked chick-peas—and on Sunday they are served in many Sifniot homes and at O Manganas. It also scores highly for atmosphere and wine. It isn't easy to find as it's down a labyrinth of lanes; just follow the Greeks.

Other places include **Zorba's** up in Kastro, which has a fine view. For seafood **Captain Andreas** on the waterfront in Kamares has a good selection of fresh temptations and, as seems to be the trend these days, an Italian restaurant, **Lorenzo's**, has opened to entice the jaded palate. Across the street **Dionysos** serves breakfast on its rooftop, with nice views of the bay (they also provide hot showers for yachties, 200 dr.). A pre-dinner ouzo, watching the sun go down, is a must at the friendly **Café Folie**, at the far end of Kamares beach; very good snacks during the day, too. Out at Platys Gialos there is a good choice of seaside restaurants serving fresh fish. For good Sifniote dishes try the **Cyklades Beach** or **Sofia**. A popular Italian restaurant here is **Mama Mia**. At any of these three 2500 dr. will buy you a full meal. If you get to Vathi, reward yourself with a fish lunch at one of the tavernas in the bay; for 2500 dr. feast on fresh fish, local cheese, salad and wine.

The local cheese, *xynomitsithra*, is a hard sheep's-milk cheese, steeped in wine and then kept in barrels; it stinks, but cheese connoisseurs may want to try it.

Sikinos

If you find the other Cyclades too cosmopolitan, or you want to try out your Greek, you can always visit Sikinos, which is small and charming, untouched by history, unaffected as yet by organized tours (although its proximity to Ios may soon change all that). The one town on Sikinos is very pretty if sleepy, there's a beach, and a few other things to see if you should begin to tire of the simple pleasures of old-fashioned island life. The main ways of getting around are on foot and by mule. Vines still cover much of the fertile areas. In ancient times it was one of several islands called Oenoe, or 'wine island'.

Connections

Daily tourist boat to Folegandros and Ios; ferry five times a week to Piraeus, four times a week to Santorini, less frequently with Paros, Naxos, Sifnos, Serifos and Syros, once a week with Kythnos, Kimolos, Crete and the Dodecanese; catamaran once a week to other Cyclades and Piraeus.

Walks Around Sikinos

The island's port, **Alopronia**, affords little shelter from the winds or for weary visitors—most facilities are up at the capital, known either as **Sikinos**, Chora or Kastro. This is the island's only real town, and an hour's walk up from the jetty, if the bus hasn't put in an appearance. Looming over the village is the ruined **monastery of Zoodochos Pigi**, fortified against the frequent pirate incursions which the island endured in the past. The 300 inhabitants are most proud, however, of their 'cathedral' with its icons by the 18th-century master Skordilis.

There are two walks to make on Sikinos, each taking about 1½ hours. The path to the northeast leads to the rather scant remains of a Classical fortress at **Paliokastro;** the second, to the southwest, will take you to **Episkopi**, where a Roman heroon of the 3rd century was converted into the Byzantine church Koimisis Theotokou; the church itself was remodelled in the 17th century after an earthquake.

Sikinos' beaches lie along the southeastern coast, from the port Alopronia to Ag. Georgiou Bay; the most popular is **Spilia**, named after the island's many caves.

© (0286–)   *Where to Stay*

expensive

The only proper accommodation is at the **Porto Sikinos**, on the beach, prettily laid out in traditional island design, with 18 rooms, bar and restaurant, © 51 220.

cheap

Only a handful of rooms are available in private houses up in Chora, where you'll also find two small tavernas. In Alopronia there are also a few rooms and simple tavernas.

Syros

Inhabitants of Syros have affectionately nicknamed their island home 'our rock', as dry and barren a piece of real estate as you can find in Greece. But at the beginning of the Greek War of Independence in 1821 it was blessed with three important qualities: a large natural harbour, the protection of the King of France, and a hardworking population. The result was Syros' capital, Ermoupolis, once the major port in Greece, and today the largest city and capital of the Cyclades. It is also the best-preserved 19th-century neo-Classical town in the whole of Greece.

Syros is an island that doesn't need tourism, and looks upon its visitors as guests rather than customers—except when it comes to *loukoumia*, better known as Turkish Delight (both Greeks and Turks claim to have invented it; no-one really knows). These sweet, gummy squares, smothered in powdered sugar, are an island speciality, and vendors stream aboard any ship that calls at Syros to peddle it to passengers, who are often eager to buy it.

History

Homer wrote that Syros was a rich, fertile isle, whose inhabitants never suffered any illness, and died only when they were struck by the gentle arrows of Apollo or Artemis after living long, happy lives. The first inhabitants may have been Phoenicians, settled at Dellagracia and at Finikas. Poseidon was the chief god of Syros, and in connection with his cult one of the first observatories in the world, a heliotrope (a kind of sundial), was constructed by the philosopher Ferekides, the teacher of Pythagoras. In Roman times the population emigrated to the site of present-day Ermoupolis, at that time known as 'the Happy' with its splendid natural harbour and two prominent hills. After the collapse of the *pax Romana*, Syros was abandoned until the 13th century, when Venetians founded the hilltop town of Ano Syros.

Because Ano Syros was Catholic, the island enjoyed the protection of the French, and remained neutral at the outbreak of the War of Independence in 1821. War refugees from Chios, Psara and Smyrna brought their Orthodox faith with them and founded settlements on the other hill, Vrondatho, and down at Syros' harbour. This new port town boomed from the start, as the premier 'warehouse' of the new Greek state where cotton from Egypt and spices from the East were stored and as the central coaling station for the entire eastern Mediterranean. When the time came to name the new town, Ermoupolis—'the city of Hermes' (the god of commerce)—was the natural choice.

For 50 years Syros ran much of the Greek economy, and great fortunes were made and spent not only on elegant mansions, but also on schools, public buildings and streets; Ermoupolis built the first theatre in modern Greece and the first high school, financed by the citizens and government; and when the Syriani died, they were so pleased with themselves that the most extravagant monuments to be seen in any Greek cemetery were erected in their memory. By the 1870s, however, oil replaced coal and Piraeus replaced Ermoupolis as Greece's major port; Syros declined, but always remained the largest city and capital of the Cyclades, supporting itself with shipyards and various industries, prospering just enough to keep its grand old buildings occupied, but not enough to tear them down to build new concrete blocks. Today Ermoupolis is a National Historical Landmark.

By air: daily flights from Athens.

By sea: daily with Mykonos, Tinos, Piraeus, Paros, Naxos and Amorgos, four–five times a week with Andros, Santorini, Ios and Rafina, three times a week with Sikinos and Folegandros, twice a week to Astypalaia, Koufonissia, Skhinoussa and Heraklia, once a week to Ikaria, Samos and Anafi; catamaran daily to Piraeus and other Cyclades.

Tourist Information `

NTOG on quay, next to the port authority in Ermoupolis. Information at Town Hall, ✆ (0281) 22 375.

Tourist police, *see* regular police, ✆ (0281) 22 610.

The Teamwork travel office in the port offers excellent guided tours of Ermoupolis.

Ermoupolis

As you sail into the **commercial port**, Ermoupolis presents an imposing sight much commented on by early travellers. Above are the two hills; Catholic Ano Syros to your left (or north), and Vrondatho on the right. The rest of the city is built on an angle in a grand amphitheatre. On the other side of the harbour are the shipyards which are now obsolete, having gone into receivership only a few years ago.

Ermoupolis' central square, **Plateia Miaoulis**, is paved with marble and lined with cafés and pizzerias, dominated by a grand **town hall**, where you can take in full-length portraits of King George I and Queen Olga painted by Prossalendis. The **Archaeology Museum**, up the steps to the left, contains proto-Cycladic and Roman finds from Syros and other islands. In front of the town hall stands a statue of Miaoulis, revolutionary hero and old sea-dog, as well as a bandstand presided over by the seven muses. Sadly, the local Philharmonic Society, owing to lack of money, not interest, no longer performs there, but the municipality is endeavouring to raise funds for its revival. To the right, behind the square, stands the **Apollon Theatre**, a copy of La Scala and the first ever opera house in Greece; until 1914 it supported a regular Italian opera season. Up the street a little way from here, the central **Union Hall**, formerly a private mansion, is one of the few places you can get into to see the elaborate ceiling and wall murals characteristic of old Ermoupolis.

The next square up holds one of the town's best churches, **Ag. Nikolaos**, boasting a carved marble iconostasis by the 19th-century sculptor Vitalis. In front of the church, a memorial topped by a stone lion, also by Vitalis, is the world's first **monument to an Unknown Warrior**. The Cyclades capitol building is near here as well. On the opposite side of the square in St. Prioiou Street, the bell tower of the church **Koimesis** is one of the landmarks of Syros; its elegant neo-Classical interior contains a rare icon painted by Dominicos Theotokopoulos, better known as **El Greco** after he left for Venice and Spain. Another fine church in Ermoupolis is the **Metamorphosis**, the Orthodox cathedral.

Crowning **Vrondatho Hill** (take the main street from behind Plateia Miaoulis) is the church of the **Anastasis** with a few old icons and superb views stretching to Tinos and Mykonos. Even better, if you have the energy, is the hour's climb up Omirou St to the medieval Catholic quarter of **Ano Syros**. On the way up don't miss the **Orthodox cemetery of Ag. Georgios**, with its elaborate marble mausoleums of Syros' wealthy shipowners and merchants. Since the Crusades, most of the families in Ano Syros have been Catholic, and some have lived in the same mansions for generations and attended the **Catholic cathedral of St George** on top of Ano Syros. A large, handsome **Capuchin convent of St Jean** was founded there in 1635 by France's Louis XIII and has archives dating from the 1400s. Another church, the 15th-century **Ag. Nikolaos**, was founded in the 15th century as a house for the poor.

A 45-minute walk from Ermoupolis leads to the pretty seaside church of **Ag. Dimitrious**, founded after the discovery of an icon there in 1936; alternatively, a 15-minute walk will take you to Dili and its **Temple of Isis** built in 200 BC. Across the harbour at **Lazaretta** stood a 5th-century BC temple of Poseidon, although the only traces of it are a few artefacts in the museum. In ancient times this was probably the Poseidonia mentioned in the *Odyssey*. Also near Ermoupolis at Pefkakia, there was a **Roman-era cemetery**, although nothing remains of the actual tombs.

Around Syros

Other ancient sites are in the north of the island. At **Grammaton Bay** (reached only by boat), a prophylactic inscription to keep ships from sinking is carved in the rock, dating back to Hellenistic times. **Kastri,** just north of Chalandriani, was settled in the Bronze Age: its walls, foundations of houses and overgrown necropolis have contributed much to the understanding of this period in the Cyclades. Signs suggest it was re-inhabited for a brief period around 8000 BC. The **cave** where the philosopher Ferekides supposedly lived in the summer is nearby; his winter cave is at Alythini. Another path in the north leads to the quiet beach at **Megas Lakkos**.

Buses from Ermoupolis travel to the other seaside resorts of Syros: **Kini**, a small fishing village with a beach and tavernas, is a popular rendezvous for sunset-watching, while **Galissas** has the best beach on the island. Further south is another beach at **Finikas** (Phoenix), originally settled by the Phoenicians and mentioned in Homer. **Vari** has become a major resort, while **Dellagracia**, better known as **Posidonia**, and **Megas Gialos** have fewer tourists. **Azolimnos** is particularly popular with the Syriani for its ouzeries and cafés, but there are no hotels or rooms. In the middle of the island, **Piskopio** claims the oldest Byzantine church on Syros, Profitis Ilias, situated in the pine-covered hills. The Orthodox convent **Ag. Barbara** has an orphanage for girls and a school of arts and crafts; the walls of the monastery church are decorated with frescoes depicting Barbara's complicated martyrdom that led to her role as the patron saint of bombardiers. Inland, **Hroussa** is a pleasant, pine-shaded village with a number of new villas, while nearby **Faneromeni** ('can be seen from everywhere') itself has panoramic views of the island. **Agathopes** is a fairly quiet, sandy beach with a couple of snack bars.

Festivals

6 December, Ag. Nikolaos in Ermoupolis; the last Sunday in May, the finding of the icon at Ag. Dimitriou; 26 October, also at Ag. Dimitriou; 24 September, an Orthodox and Catholic celebration at Faneromeni.

Every two years, in either the last week of July or the first week of August, the **Apanosyria Festival** is organized by the municipality of Ano Syros, with exhibitions of local handicrafts and performances of popular plays. Another folklore festival is held, usually in June, at **Azolimnos** with three days of dancing, wine and song.

© (0281–)   ### Where to Stay

Syros is one island where you may well be able to book a flat at a moment's notice; the Teamwork Agency, © 28 771, by the port has an extensive listing of seaside properties.

expensive

Dolphin Bay Hotel (A) on Galissas Beach is a complex with everything from volleyball to disco, © 42 924; **Sea Colours Apartments** (A) in St

Nicholas, Ermoupolis, are smart apartments with terraces and wonderful views from the old sea captains' quarter, © 28716; cheaper, also in St Nicholas, is **Xenon Ipatiais**, © 23 575. Alternatively, **Omiros Hotel** is a lovely old neo-classical mansion, once the family home of sculptor Vitalis,elegantly restored; © 24 910.

moderate

In Posidonia the **Hotel Eleana** (C), © 42 601, has all the facilities and comforts of a superior grade. The ageing but pleasant **Hermes**, near the ferry boat quay, © 28 011, is a low-priced class B; try to get a room on the top floor facing the square. It has access in the back to a windy and rocky little strand where the locals swim.

cheap

In the lower price range, there are several old houses in Ermoupolis with rooms to let. There are also quite a few hotels and pensions on Syros' beaches, at Vari, Posidonia and Finikas, all catering for longer stays, and you may be able to get a room without a reservation—rarely the case with beach hotels on the other Cyclades. There is a **campsite** at Galissas.

Eating Out

The **Folia Taverna** and the **Tembelis Taverna** are two of the classic eating places in Ermoupolis; the Folia in particular serves unusual dishes at very reasonable prices. In Ano Syro, **Lilli's** is famous for its wonderful views, and the music of bouzouki legend Markos Vamvakaris, a local boy made good. His bust is in the square named after him. Also in the high town, **Rahmos** had bouzouki music. In the port **Medusa** and **Syllivani** are both good eateries. Most beaches have low-cost tavernas.

Tinos

If Delos was the sacred island of the ancient Greeks, Tinos occupies the same place in the hearts of their modern descendants. Chances are that in ancient times Delos had much the same atmosphere as Tinos—numerous lodgings and eating places, shaded stoas (in Tinos, awnings over the street) where merchants sell *tamata* (votives) and other holy objects, and busy harbours. Delos, however, evolved into a booming free trade port, an unlikely fate for Tinos. Besides its miraculous icon, Tinos is best known for its beautiful Venetian dovecotes, of which some 600 survive, scattered across the island's great sloping terraces like little houses of whitewashed stone embroidery. Tinos may be the centre of Orthodox pilgrimage, but of all the Cyclades it has the highest percentage of Catholics; many of the island's pretty white villages have somewhat atypical campaniles for landmarks—Tinos has 1200 chapels. As the 'Lourdes of Greece', Tinos maintains its relaxed family atmosphere, very much in contrast with neighbouring Mykonos, and anyone disturbing the tranquillity will be politely but firmly placed on the first ferry out.

History

Inhabited by the Ionians in Archaic times, Tinos was occupied by the Persians in 490 BC, but set free after the Battle of Marathon. In the 4th century a sanctuary of the sea god Poseidon was founded on the island (after he chased away all its snakes) and it became a sacred place, where pilgrims would come to be cured by the god and to participate in the December festivals of the Poseidonia. There were two ancient cities on the island, both confusingly named Tinos, one at the site of the present town and the other at Xombourgo. When the war between the Romans and Mithridates of Pontus broke out in 88 BC, the latter destroyed both towns. Not much happened until the Fourth Crusade, when the Venetians built a fortress called Santa Elena at Xombourgo, using the stone of the ancient acropolis and city. It was the strongest fortress of the Cyclades, and stood impregnable to eleven assaults by the Turks. Even the terrible Barbarossa was defeated by Santa Elena and its Venetian and Greek defenders. In revenge, the frustrated Turks often pillaged and destroyed the rest of Tinos.

In 1715, long after the rest of Greece had submitted to Ottoman rule, the Turkish admiral arrived in Tinos with a massive fleet and army. After sustaining a terrible attack, the Venetians decided that this time Santa Elena would not hold out, and, to the surprise of the Greeks, surrendered. The Turks allowed the Venetians to leave in safety, but in Venice, where it was a crime to fail in the course of duty, the officers were put on trial for treason, accused of having been bribed to surrender, and executed. Meanwhile the Turks blew up a good deal of Santa Elena in case the Venetians should change their minds and come back. Tinos was thus the last territorial gain of the Ottoman Empire.

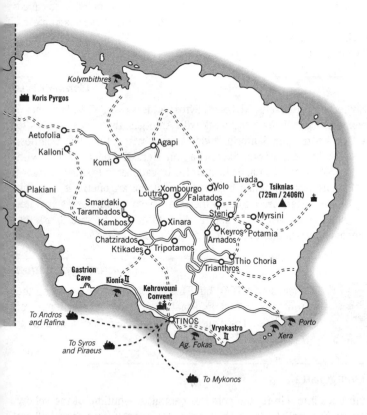

In 1822, during the Greek War of Independence, a nun of the convent Kehrovouni, Sister Pelagia, had a vision of the Virgin directing her to a certain rock where she discovered a miraculous icon of Mary and the Archangel at the

Annunciation. The icon was found to have extraordinary healing powers, and a church was soon built for it in Tinos town, called Panayia Evangelistra or Christopiliopsia. It quickly became the most important place of pilgrimage in Greece and because of its timing, a shrine of Greek nationalism; the discovery of the icon at just that moment in history helped to give the fight for independence the morale-boosting aura of a holy war. On 15 August 1940, during the huge annual celebration at the church, an Italian submarine entered the harbour of Tinos and sank the Greek cruise boat *Elli*—one of the major incidents directly before Mussolini involved Greece in World War II. Under the Colonels' regime the entire island was declared a holy place (part of that government's so-called 'moral cleansing') and the women of Tinos were required to behave at all times as if they were in church, by wearing skirts, etc., a rule quickly abolished when the junta itself went out the window.

Connections

Daily ferry from Piraeus, Mykonos, Syros, Andros and Rafina. Six times a week with Paros, five times a week with Amorgos, three times a week to the Dodecanese and Santorini, twice a week with Crete, Ios, Skiathos, Thessaloniki, Koufonissia, Shinoussa and Heraklia, once a week with Sikinos, Samos and Ikaria; daily hydrofoil or catamaran to other Cyclades and Piraeus. Note that ships from Tinos to Piraeus are often full, although surplus passengers are let on all the same. Two landing areas operate, often simultaneously, and when it's time to depart, be sure to ask the ticket agent which pier to queue up at in the tourist pens.

Tourist Information

 There's no NTOG, but Tinos Mariner travel agency on the front has helpful information and an excellent map of the island. The Tourist Police are at 5 Plateia L. Sohon, © (0283) 22 255.

Panayia Evangelistra

As your ship pulls into **Tinos**, the port and capital, the outline of the yellow church **Panayia Evangelistra** floats above the town. It's actually a short walk up Evangelistra Street, a street closed to traffic that becomes a solid mass of pilgrims on the two principal feast days of the Virgin, 15 August and 25 March. Many crawl the entire distance from the ferry to the church on all fours, with padded knees and arms. Seeing elderly women crawling in penance for the health of a loved one is a very moving and disturbing sight. The streets are full of icons and *tamata*. A red carpet covers the grand marble stair leading up to the neo-Classical church. If blind, they pledge to send an effigy of whatever they first see made from precious metal. As testimony to the miracles, there's a beautiful orange tree made of silver, fish, ships, and more besides; the church is chock full of gold and silver offerings from the grateful. Hundreds of shimmering lamps strung overhead create a magical effect, while on the floor level the church employs men who do nothing all day but remove candles from the stands so that new arrivals will have somewhere to put their own candles—the largest are the size of elephant's tusks. The pilgrims then queue up to kiss the icon itself, another work of the prolific St Luke, although its artistic merits are impossible to judge under the layers of gold, diamonds and pearls. Near the church four hostels have been built for pilgrims waiting to be healed by the icon, but there is still not enough room to house them, and the overflow camp out patiently in the courtyard.

The crypt, where Ag. Pelagia discovered the icon, is now the **Chapel of Evroseos**. Silver lines the spot in the rocks where the icon lay; the spring here, believed to be holy, is said to have curative properties. Parents from all over Greece bring their children here in August to be baptized in the font. Next to the chapel the victims of the *Elli* are interred in a mausoleum, which displays a piece of the fatal fascist torpedo.

Among the church's museums (*all open 8.30am–8.30pm*) there are: an **art gallery**, with works from the Ionian school, a reputed Rubens, a dubious Rembrandt partially hidden by the radiator, and many 19th-century works; a museum devoted to the works of the Tiniote sculptor **Antonios Soxos**, and above it the **Sculpture Museum** housing pieces by a variety of Greek sculptors such as Ioannis Boulgaros and Vitalis; old icons in the **Byzantine Museum**; and another museum containing items used in the church service.

Around Tinos Town

Parallel with Evangelistra Street, opposite a shady pine grove, the island **archaeological museum** contains artefacts from the Sanctuary of Poseidon and Amphitrite, including a sundial and a sea monster in various pieces and huge decorated storage vessels from the Archaic period.

From the port it's a short walk west to **Kionia** ('the columns'), with a beach and the **sanctuary of Poseidon and Amphitrite** which was discovered by the Belgian archaeologist Demoulin in 1902. Of the famous sanctuary the temple, the treasuries, entrances, little temple, baths, fountain of Poseidon and inns for pilgrims have been excavated. In many ways the ancient cult of the sea god and his wife Amphitrite parallels the contemporary cult of the icon—both Panayia Evangelistra and Poseidon have impressive records in rescuing sailors from storms. East of town, the closest and busiest beach is **Ag. Fokas**; a few minutes further east, at **Vryokastro**, are the walls of an ancient settlement, and a Hellenistic tower. Further east at **Xera** the beach tends to be less crowded than Ag. Fokas and Kionia, but **Porto** is now a busy resort.

Around the Island

Buses from the town pier wend their way north to the 12th-century **Kehrovouni Convent**, one of the largest in Greece. It is here that Sister Pelagia, canonized in 1971, had her two visions, in which the Virgin told her where to find the icon. You can visit her old cell and see her embalmed head. **Arnados** to the north is a charming little village, as is **Thio Choria**. From here a rough track leads down to the busy **Porto**.

In the winter Tinos turns lush and green, a colour that lingers until May when it takes on a more typical Cycladic barren brown, its hills corrugated with sun-parched terraces, relieved by the white dovecotes and their white residents. Some of the most elaborate dovecotes are in **Smardaki**, one of a cluster of small villages above Tinos town. Looming over them on a 564m hill is the famous Venetian fortress at **Xombourgo**, ruined by the Turks but still affording a superb view over Tinos' island neighbours.

First inhabited around 1000 BC, this commanding hill has a few ancient walls, although most of the stone was reused by later inhabitants, especially the Gizzi family of Venice, who built the Venetian fortress. Besides medieval houses, a fountain and three churches remain in the citadel walls. The easiest approach is from **Xinara**, seat of the Catholic arch-diocese. From here, too, you can walk to the site of one of the 8th-century BC towns called Tinos, where a large building and Geometric period temple were discovered. **Loutra**, one of the prettier villages, has a 17th-century Jesuit monastery where a school is still run by the Ursulines. From **Komi**, a long valley runs down to the sea at **Kolymbithres**, with a fine sandy beach where many people camp.

A paved road follows the mountainous ridge overlooking the southwest coast of Tinos. One possible detour descends to the valley village of **Tarambados**, with more good dovecotes; at **Kardiani** a motorable track winds down to a remote beach; otherwise, from **Isternia**, a pleasant village with plane trees, you can drive down to popular Ormos or **Ag. Nikitas beach**, the latter with rooms and tavernas. This part of Tinos is famous for its green marble, and the island has a long tradition in working the stone. Several well-known Greek artists came from or have worked in **Pyrgos**. Just by the bus stop is a small **museum** and the **residence of sculptor Giannolis Halepas**; the old grammar school, built in the first flush of Greek independence, is now a School of Fine Arts. A shop near the main square exhibits and sells students' works—Byzantine eagles are still popular motifs. Below Pyrgos the public bus continues down to the beach at **Panormos bay**, with more tavernas and rooms. **Marlas**, further north, is in the centre of the old marble quarries. From the tip of Tinos it's only a nautical mile to the island of Andros.

Festivals

15 August and 25 March at the Panayia Evangelistra, the two largest in Greece; 50 days after Greek Easter (i.e. mid-June), Ag. Triada at Kardiani; 26 October, Ag. Dimitriou in Tinos town; 21 December, Presentation of Mary at Tripotamos; 20 October, Ag. Artemiou at Falatados; 29 August, Ag. Ioannes at Komi (Catholic); 19 January, Megalomatas at Ktikades.

© *(0283–)*   ***Where to Stay***

expensive

Aeolos Bay (B) is a smart new hotel just outside the town on the beach with a pool, © 23 339. Also modern, **Tinos Beach** is close to the capital on the beach at Kionia, © 22 626; by far the largest of the island's accommodation, it also has bungalows.

moderate

Because Tinos has long been receiving pilgrims, it boasts a fine, old-fashioned hotel infrastructure not found on the other islands. Perhaps the Grande Dame of these hostelries is the **Hotel Tinion** on the left end of the harbour as you sail in, © 22 261, rated class B. A little cheaper, and with none of the frills, **Vyzantion**, 26 Alavanou, © 22 454, is nonetheless a pleasant alternative. Cheapest in this category is the **Meltemi**, 7 D. Filipoli, © 22 881, rooms have private facilities. **Aphrodite** is handy for ferries, © 22 456; inland, **Pension Favie-Souzane** © 22693 is pleasant; cheaper port pensions are **Eleana** © 22 561, and **Thalia**, © 22811. There are also nice rooms at the double-horseshoe bay of Kolymbithres.

There are quite a few rooms to rent in the town of Tinos, though little else-where; as mentioned above, it will be tough getting anything at all during the great feast days, although on 15 August sleeping outside isn't a terrible price to pay if you want to witness the greatest pilgrimage in Greece.

Eating Out

You can find inexpensive food throughout the town, though the restaurants near the ferry docks tend to be hurried and rather mediocre. In town, try **Nine Muses**, or the **Taverna I Dhrosia** at Ktikades for a meal with a view.

BC

7000–2800	Neolithic Era
4000	Precocious civilization at Palaeochoe, Limnos
3000	Milos exports obsidian
3000–2000	Early Cycladic civilization
2800–1000	Bronze Age
2600–2000	Early Minoan civilization in Crete
2000–1700	Middle Minoan: Cretan thalassocracy rules the Aegean
1700–1450	Late Minoan
1600–1150	Mycenaean civilization begins with invasion of the Peloponnese
c.1450	Eruption of Santorini's volcano decimates the Minoans; Mycenaeans occupy ruined Crete and Rhodes
1180	Traditional date of the fall of Troy (4 July)
c.1150	Beginning of the dark ages: Dorian invasion disrupts Mycenaean culture; Ionians settle Asia Minor and islands.
1000	Kos and the three cities of Rhodes join Doric Hexapolis
1100–100	Iron Age
1100–700	Geometric Period
700–500	Archaic Period
650	Aegina is first in Greece to mint coins
Late 600s	Sappho born on Lesbos
570–480	Pythagoras of Samos
500–323	Classical Age
490–479	Persian Wars end with defeat of Persian army and fleet
478	Delos becomes HQ of the Athenian-dominated Maritime League
460–377	Hippocrates of Kos
431–404	Peloponnesian War cripples Athens
378	Second Delian League
338	Philip of Macedon conquers Athens and the rest of Greece
334–323	Conquests of Alexander the Great
323–146	Hellenistic Age
146–AD 410	Roman Age

Chronology

88	Mithridates of Pontus, enemy of Rome, devastates many islands
86	Romans under Sulla destroy Athens and other Greek rebels who supported Mithridates

AD

58	St Paul visits Lindos, Rhodes
95	St John the Divine writes the Apocalypse on Patmos
391	Paganism outlawed in Roman Empire

197

410–1453	Byzantine Era
727–843	Iconoclasm in the Eastern Church
824–861	Saracen/Arab Occupation
961	Emperor Nikephoros Phokas reconquers Crete from the Saracens
1054	Pope ex-communicates Patriarch of Constantinople over differences in the creed
1088	Foundation of the Monastery on Patmos
1204	Venetians lead Fourth Crusade conquest of Contantinople and take the islands as their share of the booty
1261	Greeks retake Constantinople from Latins
1309	Knights of St John, chased out of Jerusalem, establish on Rhodes
1453	Turks begin conquest of Greece
1522	Ottomans defeat Knights of St John
1541	El Greco born on Crete
1669	Venetians lose Herakleon, Crete to the Turks after a 20-year siege
1771–74	Catherine the Great sends Russian fleet into the Aegean to harry the Sultan
1796	Napoleon captures Venice and her Ionian islands
1815–64	British rule Ionian islands
1821–27	Greek War of Independence begins
1823	Aegina made the capital of free Greece
1827	Annihilation of Turkish fleet by the British, French and Russian allies at the Battle of Navarino
1833	Otho of Bavaria becomes the first king of the Greeks
1883–1957	Cretan writer Nikos Kazantzakis
1912–13	Balkan Wars give Greece Macedonia, Crete and the Northeast Aegean Islands; the Italians pick up the Dodecanese
1922–23	Greece invades Turkey with catastrophic results
1924	Greece becomes a republic
1935	Restoration of the monarchy
1941	Nazi paratroopers complete first ever invasion by air on Crete
1945	Treaty signed returning Dodecanese islands to Greece
1948	Dodecanese islands reunite with Greece
1949	End of civil war between communists and US-backed government
1953	Earthquake shatters the Ionian islands
1967	Colonels' coup establishes a dictatorship
1974	Failure of the Junta's Cyprus adventure leads to the regime's collapse and restoration of democracy
1981	First-ever nominally socialist government (PASOK) elected
1983	Greece joins the EEC
1990	PASOK lose election to conservative New Democracy (ND)
1993	PASOK re-elected

Language

Although modern Greek, or Romaíka is a minor language spoken by few non-Greeks, it has the distinction of having caused riots and the fall of a government (in 1901). In Greece today there are basically two languages, the purist or katharevóusa and the popular or demotikí. Both are developments of ancient Greek, but although the purist is consciously Classical, the popular is as close to its ancient origins as French is to Latin. While many purist words are common in the speech of the people, the popular dominates, especially in the countryside.

Until the turn of the century all literature appeared in the purist language. What shook Athens with riots in 1901 was the appearance of the Iliad and the New Testament in the demotic. When the fury had died down a bit, more and more writers were found to be turning their pens to the demotic. Cavafy, the first great modern Greek poet, wrote in both the popular and purist. In its 'moral cleansing' of Greece the Papadopoulos government tried to revive the purist, but with little success.

Knowing the language of any country makes the stay twice as enjoyable; in Greece, especially, people spend much of the day talking. But modern Greek isn't a particularly easy language to pick by ear, and it is often spoken at great velocity (if you speak slowly someone is sure to interrupt). If you buy a modern Greek grammar, check to see if it has the demotic and not just the purist. Even if you have no desire to learn Greek, it is helpful to know at least the alphabet—so that you can find your way around—and a few basic words and phrases.

The Greek Alphabet

			Pronunciation/English Equivalent
A	α	*álfa*	short 'a' as in 'father'
B	β	*víta*	v
Γ	γ	*gámma*	gutteral *g* or *y* sound
Δ	δ	*thélta*	hard *th* as in 'though'
E	ε	*épsilon*	short 'e' as in 'bet'
Z	ζ	*zíta*	z
H	η	*íta*	long 'e' as in 'bee'
Θ	θ	*thíta*	soft *th* as in 'thin'

Ι ι		*yóta*	long 'e' as in 'bee';
			sometimes like the 'y' in 'yet'
Κ κ		*káppa*	k
Λ λ		*lámtha*	l
Μ μ		*mi*	m
Ν ν		*ni*	n
Ξ ξ		*ksi*	'x' as in 'ox'
Ο ο		*ómicron*	'o' as in 'cot'
Π π		*pi*	p
Ρ ρ		*ro*	r
Σ σ		*sígma*	s
Τ τ		*taf*	t
Υ υ		*ípsilon*	long 'e' as in 'bee'
Φ φ		*fi*	f
Χ χ		*chi*	German *ch* as in 'doch'
Ψ ψ		*psi*	*ps* as in 'stops'
Ω ω		*oméga*	'o' as in 'cot'

Dipthongs and Consonant Combinations

ΑΙ αι		short 'e' as in 'bet'
ΕΙ ει, ΟΙ οι		'i' as in 'machine'
ΟΥ ου		*oo* as in 'too'
ΑΥ αυ		*av* or *af*
ΕΥ ευ		*ev* or *ef*
ΗΥ ηυ		*iv* or *if*
ΓΓ γγ		*ng* as in 'angry'
ΓΚ γκ		hard 'g'; *ng* within word
ΝΤ ντ		'd'; *nd* within word
ΜΠ μπ		'b'; *mp* within word

Vocabulary

Yes	*né*	Ναί
	(with a short nod or tilt of the head)	
	málista (formal)	Μάλιστα
No	*óchi*	Οχι
	(with a backwards jerk of the head,	
	with a click of the tongue, smack of	
	the lips or raise of the eyebrows)	

I don't know	*then xéro* (An even greater throwing back of the head, or a display of empty hands)	Δέν ξέρω
I don't understand ... (Greek)	*then katalavéno ...* (*elliniká*)	Δέν καταλαβαίνω ... (Ελληνικά)
Does someone speak English?	*milái kanis angliká?*	Μιλάει κανείς αγγλικά;
Go away	*fíyete*	Φύγετε
Help!	*voíthia!*	Βοήθεια!
My friend	*o fílos moo* (*m*) *ee fíli moo* (*f*)	Ο φίλος μου Η φίλη μου
Please	*parakaló*	Παρακαλώ
Thank you (very much)	*evcharistó* (*pára polí*)	Ευχαριστώ (πάρα πολύ)
You're welcome	*parakaló*	Παρακαλώ
It doesn't matter	*then pirázi*	Δέν πιράζει
Alright	*en daxi*	Εν τάξι
Of course	*venéos*	Βεβαίος
Excuse me	*signómi*	Συγνώμη
Pardon?	*oríste?*	Ορίστε;
Be careful!	*proséchete!*	Προσέχεται!
Nothing	*típota*	Τίποτα
What is your name?	*pos sas léne?* (*formal*) *pos se léne?*	Πώς σάς λένε; Πώς σέ λένε;
How are you?	*ti kánete?* (*formal/pl*) *ti kanis?*	Τί κάνεται; Τί κάνεις;
Hello	*yásas, hérete* (*formal/pl*) *yásou*	Γειάσας, Χέρεται Γειάσου
Goodbye	*yásas, hérete* (*formal/pl*) *yásou, adío*	Γειάσας, Χέρεται Γειάσου, Αντίο
Good morning	*kaliméra*	Καλημέρα
Good evening	*kalispéra*	Καλησπέρα
Good night	*kaliníchta*	Καληνύχτα
What is that?	*ti íne aftó?*	Τί είναι αυτό;
What?	*ti?*	Τί;
Who?	*piós?* (*m*), *piá?* (*f*)	Ποιός; Ποιά;

Where?	poo?	Ποιός;
When?	póte?	Πότε;
why?	yiatí?	Γιατί;
how?	pos?	Πώς;

I am	íme	Είμαι
You are (*sing*)	ísse	Είσε
He, she, it is	íne	Είναι
We are	ímaste	Είμαστε
You are (*pl*)	íssaste	Είσαστε
They are	íne	Είναι

I have	écho	Εχω
You have (*sing*)	échis	Εχεις
He, she, it has	échi	Εχει
We have	échome	Εχομαι
You have (*pl*)	échete	Εχεται
They have	échoon	Εχουν

I am lost	échasa to thrómo	Εχασα το δρόμο
I am hungry	pinó	Πεινώ
I am thirsty	thipsó	Διψώ
I am tired	íme kourasménos	Είμαι κουρασμένος
I am sleepy	nistázo	Νυστάζω
I am ill	íme árostos	Είμαι άρρωστος
I am poor	íme ftochós	Είμαι φτωχός
I love you	s'agapó	Σ'αγαπώ

good	kaló	καλό
bad	kakó	κακό
so-so	étsi kétsi	έτσι κ'έτοι
slowly	sigá sigá	σιγά σιγά
fast	grígora	γρήγορα
big	megálo	μεγάλο
small	mikró	μικρό
hot	zestó	ζεστό
cold	crío	κρίο

Shops, Services, Sightseeing

I would like …	*tha íthela* …	Θά ήθελα …
where is …?	*poo íne* …?	Πού είναι …;
how much is it?	*póso káni?*	Πόσο κάνει;
bakery	*fournos*	φούρνος
	artopiíon (antiquated, above entrance)	Αρτοποιείον
bank	*trápeza*	τράπεζα
beach	*paralía*	παραλία
bed	*kreváti*	κρεβάτι
book	*vivlío*	βιβλίο
bookshop	*vivliopolío*	βιβλιοπολείο
butcher	*kreopolío*	κρεοπωλείο
church	*eklisía*	εκκλησία
cinema	*kinimatográfos*	κινηματογράφος
food	*fayitó*	φαγητό
hospital	*nosokomío*	νοσοκομείο
hotel	*xenodochío*	ξενοδοχείο
hot water	*zestó neró*	ζεστό νερό
house	*spíti*	σπίτι
kiosk	*períptero*	περίπτερο
money	*leftá*	λεφτά
museum	*moosío*	μουσείο
music	*musikí*	μουσική
newspaper (foreign)	*efimerítha* (*xéni*)	εφημερίδα (ξένη)
pharmacy	*farmakío*	φαρμακείο
police station	*astinomía*	αστυνομία
policeman	*astifílakas*	αστιφύλακας
post office	*tachithromío*	ταχυδρομείο
restaurant	*estiatório*	εστιατόριο
ruins	*archéa*	αρχαία
sea	*thálassa*	θάλασσα
shoe store	*papootsís*	παπουτσής
shower	*doush*	ντούς
student	*fititís*	φοιτητής
telephone office	*OTE*	ΟΤΕ
theatre	*théatro*	θέατρο

toilet	tooaléta	τουαλέττα
tourist policeman	astifīlakas tooristikís	αστιφύλακας τουριστικής
a walk	vólta	βόλτα

Time

What time is it?	ti óra íne?	Τί ώρα είναι;
month	mína	μήνα
week	evthomáda	εβδομάδα
day	méra	μέρα
morning	proí	πρωί
afternoon	apóyevma	απόγευμα
evening	vráthi	βράδυ
yesterday	chthés	χθές
today	símera	σήμερα
tomorrow	ávrio	αύριο
now	tóra	τώρα
later	metá	μετά
it is early	íne norís	είναι νωρίς
it is late	íne argá	είναι αργά

Travel Directions

I want to go to ...	thélo na páo sto (m), sti (f) ...	Θέλω νά πάω στό, στη ...;
How can I get to ...?	pós boró na páo sto (m), sti (f) ...?	Πώς μπορώ νά πάω στό, στη ...;
Can you give me a ride to ...?	boréte na me páte sto (m), sti (f) ...?	Μπορείτε νά μέ πάτε στό, στή ...;
Where is ...?	poo íne ...?	Πού είναι ...;
How far is it?	póso makriá íne?	Πόσο μακριά είναι;
When will the ... come?	póte tha érthi to (n), ee (f), o (m) ...?	Πότε θά έρθη τό, ή, ό ...;
When will the ... leave?	póte tha fíyí to (n), ee (f), o (m) ...?	Πότε θά φύγη τό, ή, ό ...;
From where do I catch ...?	apó poo pérno ...?	Από πού πέρνω ...;
How long does the trip take?	pósu kero pérni to taxíthi?	Πόσο καιρό πέρνει τό ταξίδι;

Please show me	parakaló thíkstemoo	Παρακαλώ δείξτε μου
How much is it?	póso káni?	Πόσο κάνει;
the (nearest) town	to horió (to pió kondinó)	Το χωριό (το πιό κοντινό)
Have a good trip	kaló taxíthi	Καλό ταξίδι
here	ethó	εδώ
there	ekí	εκεί
near	kondá	κοντά
far	makriá	μακριά
full	yemáto	γεμάτο
left	aristerá	αριστερά
right	thexiá	δεξιά
forward	brostá	μροστά
back	píso	πίσω
north	vória	βόρεια
south	nótia	νότια
east	anatoliká	ανατολικά
west	thitiká	δυτικά
corner	goniá	γωνιά
square	platía	πλατεία

Driving

where can I rent ...?	poo boró na nikiáso ...?	Πού μποπώ νά νοικιάσω ...;
a car	éna aftokínito	ένα αυτοκινητο
a motorbike	éna michanáki	ένα μηχανάκι
a bicycle	éna pothílato	ένα ποδήλατο
where can I buy petrol?	poo boró nagorásso venzíni?	Πού μπορώ ν΄αγοράσω βενζίνη;
where is a garage?	poo íne éna garáz?	Πού είναι ένα γκαράζ;
a mechanic	énan mikanikó	έναν μηχανικό
a map	enan chárti	έναν χάρτη
where is the road to ...?	poo íne o thrómos yiá ...?	Πού είναι ο δρόμος γιά ...;
where does this road lead?	poo pái aftós o thrómos?	Πού πάει αυτός ο δρόμος;
is the road good?	íne kalós o thrómos?	Είναι καλός ο δρόμος;

EXIT	*éxothos*	ΕΞΟΔΟΣ
ENTRANCE	*ísothos*	ΕΙΣΟΔΟΣ
DANGER	*kínthinos*	ΚΙΝΔΥΝΩΣ
SLOW	*arga*	ΑΡΓΑ
NO PARKING	*apagorévete ee*	ΑΠΑΓΟΡΕΥΕΤΑΙ Η
	státhmevsis	ΣΤΑΘΜΕΥΣΙΣ
KEEP OUT	*apagorévete ee*	ΑΠΑΓΟΡΕΥΕΤΑΙ Η
	ísothos	ΕΙΣΟΔΟΣ

Numbers

one	*énas* (*m*), *mía* (*f*), *éna* (*n*)	ένας, μία, ένα
two	*thío*	δύο
three	*tris* (*m, f*), *tría* (*n*)	τρείς, τρία
four	*téseris* (*m, f*), *téssera* (*n*)	τέσσερεις, τέσσερα
five	*pénde*	πέντε
six	*éxi*	έξι
seven	*eptá*	επτά
eight	*októ*	οκτώ
nine	*ennéa*	εννέα
ten	*théka*	δέκα
eleven	*éntheka*	έντεκα
twelve	*thótheka*	δώδεκα
thirteen	*thekatría*	δεκατρία
fourteen	*thekatéssera*	δεκατέσσερα
twenty	*íkosi*	είκοσι
twenty-one	*íkosi éna* (*m, n*) *mía* (*f*)	είκοσι ένα, μία
thirty	*triánda*	τριάνια
forty	*saránda*	σαράντα
fifty	*penínda*	πενήντα
sixty	*exínda*	εξήντα
seventy	*evthomínda*	ευδομήντα
eighty	*ogthónda*	ογδόντα
ninety	*enenínda*	ενενήντα
one hundred	*ekató*	εκατό
one thousand	*chília*	χίλια

Months/Days

January	*Ianooários*	Ιανουάριος
February	*Fevrooários*	Φεβρουάριος
March	*Mártios*	Μάρτιος
April	*Aprílios*	Απρίλιος
May	*Máios*	Μάιος
June	*Ioónios*	Ιούνιος
July	*Ioólios*	Ιούλιος
August	*Avgoostos*	Αύγουστος
September	*Septémvrios*	Σεπτέμβριος
October	*Októvrios*	Οκτώβριος
November	*Noémvrios*	Νοέμβριος
December	*Thekémvrios*	Δεκέμβριος

Sunday	*Kiriakí*	Κυριακή
Monday	*Theftéra*	Δευτέρα
Tuesday	*Tríti*	Τρίτη
Wednesday	*Tetárti*	Τετάρτη
Thursday	*Pémpti*	Πέμπτη
Friday	*Paraskeví*	Παρασκευή
Saturday	*Sávato*	Σάββατο

Transport

the airport	*to arothrómio*	τό αεροδρόμιο
the aeroplane	*to aropláno*	τό αεροπλάνο
the bus station	*ee stási leoforíou*	ή στάση λεωφορείου
the bus	*to leoforío*	τό λεωφορείο
the railway station	*o stathmós too trénou*	ό σταθμός τού τραίνου
the train	*to tréno*	τό τραίνο
the port	*to limáni*	τό λιμάνι
the port authority	*to limenarchío*	τό λιμεναρχείο
the ship	*to plío, to karávi*	τό πλοίο, τό καράβι
the steamship	*to vapóri*	τό βαπόρι
the car	*to aftokínito*	τό αυτοκίνητο
a ticket	*éna isitírio*	ένα εισιτήριο

The Menu

Hors d'oeuvres	Orektiká (Mezéthes)	Ορεκτικά (Μεζέδες)
yoghurt and cucumbers	tzatziki	τζατζίκι
olives	eliés	εληές
stuffed vine leaves	dolmáthes	ντολμάδες
cod's roe dip	taramosalata	ταραμοσαλάτα
mixed hors d'oeuvres	thiáfora orektiká	διάφορα ορεκτικά

Soups	Soópes	Σούπες
egg and lemon soup	avgolémono	αυγολέμονο
vegetable soup	chortósoupa	χορτόσουπα
fish soup	psarósoupa	ψαρόσουπα
giblets in egg and lemon soup	magirítsa	μαγειρίτσα

Pasta and Rice	Zimariká	Ζυμαρικά
pilaf	piláfi	πιλάφι
spaghetti	spagéti	σπαγκέτι
macaroni	makarónia	μακαρόνια

Vegetables (in oil)	Latherá	Λαδερά
potatoes	patátes	πατάτες
stuffed tomatoes	tomátes yemistés	ντομάτες γεμιστές
stuffed aubergines/ eggplants	melitzánes yemistés	μελιτζάνες γεμιστές
stuffed peppers	piperíes yemistés	πιπεριές γεμιστές
beans	fasólia	φασόλια
lentils	fakí	φακή
greens	chórta	χόρτu

Fish	Psária	Ψάρια
lobster	astakós	αστακός
little squid	kalamarákia	καλαμαράκια
octopus	achtapóthi	αχταπόδι
red mullet	barboúni	μπαρμπούνι
prawns (shrimps)	garíthes	γαρίδες
whitebait	maríthes	μυρίδες
sea bream	sinagrítha	συναγρίδα

fried cod (with garlic and vinegar sauce)	*bakaliáros (skorthaliá)*	μπακαλιάρος (σκορδαλιά)
oysters	*stríthia*	στρείδια
bass	*lithrínia*	λιθρίνια

Eggs **Avgá** **Αυγά**

ham omelette	*omeléta me zambón*	ομελέττα μέ ζαμπόν
cheese omelette	*omeléta me tirí*	ομελέττα μέ τυρί
fried (scrambled) eggs	*avgá tiganitá (brouyé)*	αυγά τηγανιτά (μπρουγέ)

Main Courses **Kíria Piáta** **Κύρια Πιάτα**

chicken	*kotópoulo*	κοτόπουλο
beefsteak	*biftéki*	μπιφτέκι
rabbit	*kounéli*	κουνέλι
meat and macaroni	*pastítsio*	παστίτσιο
meat and aubergine/ eggplant with white sauce	*mousaká*	μουσακά
liver	*seekóti*	συκώτι
veal	*moschári*	μοσχάρι
lamb	*arnáki*	αρνάκι
pork chops	*brizólas chirinés*	μπριζόλες χοιρινές
meat balls in tomato sauce	*soutsoukákia*	σουτζουκάκια
sausage	*lukániko*	λουκάνικο

Grills **Skáras** **Σχάρας**

meat on a skewer	*souvláki*	σουβλάκι
veal chops	*kotelétes*	κοτελέτες
roast chicken	*kotópoulo psistó*	κοτόπουλο ψηστό
meat balls	*keftéthes*	κεφτέδες

Salads **Salátes** **Σαλάτες**

tomatoes	*domátes*	ντομάτες
cucumber	*angoúri*	αγγούρι
Russian salad	*róssiki saláta*	ρώσσικη σαλάτα

village salad with cheese and olives	*choriatiki*	χοριάτικη
courgettes/zucchini	*kolokithákia*	κολοκυθάκια

Cheeses — **Tiriá** — **Τυριά**

cheese pie	*tirópitta*	τυρόπιττα
goat's cheese	*féta*	φέτα
hard buttery cheese	*kasséri*	κασέρι
blue cheese (roquefort)	*rokfór*	ροκφόρ
Greek 'Gruyère'	*graviéra*	γραβιέρα

Sweets — **Glyká** — **Γλυκά**

ice cream	*pagotó*	παγωτό
sugared biscuits	*kourabiéthes*	κουραμπιέδεs
hot honey fritters	*loukoumáthes*	λουκουμάδεs
sesame seed sweet	*halvá*	χαλβά
nuts and honey in fillo pastry	*baklavá*	μπακλαβά
custard in fillo pastry	*galaktoboúreko*	γαλακτομπούρεκο
yoghurt	*yiaoúrti*	γιαούρτι
rice pudding	*rizógalo*	ρυζόγαλο
shredded wheat with nuts and honey	*kataifi*	καταΐφι
custard tart	*bougátsa*	μπουγάτσα
soft almond biscuits	*amigthalotá*	αμιγδαλωτά

Fruit — **Froóta** — **Φρούτα**

pear	*achláthi*	αχλάδι
orange	*portokáli*	πορτοκάλι
apple	*mílo*	μήλο
peach	*rothákino*	ροδάκινο
melon	*pepóni*	πεπόνι
watermelon	*karpoúzi*	καρπούζι
plum	*thamáskino*	δαμάσκινο
figs	*síka*	σύκα
grapes	*stafília*	σταφύλια
banana	*banána*	μπανάνα
apricot	*veríkoko*	βερύκοκο

Miscellaneous

water (boiled)	*neró (vrastó)*	νερό (βραστό)
bread	*psomí*	ψωμί
butter	*voútiro*	βούτυρο
honey	*méli*	μέλι
jam	*marmelátha*	μαρμελάδα
salt	*aláti*	αλάτι
pepper	*pipéri*	πιπερι
sugar	*záchari*	ζάχαρη
oil	*láthi*	λάδι
vinegar	*xíthi*	ξύδι
mustard	*mustárda*	μουστάρδα
lemon	*lemóni*	λεμόνι
milk	*gála*	γάλα
tea	*tsái*	τσάϊ
chocolate	*sokoláta*	σοκολάτα
the bill/check	*logariasmó*	λογαριασμό
to your health!	*stín iyásas (formal, pl)*	στήν ηγειά σας!
	stín iyásou (sing)	στήν ηγειά σου!

accidents, moped 12
Acrisius (King of Argos) 172
air travel 2–4
  carrying bikes on planes 13
  see also under individual places
    (getting there)
Ajax of Oileus 138
Albania, refugees from 71, 103
Alexander the Great xi, 58, 59, 70
AMORGOS **94–8**, *95*
  Aegiali 94, **97**
  Ag. Anna beach 97
  Ag. Trias 97
  Amorgos capital (Chora) **96**, 97
  Apano Kastro 96
  Arkesini 96–7
  Chozoviotissa monastery 94, **96**
  eating out 98
  festivals 97
  getting there **95**, 98, 99
  history 94–5
  Katapola 96
  Keros 94
  Minoa 94, **96**
  Paradisa beach 97
  Rahida 96
  Rakhidi 96–7
  Tholaria 97
  tourist information 95
  where to stay 97–8
ANAFI ix, **99–101**
  Ag. Nikolaos 100
  around the island 100
  beaches 100

Chora 100
eating out 101
festivals 100
getting there 100
history 100
Kastro 100
Katalimatsa 100
Monastery of Panayia Kalmiotissa
  100
where to stay 100
ANDROS x, **101–7**, *102*
  Ag. Georgios cathedral 104
  Ag. Nikolaos monastery 104
  Ag. Petros 105
  Ag. Thalassini church 104
  Aladino 104
  Amolohos 106
  Apikia 104
  Archaeology Museum 104
  Arnas 105
  Batsi 105
  Bay of Korthion 105
  capital (Chora) 103–4
  Castle of the Old Woman 105
  eating out 107
  Emborios beach 103–4
  festivals 106
  Gavrion 105
  getting there 103
  history 101–3
  Kamara 103
  Kato Kastro 103
  Menites 104
  Mesaria 104

Note: Page references in **bold** indicate main references and those in
italics indicate maps. All Cycladic Islands appear in capital letters.

Index

by train 5–6
see also under individual places
gipsies 71
Gizzi 94
Goths 94
Greek Automobile Touring Club 10,
   11, 12
Greek language 61
Greek Travel Pages 10
Greek Wine Bureau 26
Green Cards 11
guesthouses 42

Hadraada, Harald 89
Hadzikyriakos-Ghikas, Nikos 78
Halepas, Giannolis 194
hasápiko dance 60
health 27–8
Hellenistic period 54
Heraklia ix
Hermes 102
Hippodamus 88
history
   modern 45–51
   see also under individual places
hitch–hiking 13
holidays, national 31–2
Homer 76, **119**
horse riding 35
hospitals 28
hotels 38–9 *see also under* individual
   places (where to stay)
houses, renting 41–2
Humbert, Cardinal 61
hydrofoils 9

Iconoclasm 61
Ignatius 155
Igoumenitsa, boats to 7
immigration 14–15

International Driving Permits 10
Ioannides (dictator) 50
Ionian islands ix
Ionic Amphictyonic league 145
IOS ix, **116–21**, *117*
   Ag. Barbara 119
   Ag. Ioannis Kalamos 118
   Ag.Theodotis Bay 118
   Apano Kambos 119
   beaches 118–19
   eating out 120–1
   getting there 116
   Gialos 116–17
   Hellinika 119
   Ios town 117–18
   Koumbara beach 117
   Manganari Bay 118
   Milopotas beach 117, **118**
   Paliokastro 118–19
   Perivolia 119
   Plakatos 119
   Psathis Bay 118
   tourist information 116
   where to stay 119–20
Iraklia x, 98, **99**
   eating out 99
   Livadi beach 99
   where to stay 99
Istanbul *see* Constantinople
Italy
   ferries to Greece 7
   war with Greece 48

Jason and the Argonauts 100
jellyfish 64
Justinian 70, 155

Kairis, Theophilos 103
kalamatianós dance 60
kamaki 43

mosquitos 64
motorbikes 12
motoring *see* cars
Motor Insurance Bureau 11
museums 29
  Athens 73–80
  Naxos 52
  photography 33
  Rhodes 54
music 29–31
Mussolini, Benito 48, 191
Mycenaean civilization xi
MYKONOS ix, **138–44**, *139*
  Ano Mera 141
  Archaeology Museum 140
  around Mykonos 140–1
  Athenian School of Fine Arts 42
  Chora 140
  Dimastos 141
  diving schools 34
  eating out 143
  Elia beach 141
  Folklore Museum 140
  Garden of Rapaki 141
  getting there 2, 4, **139**
  history 138
  mythology 138
  Nautical Museum 140
  nightlife 143–4
  Ornos 141
  Panayia Paraportiani 140
  Panormos Bay 141
  Paradise nudist beach 141
  Platis Yialos 141
  Portes 141
  Psarou 141
  Super Paradise nudist beach 141
  Tourist Police **139**, 140
  Tourliani Monastery 141
  Tragonisi 141

  where to stay 141–2
mythology, *see under* individual places

NAXOS ix, 94, **144–52**, *147*
  Ag. Anna beach 148
  Ag. Diasoritis church 150
  Ag. Georgios beach 148
  Ag. Ioannis Gyroulas 149
  Ag. Mamas 149
  Ag. Prokopios beach 148
  Ag. Thaleleos 149
  Apano Kastro 150
  Apiranthos 150
  Apollon 150
  Archaeology Museum 148
  beaches 148–9
  Belonia 149
  Bourgos 146
  Catholic Cathedral 148
  Chalki 149–50
  Church of Panayia Pantansassa 148
  Delion 144, 148
  eating out 152
  festivals 151
  Filoti 150
  Francopoulo 150
  Galanado 149
  Galini 151
  getting there 4, 98, 99, **146**
  Grotta 148
  harbour mole 148
  history 144–5
  Ipsiloteras 151
  Kastraki beach 149
  Kastro 146
  Koimisis tis Theotokou 150
  Komiaki 150
  Koronos 150
  kouros 150–1
  Kourounochori 149